# 마이갓 5 Step 모의고사 공부법

**1** ●Vocabulary 필수 단어 암기 & Test
① 단원별 필수 단어 암기 ② 영어 → 한글 Test ③ 한글 → 영어 Test

**2** ●Text 지문과 해설
① 전체 지문 해석 ② 페이지별 필기 공간 확보 ③ N회독을 통한 지문 습득

**3** ●Practice 1 빈칸 시험 (w/ 문법 힌트)
① 해석 없는 반복 빈칸 시험 ② 문법 힌트를 통한 어법 숙지
③ 주요 문법과 암기 내용 최종 확인

**4** ●Practice 2 빈칸 시험 (w/ 해석)
① 주요 내용/어법/어휘 빈칸 ② 한글을 통한 내용 숙지
③ 반복 시험을 통한 빈칸 암기

**5** ●Quiz 객관식 예상문제를 콕콕!
① 수능형 객관식 변형문제 ② 100% 자체 제작 변형문제 ③ 빈출 내신 문제 유형 연습

영어 내신의 끝
**마이갓 모의고사** 고1,2
1 등급을 위한 5단계 노하우
2 모의고사 연도 및 시행월 별 완전정복
3 내신변형 완전정복

영어 내신의 끝
**마이갓 교과서** 고1,2
1 등급을 위한 10단계 노하우
2 교과서 레슨별 완전정복
3 영어 영역 마스터를 위한 지름길

마이갓 교재
보듬책방 온라인 스토어 (https://smartstore.naver.com/bdbooks)

KB134134

# 마이갓 10 Step 영어 내신 공부법

## Vocabulary

**필수 단어 암기 & Test**
① 단원별 필수 단어 암기
② 영어 → 한글 Test
③ 한글 → 영어 Test

## Grammar

**단원별 중요 문법과 연습 문제**
① 기초 문법 설명
② 교과서 적용 예시 소개
③ 기초/ Advanced Test

## Text

**지문과 해설**
① 전체 지문 해석
② 페이지별 필기 공간 확보
③ N회독을 통한 지문 습득

## Practice 3

**빈칸 시험 (w/ 해석)**
① 주요 내용/어법/어휘 빈칸
② 한글을 통한 내용 숙지
③ 반복 시험을 통한 빈칸 암기

## Practice 2

**빈칸 시험 (w/ 해석)**
① 주요 내용/어법/어휘 빈칸
② 한글을 통한 내용 숙지
③ 반복 시험을 통한 빈칸 암기

## Practice 1

**어휘 & 어법 선택 시험**
① 시험에 나오는 어법 어휘 공략
② 중요 어법/어휘 선택형 시험
③ 반복 시험을 통한 포인트 숙지

## Quiz

**객관식 예상문제를 콕콕!**
① 수능형 객관식 변형문제
② 100% 자체 제작 변형문제
③ 빈출 내신 문제 유형 연습

## Final Test

**주관식 서술형 예상문제**
① 어순/영작/어법 등
   주관식 서술형 문제 대비!
② 100% 자체 제작 변형문제

## 전체 영작 연습

**직접 영작 해보기**
① 주어진 단어를 활용한
   전체 서술형 영작 훈련
② 쓰기를 통한 내용 암기

## 학교 기출 문제

**지문과 해설**
① 단원별 실제 학교 기출
   문제 모음
② 객관식부터 서술형까지
   완벽 커버!

21년 고2
3월 모의고사

마
이
갓

연습과 실전 모두 잡는 내신대비 완벽
| workbook |

보듬영어

# 2021 고2

# 3월

## WORK BOOK

———

**2021년 고2 3월 모의고사 내신대비용 WorkBook & 변형문제**

# CONTENTS

2021 고2 3월 WORK BOOK

# Voca

| ❶ voca | ❷ text | ❸ [ / ] | ❹ ___ | ❺ quiz 1 | ❻ quiz 2 | ❼ quiz 3 | ❽ quiz 4 | ❾ quiz 5 | ❿ quiz 6 |
|---|---|---|---|---|---|---|---|---|---|

| | | | | | | |
|---|---|---|---|---|---|---|
| 18 | on behalf of | ~을 대표하여 | | organization | 조직, 단체 | |
| | residents' association | 입주민 조합 | | risk | 위태롭게 하다 | |
| | recycling | 재활용 | | adopt | 채택하다 | |
| | thanks to | ~의 덕분에,때문에 | | mentality | 사고방식 | |
| | given | 정해진 | | disassociated | 분리된 | |
| | messy | 어지러운 | | bonded | 결속되어 있는 | |
| | decide on | ~을 결정하다 | | job security | 직업 안정성 | |
| | apartment complex | 아파트 단지 | | management | 경영진 | |
| | cooperation | 협조 | | assessment | 평가 | |
| | in advance | 미리,사전에 | | on one's own | 독자적으로 | |
| | participation | 참여 | | determine | 판정하다,결정하다 | |
| 19 | due to | ~하기로 한(예정된) | | advance | 발전시키다 | |
| | give a presentation | 보고하다,발표하다 | | career | 경력 | |
| | chilly | 차가운 | 21 | precisely | 정확히 | |
| | creep over | ~을 엄습하다 | | rehearsal | 예행연습 | |
| | still | 정지한 | | stage | (집회 등을) 조직하다 | |
| | trap | 가두다 | | prior | 사전의 | |
| | gaze at | ~을 보다,응시하다 | | mirror | 그대로 반영하다 | |
| | blur | 흐릿한 형체 | | sprint | 단거리 달리기 경주 | |
| 20 | insider | 내부자 | | get into shape | 몸 상태를 좋게 만들다 | |
| | outsider | 외부인 | | endurance | 지구력 | |
| | challenge | 이의를 제기하다 | | optimal | 최적의 | |
| | characteristic | 특성 | | predetermined | 미리 정해진 | |
| | perspective | 관점 | | assume | 가정하다 | |
| | point out | ~을 지적하다 | | a range of | 다양한 | |

# 2021년 고2 3월 모의고사 내신대비용 Workbook & 변형문제

## Voca

| ① voca | ② text | ③ [ / ] | ④ ____ | ⑤ quiz 1 | ⑥ quiz 2 | ⑦ quiz 3 | ⑧ quiz 4 | ⑨ quiz 5 | ⑩ quiz 6 |
|---|---|---|---|---|---|---|---|---|---|

| | | | | | | | | | |
|---|---|---|---|---|---|---|---|---|---|
| | disaster | 재앙 | | | myth | 잘못된 통념 | | | |
| 22 | ecosystem | 생태계 | | | arrangement | (사는) 모습, (생활) 방식 | | | |
| | sound | 건전한 | 23 | | modern | 근대의,현대의 | | | |
| | conservationist | 환경 보호주의자 | | | era | 시대 | | | |
| | principle | 원칙 | | | be attributed to | ~에 기인한 것으로 여기다 | | | |
| | minimize | 최소화하다 | | | novel | 새로운 | | | |
| | disruption | (환경) 파괴 | | | originate | 유래하다 | | | |
| | confused with | ~과 혼동되는 | | | exist | 존재하다 | | | |
| | suppose | 전제로~하다 | | | divine | 신의 | | | |
| | not to say | ~이라고까지는 할 수 없어도 | | | verb | 동사 | | | |
| | notion | 개념 | | | inspire | 영감을 주다 | | | |
| | misleading | 잘못된 인식을 주는 | | | reflect | 반영하다 | | | |
| | static | 정적인 | | | argue | 주장하다 | | | |
| | dynamic | 역동적인 | | | possessed by | ~에 사로잡힌 | | | |
| | endure | 지속되다 | | | descend | 내려오다 | | | |
| | apparently | 겉보기에는 | | | imitate | 모방하다 | | | |
| | in comparison with | ~과 비교해 보면 | | | reveal | 드러내다 | | | |
| | adapt to | ~에 적응하다 | | | sacred | 신성한 | | | |
| | consequent | 결과적인 | | | quality | 특성 | | | |
| | inhabitant | 서식자,거주자 | | | pale imitation | 어설프게 흉내 낸 것 | | | |
| | lifespan | 수명 | | | perfection | 완벽함 | | | |
| | eventually | 결국 | | | blindly | 맹목적으로 | | | |
| | community | (동식물의) 군집 | | | underlying | 근저에 있는 | | | |
| | circumstances | 환경 | | | compromise | 타협 | | | |
| | constantly | 항상 | | | abstraction | 추상 | | | |

# Voca

| | | | | |
|---|---|---|---|---|
| | accuracy | 정확성 | point of view | 관점 |
| | creativity | 창의성 | illustrate | 설명하다 |
| | superhuman | 초인적인 | philosophy | 철학 |
| | pure | 순수한 | at a distance | 멀리서/거리를두고 |
| 24 | mistakenly | 잘못하여, 틀리게 | employ | 이용하다 |
| | hypothesis | 가설 | subject | 대상 |
| | guarantee | 보장하다 | straightforwardly | 있는 그대로, 솔직하게 |
| | slow down | ~을 둔화시키다 | positioning | 위치 선정 |
| | reaction | 반응 | comment on | ~에 관해 논평하다 |
| | shore | 해변 | interpret | 해석하다 |
| | established facts | 기정 사실 | unfold | 전개되다 |
| | venture into | ~로 과감히 들어가 보다 | impersonal | 냉담한 |
| | prediction | 예측 | unnoticeable | 눈에띄지 않게 |
| | alley | 골목길 | take place | 개최되다[일어나다] |
| | blind | 막다른 | viewpoint | 관점[시각]<br>(무엇을 바라보는) 방향 |
| 29 | reflect on | ~에 관해 곰곰이 생각하다 | 31 formidable | 강력한 |
| | inclusivity | 포용성 | institution | 단체, 기관, 협회 |
| | ultimately | 궁극적으로 | trace back to | ~로 거슬러 올라가다 |
| | collaboration | 협력 | primitive | 원시적인 |
| | typically | 보통, 일반적으로 | hide | 가죽 |
| | rule | 지배하다 | gut | 내장 |
| | exclusivity | 배타성 | aggression | 공격, 공격성 |
| | senior | 상급의 | awe - inspiring | 경외심을 자아내는 |
| | inadequate | 부적절한 | assertiveness | 당당함, 자기 주장 |
| 30 | objective | 객관적인 | predatory | 공격적인, 포식동물 같은 |

# Voca

| ❶ voca | ❷ text | ❸ [ / ] | ❹ ___ | ❺ quiz 1 | ❻ quiz 2 | ❼ quiz 3 | ❽ quiz 4 | ❾ quiz 5 | ❿ quiz 6 |

| | leading | 주요한, 일류의 | 34 | profit | 수익, 이익 |
|---|---|---|---|---|---|
| | summon up | ~을 떠올리다 | | reconsider | 재고하다 |
| | band | 무리 | | motive | 동기 |
| | dominance | 지배, 우월함 | | produce | 농산물 |
| **32** | evolve | 진화하다 | | manufacture | 제조하다 |
| | perceive | 인식하다 | | loyalty card | 고객 우대 카드 |
| | unusualness | 특이함, 특이성 | | track | 추적하다 |
| | encode | (정보를 특정한 형식으로) 입력하다 | | analytics | 분석,분석학 |
| | neurologist | 신경학자 | | slice | 쪼개다, 자르다 |
| | stimulation | 자극 | | currency | 통화, 화폐 |
| | expose | 노출하다 | | capitalist system | 자본주의 체제 |
| | demonstration | 실연, 직접 보여 줌 | | machine learning | 기계 학습 |
| | enthusiasm | 열의, 열성 | | maximize | 최대화하다 |
| | working memory | 작동 기억 | | surveillance | 관찰, 감시 |
| | devoted to | ~을 전담하는 | 35 | academic | 대학 교수 |
| | perceptual | 지각의 | | ethically | 윤리적으로 |
| | feed | 충족하다 | | manipulate | 조종하다, 조작하다 |
| | exploratory | 탐구적인 | | admit to | ~한 것을 인정하다 |
| **33** | psychological | 심리학적인 | | competitor | 경쟁자 |
| | naturally | 물론, 당연히, 자연스럽게 | | peer | 또래 친구 |
| | divide | 나누다 | | unfavorable | 부정적인, 바람직하지 못한 |
| | cognitive | 인식의 | | thereby | 그로 인해 |
| | retain | 기억하다, 보유하다 | | play on | (감정 등을) 이용하다 |
| | festivities | 만찬, 축제 행사 | | vulnerability | 취약성 |
| | sommelier | 소믈리에 | | inadequateness | 부적절함, 불충분함 |

# Voca

| | | | | | |
|---|---|---|---|---|---|
| | contribute to | ~에 기여하다, ~의 원인이 되다 | | deterrent | 억제책 |
| | fixated | 집착하는 | 38 | external | 외부의 |
| | gratification | 만족(감) | | spin on one's axis | 자전하다, 축을 중심으로 돌다 |
| 36 | graduate | 졸업생 | | verify | 검증하다, 확인하다 |
| | corresponding | 상응하는, 대응하는 | | criterion | 기준 (복수-criteria) |
| | relaxation | 휴식 | | sphere | 구 |
| | life expectancy | 평균 수명 | | meta - physical | 형이상학의 |
| | take over | ~을 장악하다 | | present challenge a | 난제가 되다 |
| | correlated with | ~과 서로 관련된 | | verification | 검증, 확인 |
| | at first glance | 처음 봐서는 | | falsify | 거짓임을 입증하다 |
| | imply | 의미하다 | 39 | instinct | 본능 |
| | at all costs | 무슨 수를 써서라도 | | generalize | 일반화하다 |
| | conclude | 결론[판단]을 내리다 | | distort | (사실을) 왜곡하다 |
| | expectancy | (특히 좋거나 신나는 일에 대한) 기대 | | categorize | (개개의 범주로) 분류하다 |
| | per se | 그 자체로 | | unconsciously | 무의식적으로 |
| 37 | fairness | 공정성 | | prejudiced | 편견을 가진 |
| | taxation | 과세 | | enlightened | 계몽된 |
| | fall on | ~에게 부과되다, (책임 등이) 맡겨지다 | | function | (정상적으로) 활동하다 |
| | sin tax | 죄악세 | | group together | ~을 하나로 묶다 |
| | disapproval | 반대, 못마땅해 함 | | jump to a conclusion | 성급하게 결론을 내리다 |
| | engage in | ~을 하다 | | unusual | 드문 |
| | carbon emission | 탄소 배출 | 40 | briefly | 잠시, 짧게 |
| | dimension | 차원 | | memorize | 암기하다 |
| | explicit | 명백한 | | digit | 자릿수 |
| | revenue | 세입,세수 | | opt for | ~을 선택하다 |

# Voca

| ❶ voca | ❷ text | ❸ [ / ] | ❹ _____ | ❺ quiz 1 | ❻ quiz 2 | ❼ quiz 3 | ❽ quiz 4 | ❾ quiz 5 | ❿ quiz 6 |
|---|---|---|---|---|---|---|---|---|---|

|  | | | | | |
|---|---|---|---|---|---|
| | impulse | (마음의) 충동 | out of sight | 보이지 않는 곳에 | |
| | intellective | 지적인 | uneasy | 불안한 | |
| | distraction | 주의를 산만하게 하는 것 | in a little while | 잠시 후에 | |
| | reflective | 숙고하는 | as for | ~에 관해서라면 | |
| | reflexive | 반사적인 | miserable | 몹시 불행한,비참한 | |
| | load | 부담, 무거운 짐 | utter | (목소리를)내다 | |
| | varied | 다양한 | at once | 즉시,당장 | |
| 41~42 | self - worth | 자부심 | cheerful | 기운찬 | |
| | associate ~ with | ~을...와 관련시키다 | | | |
| | rooted in | ~에 뿌리를 둔 | | | |
| | descriptive | 설명하는 | | | |
| | unreasonable | 부당한 | | | |
| | certification test | 자격 시험 | | | |
| | reaffirm | 재확인하다 | | | |
| | attend to | ~에 주의를 기울이다 | | | |
| | rationalize | 합리화하다 | | | |
| | variable | 변수 | | | |
| | dedication | 헌신 | | | |
| | meet ~ head on | ~에 정면으로 맞서다 | | | |
| | virtue | 미덕 | | | |
| | term | 말 | | | |
| | compound | 악화시키다 | | | |
| | relieve | 완화시키다 | | | |
| 43~45 | seize | 움켜쥐다 | | | |
| | ill | 아픈 | | | |

보듬영어

영 → 한

# Voca test

| ❶ voca | ❷ text | ❸ [ / ] | ❹ ___ | ❺ quiz 1 | ❻ quiz 2 | ❼ quiz 3 | ❽ quiz 4 | ❾ quiz 5 | ❿ quiz 6 |
|--------|--------|---------|--------|----------|----------|----------|----------|----------|----------|
| **18** on behalf of | | | | organization | | | | | |
| residents' association | | | | risk | | | | | |
| recycling | | | | adopt | | | | | |
| thanks to | | | | mentality | | | | | |
| given | | | | disassociated | | | | | |
| messy | | | | bonded | | | | | |
| decide on | | | | job security | | | | | |
| apartment complex | | | | management | | | | | |
| cooperation | | | | assessment | | | | | |
| in advance | | | | on one's own | | | | | |
| participation | | | | determine | | | | | |
| **19** due to | | | | advance | | | | | |
| give a presentation | | | | career | | | | | |
| chilly | | **21** precisely | | | | | | | |
| creep over | | | | rehearsal | | | | | |
| still | | | | stage | | | | | |
| trap | | | | prior | | | | | |
| gaze at | | | | mirror | | | | | |
| blur | | | | sprint | | | | | |
| **20** insider | | | | get into shape | | | | | |
| outsider | | | | endurance | | | | | |
| challenge | | | | optimal | | | | | |
| characteristic | | | | predetermined | | | | | |
| perspective | | | | assume | | | | | |
| point out | | | | a range of | | | | | |

영 → 한

# Voca test

| | | | | |
|---|---|---|---|---|
| | disaster | | | myth |
| 22 | ecosystem | | | arrangement |
| | sound | 23 | | modern |
| | conservationist | | | era |
| | principle | | | be attributed to |
| | minimize | | | novel |
| | disruption | | | originate |
| | confused with | | | exist |
| | suppose | | | divine |
| | not to say | | | verb |
| | notion | | | inspire |
| | misleading | | | reflect |
| | static | | | argue |
| | dynamic | | | possessed by |
| | endure | | | descend |
| | apparently | | | imitate |
| | in comparison with | | | reveal |
| | adapt to | | | sacred |
| | consequent | | | quality |
| | inhabitant | | | pale imitation |
| | lifespan | | | perfection |
| | eventually | | | blindly |
| | community | | | underlying |
| | circumstances | | | compromise |
| | constantly | | | abstraction |

# Voca test

| ① voca | ❷ text | ❸ [ / ] | ❹ ___ | ❺ quiz 1 | ❻ quiz 2 | ❼ quiz 3 | ❽ quiz 4 | ❾ quiz 5 | ❿ quiz 6 |
|---|---|---|---|---|---|---|---|---|---|
| | accuracy | | | | point of view | | | | |
| | creativity | | | | illustrate | | | | |
| | superhuman | | | | philosophy | | | | |
| | pure | | | | at a distance | | | | |
| **24** | mistakenly | | | | employ | | | | |
| | hypothesis | | | | subject | | | | |
| | guarantee | | | | straightforwardly | | | | |
| | slow down | | | | positioning | | | | |
| | reaction | | | | comment on | | | | |
| | shore | | | | interpret | | | | |
| | established facts | | | | unfold | | | | |
| | venture into | | | | impersonal | | | | |
| | prediction | | | | unnoticeable | | | | |
| | alley | | | | take place | | | | |
| | blind | | | | viewpoint | | | | |
| **29** | reflect on | | **31** | | formidable | | | | |
| | inclusivity | | | | institution | | | | |
| | ultimately | | | | trace back to | | | | |
| | collaboration | | | | primitive | | | | |
| | typically | | | | hide | | | | |
| | rule | | | | gut | | | | |
| | exclusivity | | | | aggression | | | | |
| | senior | | | | awe - inspiring | | | | |
| | inadequate | | | | assertiveness | | | | |
| **30** | objective | | | | predatory | | | | |

영 → 한

# Voca test

| ❶ voca | ❷ text | ❸ [ / ] | ❹ _____ | ❺ quiz 1 | ❻ quiz 2 | ❼ quiz 3 | ❽ quiz 4 | ❾ quiz 5 | ❿ quiz 6 |
|---|---|---|---|---|---|---|---|---|---|
| | leading | | | | | | | | |
| | summon up | | | | | | | | |
| | band | | | | | | | | |
| | dominance | | | | | | | | |
| 32 | evolve | | | | | | | | |
| | perceive | | | | | | | | |
| | unusualness | | | | | | | | |
| | encode | | | | | | | | |
| | neurologist | | | | | | | | |
| | stimulation | | | | | | | | |
| | expose | | | | | | | | |
| | demonstration | | | | | | | | |
| | enthusiasm | | | | | | | | |
| | working memory | | | | | | | | |
| | devoted to | | | | | | | | |
| | perceptual | | | | | | | | |
| | feed | | | | | | | | |
| | exploratory | | | | | | | | |
| 33 | psychological | | | | | | | | |
| | naturally | | | | | | | | |
| | divide | | | | | | | | |
| | cognitive | | | | | | | | |
| | retain | | | | | | | | |
| | festivities | | | | | | | | |
| | sommelier | | | | | | | | |
| 34 | profit | | | | | | | | |
| | reconsider | | | | | | | | |
| | motive | | | | | | | | |
| | produce | | | | | | | | |
| | manufacture | | | | | | | | |
| | loyalty card | | | | | | | | |
| | track | | | | | | | | |
| | analytics | | | | | | | | |
| | slice | | | | | | | | |
| | currency | | | | | | | | |
| | capitalist system | | | | | | | | |
| | machine learning | | | | | | | | |
| | maximize | | | | | | | | |
| | surveillance | | | | | | | | |
| 35 | academic | | | | | | | | |
| | ethically | | | | | | | | |
| | manipulate | | | | | | | | |
| | admit to | | | | | | | | |
| | competitor | | | | | | | | |
| | peer | | | | | | | | |
| | unfavorable | | | | | | | | |
| | thereby | | | | | | | | |
| | play on | | | | | | | | |
| | vulnerability | | | | | | | | |
| | inadequateness | | | | | | | | |

보듬영어

영 → 한

# Voca test

| ❶ voca | ❷ text | ❸ [ / ] | ❹ ____ | ❺ quiz 1 | ❻ quiz 2 | ❼ quiz 3 | ❽ quiz 4 | ❾ quiz 5 | ❿ quiz 6 |
|---|---|---|---|---|---|---|---|---|---|

| | | | | |
|---|---|---|---|---|
| | contribute to | | | deterrent |
| | fixated | | 38 | external |
| | gratification | | | spin on one's axis |
| 36 | graduate | | | verify |
| | corresponding | | | criterion |
| | relaxation | | | sphere |
| | life expectancy | | | meta – physical |
| | take over | | | present a challenge |
| | correlated with | | | verification |
| | at first glance | | | falsify |
| | imply | | 39 | instinct |
| | at all costs | | | generalize |
| | conclude | | | distort |
| | expectancy | | | categorize |
| | per se | | | unconsciously |
| 37 | fairness | | | prejudiced |
| | taxation | | | enlightened |
| | fall on | | | function |
| | sin tax | | | group together |
| | disapproval | | | jump to a conclusion |
| | engage in | | | unusual |
| | carbon emission | | 40 | briefly |
| | dimension | | | memorize |
| | explicit | | | digit |
| | revenue | | | opt for |

영 → 한

# Voca test

| ① voca | ② text | ③ [ / ] | ④ ___ | ⑤ quiz 1 | ⑥ quiz 2 | ⑦ quiz 3 | ⑧ quiz 4 | ⑨ quiz 5 | ⑩ quiz 6 |
|---|---|---|---|---|---|---|---|---|---|
| | impulse | | out of sight | | | | | | |
| | intellective | | uneasy | | | | | | |
| | distraction | | in a little while | | | | | | |
| | reflective | | as for | | | | | | |
| | reflexive | | miserable | | | | | | |
| | load | | utter | | | | | | |
| | varied | | at once | | | | | | |
| 41~42 | self – worth | | cheerful | | | | | | |
| | associate ~ with | | | | | | | | |
| | rooted in | | | | | | | | |
| | descriptive | | | | | | | | |
| | unreasonable | | | | | | | | |
| | certification test | | | | | | | | |
| | reaffirm | | | | | | | | |
| | attend to | | | | | | | | |
| | rationalize | | | | | | | | |
| | variable | | | | | | | | |
| | dedication | | | | | | | | |
| | meet ~ head on | | | | | | | | |
| | virtue | | | | | | | | |
| | term | | | | | | | | |
| | compound | | | | | | | | |
| | relieve | | | | | | | | |
| 43~45 | seize | | | | | | | | |
| | ill | | | | | | | | |

한 → 영

## Voca test

| ① voca | ② text | ③ [ / ] | ④ _____ | ⑤ quiz 1 | ⑥ quiz 2 | ⑦ quiz 3 | ⑧ quiz 4 | ⑨ quiz 5 | ⑩ quiz 6 |
|---|---|---|---|---|---|---|---|---|---|
| 18 | | | ~을 대표하여 | | | | 조직, 단체 | | |
| | | | 입주민 조합 | | | | 위태롭게 하다 | | |
| | | | 재활용 | | | | 채택하다 | | |
| | | | ~의 덕분에,때문에 | | | | 사고방식 | | |
| | | | 정해진 | | | | 분리된 | | |
| | | | 어지러운 | | | | 결속되어 있는 | | |
| | | | ~을 결정하다 | | | | 직업 안정성 | | |
| | | | 아파트 단지 | | | | 경영진 | | |
| | | | 협조 | | | | 평가 | | |
| | | | 미리,사전에 | | | | 독자적으로 | | |
| | | | 참여 | | | | 판정하다,결정하다 | | |
| 19 | | | ~하기로 한(예정된) | | | | 발전시키다 | | |
| | | | 보고하다,발표하다 | | | | 경력 | | |
| | | | 차가운 | 21 | | | 정확히 | | |
| | | | ~을 엄습하다 | | | | 예행연습 | | |
| | | | 정지한 | | | | (집회 등을) 조직하다 | | |
| | | | 가두다 | | | | 사전의 | | |
| | | | ~을 보다,응시하다 | | | | 그대로 반영하다 | | |
| | | | 흐릿한 형체 | | | | 단거리 달리기 경주 | | |
| 20 | | | 내부자 | | | | 몸 상태를 좋게 만들다 | | |
| | | | 외부인 | | | | 지구력 | | |
| | | | 이의를 제기하다 | | | | 최적의 | | |
| | | | 특성 | | | | 미리 정해진 | | |
| | | | 관점 | | | | 가정하다 | | |
| | | | ~을 지적하다 | | | | 다양한 | | |

한 ➡ 영

# Voca test

① voca  ② text  ③ [ / ]  ④ _____  ⑤ quiz 1  ⑥ quiz 2  ⑦ quiz 3  ⑧ quiz 4  ⑨ quiz 5  ⑩ quiz 6

| | | | |
|---|---|---|---|
| | 재앙 | | 잘못된 통념 |
| 22 | 생태계 | | (사는) 모습, (생활) 방식 |
| | 건전한 | 23 | 근대의,현대의 |
| | 환경 보호주의자 | | 시대 |
| | 원칙 | | ~에 기인한 것으로 여기다 |
| | 최소화하다 | | 새로운 |
| | (환경) 파괴 | | 유래하다 |
| | ~과 혼동되는 | | 존재하다 |
| | 전제로~하다 | | 신의 |
| | ~이라고까지는 할 수 없어도 | | 동사 |
| | 개념 | | 영감을 주다 |
| | 잘못된 인식을 주는 | | 반영하다 |
| | 정적인 | | 주장하다 |
| | 역동적인 | | ~에 사로잡힌 |
| | 지속되다 | | 내려오다 |
| | 겉보기에는 | | 모방하다 |
| | ~과 비교해 보면 | | 드러내다 |
| | ~에 적응하다 | | 신성한 |
| | 결과적인 | | 특성 |
| | 서식자,거주자 | | 어설프게 흉내 낸 것 |
| | 수명 | | 완벽함 |
| | 결국 | | 맹목적으로 |
| | (동식물의) 군집 | | 근저에 있는 |
| | 환경 | | 타협 |
| | 항상 | | 추상 |

# Voca test

| ❶ voca | ❷ text | ❸ [ / ] | ❹ ____ | ❺ quiz 1 | ❻ quiz 2 | ❼ quiz 3 | ❽ quiz 4 | ❾ quiz 5 | ❿ quiz 6 |
|---|---|---|---|---|---|---|---|---|---|

| | | 정확성 | | | | 관점 |
|---|---|---|---|---|---|---|
| | | 창의성 | | | | 설명하다 |
| | | 초인적인 | | | | 철학 |
| | | 순수한 | | | | 멀리서/거리를두고 |
| 24 | | 잘못하여,틀리게 | | | | 이용하다 |
| | | 가설 | | | | 대상 |
| | | 보장하다 | | | | 있는 그대로,솔직하게 |
| | | ~을 둔화시키다 | | | | 위치 선정 |
| | | 반응 | | | | ~에 관해 논평하다 |
| | | 해변 | | | | 해석하다 |
| | | 기정 사실 | | | | 전개되다 |
| | | ~로 과감히 들어가 보다 | | | | 냉담한 |
| | | 예측 | | | | 눈에띄지 않게 |
| | | 골목길 | | | | 개최되다[일어나다] |
| | | 막다른 | | | | 관점[시각] (무엇을 바라보는) 방향 |
| 29 | | ~에 관해 곰곰이 생각하다 | 31 | | | 강력한 |
| | | 포용성 | | | | 단체, 기관, 협회 |
| | | 궁극적으로 | | | | ~로 거슬러 올라가다 |
| | | 협력 | | | | 원시적인 |
| | | 보통,일반적으로 | | | | 가죽 |
| | | 지배하다 | | | | 내장 |
| | | 배타성 | | | | 공격,공격성 |
| | | 상급의 | | | | 경외심을 자아내는 |
| | | 부적절한 | | | | 당당함, 자기 주장 |
| 30 | | 객관적인 | | | | 공격적인, 포식동물 같은 |

한 → 영

# Voca test

| ❶ voca | ❷ text | ❸ [ / ] | ❹ _____ | ❺ quiz 1 | ❻ quiz 2 | ❼ quiz 3 | ❽ quiz 4 | ❾ quiz 5 | ❿ quiz 6 |
|---|---|---|---|---|---|---|---|---|---|
| | | | 주요한, 일류의 | 34 | 수익, 이익 | | | | |
| | | | ~을 떠올리다 | | 재고하다 | | | | |
| | | | 무리 | | 동기 | | | | |
| | | | 지배, 우월함 | | 농산물 | | | | |
| 32 | | | 진화하다 | | 제조하다 | | | | |
| | | | 인식하다 | | 고객 우대 카드 | | | | |
| | | | 특이함, 특이성 | | 추적하다 | | | | |
| | | | (정보를 특정한 형식으로) 입력하다 | | 분석,분석학 | | | | |
| | | | 신경학자 | | 쪼개다, 자르다 | | | | |
| | | | 자극 | | 통화, 화폐 | | | | |
| | | | 노출하다 | | 자본주의 체제 | | | | |
| | | | 실연, 직접 보여 줌 | | 기계 학습 | | | | |
| | | | 열의, 열성 | | 최대화하다 | | | | |
| | | | 작동 기억 | | 관찰, 감시 | | | | |
| | | | ~을 전담하는 | 35 | 대학 교수 | | | | |
| | | | 지각의 | | 윤리적으로 | | | | |
| | | | 충족하다 | | 조종하다, 조작하다 | | | | |
| | | | 탐구적인 | | ~한 것을 인정하다 | | | | |
| 33 | | | 심리학적인 | | 경쟁자 | | | | |
| | | | 물론, 당연히, 자연스럽게 | | 또래 친구 | | | | |
| | | | 나누다 | | 부정적인, 바람직하지 못한 | | | | |
| | | | 인식의 | | 그로 인해 | | | | |
| | | | 기억하다, 보유하다 | | (감정 등을) 이용하다 | | | | |
| | | | 만찬, 축제 행사 | | 취약성 | | | | |
| | | | 소믈리에 | | 부적절함, 불충분함 | | | | |

한 → 영

# Voca test

| ❶ voca | ❷ text | ❸ [ / ] | ❹ ____ | ❺ quiz 1 | ❻ quiz 2 | ❼ quiz 3 | ❽ quiz 4 | ❾ quiz 5 | ❿ quiz 6 |
|---|---|---|---|---|---|---|---|---|---|
| | | | ~에 기여하다, ~의 원인이 되다 | | | | | | |
| | | | 집착하는 | 38 | | | | | |
| | | | 만족(감) | | | | | | |
| 36 | | | 졸업생 | | | | | | |
| | | | 상응하는, 대응하는 | | | | | | |
| | | | 휴식 | | | | | | |
| | | | 평균 수명 | | | | | | |
| | | | ~을 장악하다 | | | | | | |
| | | | ~과 서로 관련된 | | | | | | |
| | | | 처음 봐서는 | | | | | | |
| | | | 의미하다 | 39 | | | | | |
| | | | 무슨 수를 써서라도 | | | | | | |
| | | | 결론[판단]을 내리다 | | | | | | |
| | | | (특히 좋거나 신나는 일에 대한) 기대 | | | | | | |
| | | | 그 자체로 | | | | | | |
| 37 | | | 공정성 | | | | | | |
| | | | 과세 | | | | | | |
| | | | ~에게 부과되다, (책임 등이) 맡겨지다 | | | | | | |
| | | | 죄악세 | | | | | | |
| | | | 반대, 못마땅해 함 | | | | | | |
| | | | ~을 하다 | | | | | | |
| | | | 탄소 배출 | 40 | | | | | |
| | | | 차원 | | | | | | |
| | | | 명백한 | | | | | | |
| | | | 세입,세수 | | | | | | |

| ❹ ____ |
|---|
| 억제책 |
| 외부의 |
| 자전하다, 축을 중심으로 돌다 |
| 검증하다, 확인하다 |
| 기준 (복수-criteria) |
| 구 |
| 형이상학의 |
| 난제가 되다 |
| 검증, 확인 |
| 거짓임을 입증하다 |
| 본능 |
| 일반화하다 |
| (사실을) 왜곡하다 |
| (개개의 범주로) 분류하다 |
| 무의식적으로 |
| 편견을 가진 |
| 계몽된 |
| (정상적으로) 활동하다 |
| ~을 하나로 묶다 |
| 성급하게 결론을 내리다 |
| 드문 |
| 잠시, 짧게 |
| 암기하다 |
| 자릿수 |
| ~을 선택하다 |

한 → 영

Voca test

| ❶ voca | ❷ text | ❸ [ / ] | ❹ ____ | ❺ quiz 1 | ❻ quiz 2 | ❼ quiz 3 | ❽ quiz 4 | ❾ quiz 5 | ❿ quiz 6 |
|---|---|---|---|---|---|---|---|---|---|
| | | (마음의) 충동 | | | | | 보이지 않는 곳에 | | |
| | | 지적인 | | | | | 불안한 | | |
| | | 주의를 산만하게 하는 것 | | | | | 잠시 후에 | | |
| | | 숙고하는 | | | | | ~에 관해서라면 | | |
| | | 반사적인 | | | | | 몹시 불행한,비참한 | | |
| | | 부담, 무거운 짐 | | | | | (목소리를)내다 | | |
| | | 다양한 | | | | | 즉시,당장 | | |
| 41~42 | | 자부심 | | | | | 기운찬 | | |
| | | ~을...와 관련시키다 | | | | | | | |
| | | ~에 뿌리를 둔 | | | | | | | |
| | | 설명하는 | | | | | | | |
| | | 부당한 | | | | | | | |
| | | 자격 시험 | | | | | | | |
| | | 재확인하다 | | | | | | | |
| | | ~에 주의를 기울이다 | | | | | | | |
| | | 합리화하다 | | | | | | | |
| | | 변수 | | | | | | | |
| | | 헌신 | | | | | | | |
| | | ~에 정면으로 맞서다 | | | | | | | |
| | | 미덕 | | | | | | | |
| | | 말 | | | | | | | |
| | | 악화시키다 | | | | | | | |
| | | 완화시키다 | | | | | | | |
| 43~45 | | 움켜쥐다 | | | | | | | |
| | | 아픈 | | | | | | | |

# 2021 고2 3월 모의고사

❶ voca　❷ text　❸ [ / ]　❹ ＿＿　❺ quiz 1　❻ quiz 2　❼ quiz 3　❽ quiz 4　❾ quiz 5　❿ quiz 6

## 18 목적

My name is Anthony Thompson and I am writing on behalf of the residents' association. Our recycling program has been

working well thanks to your participation. However, a problem has recently occurred that needs your attention. Because there is

no given day for recycling, residents are putting their recycling out at any time. This makes the recycling area messy, which

requires extra labor and cost. To deal with this problem, the residents' association has decided on a day to recycle. I would like

to let you know that you can put out your recycling on Wednesdays only. I am sure it will make our apartment complex look

much more pleasant. Thank you in advance for your cooperation.

제 이름은 Anthony Thompson이고 저는 입주민 조합을 대표하여 편지를 쓰고 있습니다. 우리의 재활용 프로그램은 여러분의 참여 덕분에 잘 운영되고 있습니다. 그런데 최근에 여러분의 관심이 필요한 문제가 생겼습니다. 재활용을 위해 정해진 날이 없어서 입주민들은 아무 때나 자신들의 재활용품을 내놓습니다. 이것이 재활용 구역을 어지럽혀서 추가 노동과 비용이 필요하게 합니다. 이 문제를 처리하기 위해서 입주민 조합은 재활용하는 날을 결정했습니다. 수요일에만 여러분의 재활용품을 내놓을 수 있다는 것을 알려드리고 싶습니다. 그것이 우리 아파트 단지를 훨씬 더 쾌적해 보이게 만들 것이라고 저는 확신합니다. 여러분의 협조에 미리 감사드립니다.

## 19 심경

It was a day I was due to give a presentation at work, not something I'd do often. As I stood up to begin, I froze. A chilly

'pins-and-needles' feeling crept over me, starting in my hands. Time seemed to stand still as I struggled to start speaking, and I

felt a pressure around my throat, as though my voice was trapped and couldn't come out. Gazing around at the blur of faces, I

realized they were all waiting for me to begin, but by now I knew I couldn't continue.

내가 직장에서 발표를 하기로 한 날이었고 내가 자주 하곤 했던 것이 아니었다. 시작하려고 일어섰을 때 나는 얼어붙었다. '핀과 바늘로 찌르는 듯한' 차가운 느낌이 손에서 시작해서 나를 엄습했다. 내가 말하기 시작하려고 애쓸 때 시간이 정지해 있는 것 같았고 나는 목 부근에서 압박감을 느꼈는데 마치 내 목소리가 갇혀서 빠져나올 수 없는 것 같았다. 흐릿한 형체의 얼굴들을 둘러보며 나는 그들이 모두 내가 시작하기를 기다리고 있다는 것을 깨달았지만 그때쯤 나는 내가 계속할 수 없다는 것을 알았다.

# 20 주장

No matter what your situation, whether you are an insider or an outsider, you need to become the voice that challenges yesterday's answers. Think about the characteristics that make outsiders valuable to an organization. They are the people who have the perspective to see problems that the insiders are too close to really notice. They are the ones who have the freedom to point out these problems and criticize them without risking their job or their career. Part of adopting an outsider mentality is forcing yourself to look around your organization with this disassociated, less emotional perspective. If you didn't know your coworkers and feel bonded to them by your shared experiences, what would you think of them? You may not have the job security or confidence to speak your mind to management, but you can make these "outsider" assessments of your organization on your own and use what you determine to advance your career.

여러분의 상황이 어떠하든, 여러분이 내부자이건 외부자이건, 여러분은 어제의 정답에 이의를 제기하는 목소리가 될 필요가 있다. 외부자를 조직에게 가치 있게 만드는 특성들에 관해 생각해 보라. 그들은 내부자가 너무 가까이 있어서 정말 알아차릴 수 없는 문제들을 볼 수 있는 관점을 가진 사람들이다. 그들은 자신의 일자리나 자신의 경력을 위태롭게 하지 않고 이런 문제들을 지적하고 그것들을 비판할 수 있는 자유를 가진 사람들이다. 외부자의 사고방식을 채택하는 것의 일부는 이렇게 분리된, 덜 감정적인 관점으로 여러분의 조직을 스스로 둘러보게 하는 것이다. 여러분이 자신의 동료를 모르고 여러분의 공유된 경험에 의해 그들에게 결속되어 있다고 느끼지 않는다면 여러분은 그들에 관해 어떻게 생각하겠는가? 여러분이 자신의 생각을 경영진에게 말할 직업 안정성이나 자신감을 갖고 있지 않을지도 모르지만 여러분은 자신의 조직에 관해 이런 '외부자의' 평가를 독자적으로 할 수 있고 여러분이 판정한 것을 자신의 경력을 발전시키기 위해 이용할 수 있다.

# 21 추론

The known fact of contingencies, without knowing precisely what those contingencies will be, shows that disaster preparation is not the same thing as disaster rehearsal. No matter how many mock disasters are staged according to prior plans, the real disaster will never mirror any one of them. Disaster-preparation planning is more like training for a marathon than training for a high-jump competition or a sprinting event. Marathon runners do not practice by running the full course of twenty-six miles; rather, they get into shape by running shorter distances and building up their endurance with cross-training. If they have prepared successfully, then they are in optimal condition to run the marathon over its predetermined course and length, assuming a range of weather conditions, predicted or not. This is normal marathon preparation.

비상사태에 관해 이미 알려진 사실은, 그 비상사태가 어떤 것이 될 것인지 정확히 아는 것이 없이, 재난 대비가 재난 예행연습과 똑같은 것이 아니라는 것을 보여 준다. 아무리 많은 모의 재난이 사전 계획에 따라 조직되더라도 실제 재난은 그런 것들 중 어느 하나라도 그대로 반영하지 않을 것이다. 재난 대비 계획 세우기는 높이뛰기 시합이나 단거리 달리기 경주를 위해 훈련하는 것이라기보다는 마라톤을 위해 훈련하는 것과 더 비슷하다. 마라톤 선수들은 26마일 전체 코스를 달리는 것으로 연습하는 것이 아니라 오히려 더 짧은 거리를 달리고 여러 가지 운동을 조합하여 행하는 훈련법으로 자신의 지구력을 강화함으로써 몸 상태를 좋게 만든다. 만약 그들이 성공적으로 준비했다면 그들은 마라톤의 미리 정해진 코스와 길이에 걸쳐 예상되었든 아니든 다양한 기상 조건을 가정하면서 마라톤을 달릴 수 있는 최적의 상태에 있다. 이것이 보통의 마라톤 준비이다.

## 22 요지

Fears of damaging ecosystems are based on the sound conservationist principle that we should aim to minimize the disruption we cause, but there is a risk that this principle may be confused with the old idea of a 'balance of nature.' This supposes a perfect order of nature that will seek to maintain itself and that we should not change. It is a romantic, not to say idyllic, notion, but deeply misleading because it supposes a static condition. Ecosystems are dynamic, and although some may endure, apparently unchanged, for periods that are long in comparison with the human lifespan, they must and do change eventually. Species come and go, climates change, plant and animal communities adapt to altered circumstances, and when examined in fine detail such adaptation and consequent change can be seen to be taking place constantly. The 'balance of nature' is a myth. Our planet is dynamic, and so are the arrangements by which its inhabitants live together.

생태계를 손상하는 것에 대한 두려움은 우리가 초래하는 (환경) 파괴를 최소화하는 것을 목표로 해야 한다는 건전한 환경 보호주의자 원칙을 바탕으로 하지만, 이 원칙이 '자연의 균형'이라는 오래된 생각과 혼동될지도 모른다는 위험이 있다. 이것은 그 자체를 유지하려고 노력하고 우리가 바꾸어서는 안 되는 완벽한 자연의 질서를 전제로 한다. 그것은 목가적이라고까지는 할 수 없어도 낭만적인 개념이지만 정적인 상태를 전제로 하기 때문에 매우 잘못된 인식을 준다. 생태계는 역동적이고, 일부는 겉보기에는 변하지 않는 채로 인간의 수명과 비교해 보면 오랜 기간 동안 지속될지 모르지만, 그것은 결국 변할 것임에 틀림없고 정말 변한다. 생물 종(種)들은 생겼다 사라지고 기후는 변하며 동식물 군집은 달라진 환경에 적응하고 미세하게 자세히 검토하면 그런 적응과 결과적인 변화는 항상 일어나고 있는 것으로 보일 수 있다. '자연의 균형'은 잘못된 통념이다. 지구는 역동적이고 지구의 서식자들이 함께 사는 모습[생활 방식]도 그러하다.

## 23 주제

Before the modern scientific era, creativity was attributed to a superhuman force; all novel ideas originated with the gods. After all, how could a person create something that did not exist before the divine act of creation? In fact, the Latin meaning of the verb "inspire" is "to breathe into," reflecting the belief that creative inspiration was similar to the moment in creation when God first breathed life into man. Plato argued that the poet was possessed by divine inspiration, and Plotin wrote that art could only be beautiful if it descended from God. The artist's job was not to imitate nature but rather to reveal the sacred and transcendent qualities of nature. Art could only be a pale imitation of the perfection of the world of ideas. Greek artists did not blindly imitate what they saw in reality; instead they tried to represent the pure, true forms underlying reality, resulting in a sort of compromise between abstraction and accuracy.

근대의 과학적인 시대 이전에 창의성은 초인적인 힘에 기인한 것으로 여겼는데 모든 새로운 생각은 신에게서 유래했다. 결국 신의 창조 행위 이전에 존재하지 않았던 것을 어떻게 인간이 만들 수 있었겠는가? 사실, '영감을 주다'라는 동사의 라틴어의 의미는 '숨결을 불어넣다'이고 창의적 영감은 신이 처음에 인간에게 생명을 불어 넣었을 때 창조의 순간과 비슷했다는 믿음을 반영한다. Plato는 시인은 신이 내린 영감에 사로잡혔다고 주장했고 Plotin은 예술은 그것이 신으로부터 내려온 경우에만 아름다울 수 있다고 썼다. 예술가의 일은 자연을 모방하는 것이라기보다는 오히려 자연의 신성하고 초월적인 특성을 드러내는 것이었다. 예술은 관념[이데아]의 세계의 완벽함을 어설프게 흉내 낸 것에 불과한 것일 수 있었다. 그리스의 예술가들은 그들이 현실에서 본 것을 맹목적으로 모방하지 않았고 그 대신 현실의 근저에 있는 순수하고 진정한 형태를 나타내려고 애썼는데 그 결과 추상과 정확성 간의 일종의 타협을 발생시켰다.

## 24 제목

Some beginning researchers mistakenly believe that a good hypothesis is one that is guaranteed to be right (e.g., alcohol will slow down reaction time). However, if we already know your hypothesis is true before you test it, testing your hypothesis won't tell us anything new. Remember, research is supposed to produce new knowledge. To get new knowledge, you, as a researcher-explorer, need to leave the safety of the shore (established facts) and venture into uncharted waters (as Einstein said, "If we knew what we were doing, it would not be called research, would it?"). If your predictions about what will happen in these uncharted waters are wrong, that's okay: Scientists are allowed to make mistakes (as Bates said, "Research is the process of going up alleys to see if they are blind"). Indeed, scientists often learn more from predictions that do not turn out than from those that do.

일부 처음 시작하는 연구자들은 좋은 가설은 옳다는 것이 보장된 것이라고 잘못 믿는다(예를 들면, '알코올은 반응 시간을 둔화시킬 것이다.'). 하지만 여러분의 가설을 여러분이 검사해 보기 전에 그것이 사실이라고 이미 우리가 알고 있다면 여러분의 가설을 검사하는 것은 우리에게 아무런 새로운 것도 말해 주지 않을 것이다. 연구란 '새로운' 지식을 생산해야 한다는 것을 기억하라. 새로운 지식을 얻기 위해서 연구자이자 탐험가로서 여러분은 해변의 안전함(기정 사실)을 떠나 미개척 영역으로 과감히 들어가 볼 필요가 있다(아인슈타인이 말했듯이, "우리가 무엇을 하고 있는지 안다면 그것은 연구라고 불리지 않을 것이다, 그렇지?"). 이런 미개척 영역에서 무엇이 일어날 것인지에 관한 여러분의 예측이 틀린다면 그것은 괜찮다. 과학자는 실수를 저지르도록 허용되어 있다(Bates가 말했듯이, "연구는 막다른 길인지 보려고 골목길을 올라가 보는 과정이다."). 정말로 과학자는 흔히 결과를 내는 예측들보다는 결과를 내지 않는 예측들로부터 더 많이 배운다.

## 29 어법

While reflecting on the needs of organizations, leaders, and families today, we realize that one of the unique characteristics is inclusivity. Why? Because inclusivity supports what everyone ultimately wants from their relationships: collaboration. Yet the majority of leaders, organizations, and families are still using the language of the old paradigm in which one person — typically the oldest, most educated, and/or wealthiest — makes all the decisions, and their decisions rule with little discussion or inclusion of others, resulting in exclusivity. Today, this person could be a director, CEO, or other senior leader of an organization. There is no need for others to present their ideas because they are considered inadequate. Yet research shows that exclusivity in problem solving, even with a genius, is not as effective as inclusivity, where everyone's ideas are heard and a solution is developed through collaboration.

오늘날 조직, 지도자, 그리고 가족의 요구에 관해 곰곰이 생각할 때 우리는 독특한 특성 중 하나가 포용성이라는 것을 깨닫는다. 왜 그런가? 포용성은 모든 사람이 자신의 관계에서 궁극적으로 원하는 것인 협력을 뒷받침하기 때문이다. 그러나 대다수의 지도자, 조직, 그리고 가족은 여전히 오래된 패러다임의 언어를 사용하고 있고, 거기서는 한 사람이, 보통 가장 연장자, 가장 교육을 많이 받은 사람, 그리고 / 또는 가장 부유한 사람인데, 모든 결정을 내리고 토론이나 다른 사람을 포함시키는 것이 거의 없이 그들의 결정이 지배하고 결과적으로 배타성을 초래한다. 오늘날 이 사람은 어떤 조직의 관리자, 최고 경영자, 또는 다른 상급 지도자일 수 있다. 다른 사람들이 자신의 생각을 제시할 필요가 없는데 왜냐하면 그것은 부적절한 것으로 여겨지기 때문이다. 그러나 연구에 따르면 문제 해결에 있어서 배타성은, 심지어 천재와 함께하는 것이더라도, 포용성만큼 효과적이지 않은데, 포용성이 있는 경우에는 모든 사람의 생각을 듣게 되고 해결책은 협력을 통해 발전된다.

## 30 어휘

The objective point of view is illustrated by John Ford's "philosophy of camera." Ford considered the camera to be a window and the audience to be outside the window viewing the people and events within. We are asked to watch the actions as if they were taking place at a distance, and we are not asked to participate. The objective point of view employs a static camera as much as possible in order to produce this window effect, and it concentrates on the actors and the action without drawing attention to the camera. The objective camera suggests an emotional distance between camera and subject; the camera seems simply to be recording, as straightforwardly as possible, the characters and actions of the story. For the most part, the director uses natural, normal types of camera positioning and camera angles. The objective camera does not comment on or interpret the action but merely records it, letting it unfold. We see the action from the viewpoint of an impersonal observer. If the camera moves, it does so unnoticeably, calling as little attention to itself as possible.

객관적인 관점은 John Ford의 '카메라의 철학'에 의해 설명된다. Ford는 카메라를 창문이라고 생각했고 관객은 창문 안에 있는 사람과 사건을 바라보면서 창문 밖에 있다고 생각했다. 우리는 사건들이 멀리서 일어나고 있는 것처럼 그것들을 바라보도록 요청받고, 참여하도록 요청받지 않는다. 객관적인 관점은 이런 창문 효과를 만들기 위해 정적인 카메라를 가능한 한 많이 이용하고, 그것은 카메라에 관심을 끄는 것 없이 배우와 사건에 집중한다. 객관적인 카메라는 카메라와 대상 간의 감정적인 거리를 보여 주는데, 카메라는 이야기의 등장인물과 사건을 가능한 한 있는 그대로 그저 기록하고 있는 것으로 보인다. 대부분의 경우, 감독은 자연스럽고 일반적인 종류의 카메라 위치 선정과 카메라 각도를 사용한다. 객관적인 카메라는 사건에 관해 논평하거나 해석하지 않고 그것이 전개되게 하면서 그저 그것을 기록한다. 우리는 냉담한 관찰자의 관점에서 사건을 본다. 만약 카메라가 움직인다면 그것은 눈에 띄지 않게, 가능한 한 자신[카메라]에게 거의 관심을 불러일으키지 않으면서, 그렇게 한다.

## 31 빈칸

Even the most respectable of all musical institutions, the symphony orchestra, carries inside its DNA the legacy of the hunt. The various instruments in the orchestra can be traced back to these primitive origins — their earliest forms were made either from the animal (horn, hide, gut, bone) or the weapons employed in bringing the animal under control (stick, bow). Are we wrong to hear this history in the music itself, in the formidable aggression and awe-inspiring assertiveness of those monumental symphonies that remain the core repertoire of the world's leading orchestras? Listening to Beethoven, Brahms, Mahler, Bruckner, Berlioz, Tchaikovsky, Shostakovich, and other great composers, I can easily summon up images of bands of men starting to chase animals, using sound as a source and symbol of dominance, an expression of the will to predatory power.

심지어 모든 음악 단체 중 가장 훌륭한 단체인 교향악단도 자신의 DNA 안에 사냥의 유산을 지니고 있다. 교향악단에 있는 다양한 악기들은 다음의 원시적인 기원으로 거슬러 올라갈 수 있는데, 그것들의 초기 형태는 동물(뿔, 가죽, 내장, 뼈) 또는 동물을 진압하기 위해 사용된 무기(막대, 활)로 만들어졌다. 음악 그 자체에서, 세계의 주요한 교향악단의 핵심 레퍼토리로 남아 있는 기념비적인 교향곡들의 강력한 공격성과 경외감을 자아내는 당당함에서 이러한 역사를 듣는다면 우리가 틀린 것인가? 베토벤, 브람스, 말러, 브루크너, 베를리오즈, 차이코프스키, 쇼스타코비치 및 다른 위대한 작곡가들의 음악을 들으며, 나는 소리를 지배의 원천이자 상징으로, 공격적인 힘에 대한 의지의 표현으로 사용하면서 동물을 쫓기 시작하는 사람들 무리의 이미지를 쉽게 떠올릴 수 있다.

# 32 빈칸

Our brains have evolved to remember unexpected events because basic survival depends on the ability to perceive causes and predict effects. If the brain predicts one event and experiences another, the unusualness will be especially interesting and will be encoded accordingly. Neurologist and classroom teacher Judith Willis has claimed that surprise in the classroom is one of the most effective ways of teaching with brain stimulation in mind. If students are exposed to new experiences via demonstrations or through the unexpected enthusiasm of their teachers or peers, they will be much more likely to connect with the information that follows. Willis has written that encouraging active discovery in the classroom allows students to interact with new information, moving it beyond working memory to be processed in the frontal lobe, which is devoted to advanced cognitive functioning. Preference for novelty sets us up for learning by directing attention, providing stimulation to developing perceptual systems, and feeding curious and exploratory behavior.

우리의 뇌는 예상치 못한 사건들을 기억하도록 진화해 왔는데, 왜냐하면 기본적인 생존이 원인을 인식하고 결과를 예측하는 능력에 달려 있기 때문이다. 만약 뇌가 어떤 사건을 예측하고 (그것과) 다른 사건을 경험한다면, 그 특이함은 특히 흥미로울 것이고 그에 따라 (뇌 속의 정보로) 입력될 것이다. 신경학자이자 학급 교사인 Judith Willis는 교실에서의 놀라움은 뇌 자극을 염두에 두고 가르치는 가장 효과적인 방법 중 하나라고 주장했다. 학생들이 실연, 혹은 교사나 또래 친구의 예상치 못한 열의를 통해 새로운 경험에 노출되면, 그들은 뒤따르는 정보와 연결될 가능성이 훨씬 더 클 것이다. Willis는 교실에서의 능동적인 발견을 장려하는 것이 학생들로 하여금 새로운 정보와 상호 작용하게 해 주어서, 그것(새로운 정보)이 작동 기억을 넘어 고도의 인지 기능을 전담하는 (대뇌의) 전두엽에서 처리되도록 한다고 기술했다. 새로움에 대한 선호는, 주의를 이끌고, 지각 체계를 발전시키는 데 자극을 제공하며, 호기심 많고 탐구적인 행동을 충족함으로써 우리를 학습하도록 준비시킨다.

---

# 33 빈칸

Psychological research has shown that people naturally divide up cognitive labor, often without thinking about it. Imagine you're cooking up a special dinner with a friend. You're a great cook, but your friend is the wine expert, an amateur sommelier. A neighbor drops by and starts telling you both about the terrific new wines being sold at the liquor store just down the street. There are many new wines, so there's a lot to remember. How hard are you going to try to remember what the neighbor has to say about which wines to buy? Why bother when the information would be better retained by the wine expert sitting next to you? If your friend wasn't around, you might try harder. After all, it would be good to know what a good wine would be for the evening's festivities. But your friend, the wine expert, is likely to remember the information without even trying.

심리학 연구에 따르면, 사람들은 자연스럽게 인지 노동을 나누는데, 흔히 그것에 대해서 별 생각 없이 그렇게 한다. 여러분이 친구와 함께 특별한 저녁식사를 요리하고 있다고 상상해 보라. 여러분은 요리를 잘하지만, 친구는 아마추어 소믈리에라고 할 수 있는 와인 전문가이다. 이웃이 들르더니 여러분 두 사람에게 거리를 따라가면 바로 있는 주류 가게에서 파는 기막히게 좋은 새로운 와인에 대해 말하기 시작한다. 많은 새로운 와인이 있어서 기억해야 할 것이 많다. 어떤 와인을 사야 하는지에 관해 이웃이 할 말을 기억하기 위해 여러분은 얼마나 열심히 노력할까? 여러분 옆에 앉아 있는 와인 전문가가 그 정보를 더 잘 기억하고 있는데 무엇 하러 그러겠는가? 여러분의 친구가 곁에 없다면 더 열심히 애쓸지도 모른다. 어쨌든 저녁 만찬을 위해 뭐가 좋은 와인이 될지 아는 것은 좋은 일일 것이다. 하지만, 와인 전문가인 여러분의 친구는 애쓰지도 않고 그 정보를 기억하기가 쉽다.

## 34 빈칸

Even companies that sell physical products to make profit are forced by their boards and investors to reconsider their underlying motives and to collect as much data as possible from consumers. Supermarkets no longer make all their money selling their produce and manufactured goods. They give you loyalty cards with which they track your purchasing behaviors precisely. Then supermarkets sell this purchasing behavior to marketing analytics companies. The marketing analytics companies perform machine learning procedures, slicing the data in new ways, and resell behavioral data back to product manufacturers as marketing insights. When data and machine learning become currencies of value in a capitalist system, then every company's natural tendency is to maximize its ability to conduct surveillance on its own customers because the customers are themselves the new value-creation devices.

수익을 내기 위해 물적 제품을 판매하는 기업조차도 이사회와 투자자에 의해 어쩔 수 없이 자신의 근원적인 동기를 재고하게 되고 고객에게서 가능한 한 많은 정보를 수집하게 된다. 슈퍼마켓은 더 이상 자신의 농산물과 제조된 물품을 판매해서 자신의 모든 돈을 버는 것이 아니다. 그들은 여러분의 구매 행동을 정밀하게 추적하게 해 주는 고객 우대 카드를 여러분에게 준다. 그러고 나서 슈퍼마켓은 이 구매 행위를 마케팅 분석 기업에 판매한다. 마케팅 분석 기업은 기계 학습 절차를 수행하고 그 정보를 새로운 방식으로 쪼개서 행동 정보를 제품 제조 기업에 통찰력 있는 마케팅 정보로 다시 되판다. 정보와 기계 학습이 자본주의 체제에서 가치 있는 통화가 될 때, 고객 자체가 새로운 가치 창출 장치이기 때문에 모든 기업의 자연스러운 경향은 자신의 고객을 관찰하는 능력을 최대화하는 것이다.

## 35 무관

Academics, politicians, marketers and others have in the past debated whether or not it is ethically correct to market products and services directly to young consumers. This is also a dilemma for psychologists who have questioned whether they ought to help advertisers manipulate children into purchasing more products they have seen advertised. Advertisers have admitted to taking advantage of the fact that it is easy to make children feel that they are losers if they do not own the 'right' products. Clever advertising informs children that they will be viewed by their peers in an unfavorable way if they do not have the products that are advertised, thereby playing on their emotional vulnerabilities. The constant feelings of inadequateness created by advertising have been suggested to contribute to children becoming fixated with instant gratification and beliefs that material possessions are important.

지금까지 대학 교수, 정치인, 마케팅 담당자, 그리고 그 외의 사람들은 제품과 서비스를 어린 소비자들에게 직접 판촉하는 것이 윤리적으로 옳은지 그렇지 않은지를 논쟁해 왔다. 이것은 또한, 광고주들이 아이들을 조종해서 광고되는 것을 그들이 본 더 많은 제품을 구매하게 하는 것을 도와야 하는지 의문을 제기하는 심리학자들에게도 딜레마이다. 광고주들은 아이들이 그 '적절한' 제품을 소유하고 있지 않으면 자신이 패배자라고 느끼게 만드는 것이 쉽다는 사실을 이용한 것을 인정했다. 영리한 광고는 아이들에게 만약 그들이 광고되는 제품을 가지고 있지 않으면 자신의 또래 친구들에게 부정적으로 보일 것이라고 알려 주고, 그로 인해 아이들의 정서적인 취약성을 이용한다. 광고가 만들어 내는, 끊임없이 부적절하다고 느끼는 감정은, 아이들이 즉각적인 만족감과 물질적 소유물이 중요하다는 믿음에 집착하게 되는 데 기여한다고 언급되어 왔다.

# 36 순서

Once we recognize the false-cause issue, we see it everywhere. For example, a recent long-term study of University of Toronto medical students concluded that medical school class presidents lived an average of 2.4 years less than other medical school graduates. At first glance, this seemed to imply that being a medical school class president is bad for you. Does this mean that you should avoid being medical school class president at all costs? Probably not. Just because being class president is correlated with shorter life expectancy does not mean that it causes shorter life expectancy. In fact, it seems likely that the sort of person who becomes medical school class president is, on average, extremely hard-working, serious, and ambitious. Perhaps this extra stress, and the corresponding lack of social and relaxation time — rather than being class president per se — contributes to lower life expectancy. If so, the real lesson of the study is that we should all relax a little and not let our work take over our lives.

일단 잘못 파악한 원인 문제를 우리가 인식하면, 우리는 그것을 어디에서나 보게 된다. 예를 들어, 토론토 대학의 의대생들에 대한 최근의 장기간의 연구는 의대 학년 대표들이 다른 의대 졸업생들보다 평균 2.4년 더 적게 살았다는 결론을 내렸다. 처음 봐서는, 이것이 의대 학년 대표인 것이 여러분에게 해롭다는 것을 의미하는 것처럼 보였다. 이것은 여러분이 무슨 수를 써서라도 의대 학년 대표가 되는 것을 피해야 한다는 것을 의미하는가? 아마도 그렇지는 않을 것이다. 단지 학년 대표인 것이 더 짧은 평균 수명과 서로 관련된다고 해서 그것이 더 짧은 평균 수명을 '유발한다'는 의미는 아니다. 사실, 아마도 의대 학년 대표가 되는 그런 부류의 사람은 평균적으로 몹시 열심히 공부하고, 진지하며, 야망이 있는 것 같다. 의대 학년 대표인 것 그 자체라기보다 아마도 이러한 가중된 스트레스와 그에 상응하는 사교와 휴식 시간의 부족이 더 짧은 평균 수명의 원인인 것 같다. 만약 그렇다면, 이 연구의 진정한 교훈은 우리 모두가 약간의 휴식을 취해야 하고 우리의 일이 우리의 삶을 장악하게 해서는 안 된다는 것이다.

---

# 37 순서

We commonly argue about the fairness of taxation — whether this or that tax will fall more heavily on the rich or the poor. But the expressive dimension of taxation goes beyond debates about fairness, to the moral judgements societies make about which activities are worthy of honor and recognition, and which ones should be discouraged. Sometimes, these judgements are explicit. Taxes on tobacco, alcohol, and casinos are called "sin taxes" because they seek to discourage activities considered harmful or undesirable. Such taxes express society's disapproval of these activities by raising the cost of engaging in them. Proposals to tax sugary sodas (to combat obesity) or carbon emissions (to address climate change) likewise seek to change norms and shape behavior. Not all taxes have this aim. We do not tax income to express disapproval of paid employment or to discourage people from engaging in it. Nor is a general sales tax intended as a deterrent to buying things. These are simply ways of raising revenue.

우리는 흔히 과세의 공정성, 즉 이런 저런 세금이 부자들에게 더 과중하게 부과될 것인지 아니면 가난한 사람들에게 그럴 것인지에 관해 논한다. 그러나 과세의 표현적 차원은 공정성에 대한 논쟁을 넘어, 어떤 활동이 명예와 인정을 받을 가치가 있고 어떤 활동이 억제되어야 하는지에 대해 사회가 내리는 도덕적 판단에까지 이른다. 때때로 이러한 판단은 명백하다. 담배, 술, 그리고 카지노에 대한 세금은 해롭거나 바람직하지 않은 것으로 간주되는 활동들을 억제하려고 하기 때문에 '죄악세'라고 불린다. 그런 세금은 이러한 활동을 하는 데 드는 비용을 증가시킴으로써 그것에 대한 사회의 반대를 표현한다. 마찬가지로 (비만에 맞서기 위해) 설탕이 든 탄산음료에 세금을 부과하는 제안이나 (기후 변화에 대처하기 위해) 탄소 배출에 세금을 부과하는 제안은 규범을 바꾸고 행동을 형성하려 한다. 모든 세금이 이런 목적을 가진 것은 아니다. 우리는 유급 고용에 대한 반대를 표명하거나 사람들이 그것을 하는 것을 막기 위해 소득에 세금을 부과하는 것은 아니다. 일반 판매세 역시 물건을 사는 것의 억제책으로서 의도된 것이 아니다. 이것들은 단순히 세입을 올리는 방법이다.

## 38 삽입

Most beliefs — but not all — are open to tests of verification. This means that beliefs can be tested to see if they are correct or false. Beliefs can be verified or falsified with objective criteria external to the person. There are people who believe the Earth is flat and not a sphere. Because we have objective evidence that the Earth is in fact a sphere, the flat Earth belief can be shown to be false. Also, the belief that it will rain tomorrow can be tested for truth by waiting until tomorrow and seeing whether it rains or not. However, some types of beliefs cannot be tested for truth because we cannot get external evidence in our lifetimes (such as a belief that the Earth will stop spinning on its axis by the year 9999 or that there is life on a planet 100-million light-years away). Also, meta-physical beliefs (such as the existence and nature of a god) present considerable challenges in generating evidence that everyone is willing to use as a truth criterion.

전부는 아니지만 대부분의 믿음은 검증 시험을 받을 수 있다. 이것은 믿음이 옳거나 그른지를 확인하기 위해 시험될 수 있다는 것을 의미한다. 믿음은 그 사람의 외부에 있는 객관적인 기준을 통해 진실임이 입증되거나 거짓임이 입증될 수 있다. 지구가 평평하고 구가 아니라고 믿는 사람들이 있다. 우리는 지구가 사실은 구라는 객관적인 증거를 가지고 있기 때문에, 지구가 평평하다는 믿음은 거짓임이 증명될 수 있다. 또한, 내일 비가 올 것이라는 믿음은 내일까지 기다려 비가 오는지 안 오는지 봄으로써 진실인지 확인될 수 있다. 하지만, (9999년이 되면 지구가 자전하는 것을 멈출 것이라는 믿음이나 1억 광년 떨어진 행성에 생명체가 있다는 것 같은) 어떤 종류의 믿음은 우리가 일생 동안 외부 증거를 얻을 수 없기 때문에 진실인지 확인될 수 없다. 또한, (신의 존재와 본질과 같은) 형이상학적 믿음은 모든 사람이 진리 기준으로 기꺼이 사용할 증거를 만드는 데 있어서 상당한 난제가 된다.

## 39 삽입

Everyone automatically categorizes and generalizes all the time. Unconsciously. It is not a question of being prejudiced or enlightened. Categories are absolutely necessary for us to function. They give structure to our thoughts. Imagine if we saw every item and every scenario as truly unique — we would not even have a language to describe the world around us. But the necessary and useful instinct to generalize can distort our world view. It can make us mistakenly group together things, or people, or countries that are actually very different. It can make us assume everything or everyone in one category is similar. And, maybe, most unfortunate of all, it can make us jump to conclusions about a whole category based on a few, or even just one, unusual example.

모든 사람들은 항상 자동적으로 분류하고 일반화한다. 무의식적으로 (그렇게 한다). 그것은 편견을 갖고 있다거나 계몽되어 있다는 것의 문제가 아니다. 범주는 우리가 (정상적으로) 활동하는 데 반드시 필요하다. 그것들은 우리의 사고에 체계를 준다. 만일 우리가 모든 품목과 모든 있을 법한 상황을 정말로 유일무이한 것으로 본다고 상상해 보라. 그러면 우리는 우리 주변의 세계를 설명할 언어조차 갖지 못할 것이다. 그러나 필요하고 유용한 일반화하려는 본능은 우리의 세계관을 왜곡할 수 있다. 그것은 우리가 실제로는 아주 다른 사물들이나, 사람들, 혹은 나라들을 하나로 잘못 묶게 만들 수 있다. 그것은 우리가 하나의 범주 안에 있는 모든 것이나 모든 사람이 비슷하다고 가정하게 만들 수 있다. 그리고 어쩌면 모든 것 중에서 가장 유감스러운 것은, 그것이 우리로 하여금 몇 가지, 또는 심지어 고작 하나의 특이한 사례를 바탕으로 전체 범주에 대해 성급하게 결론을 내리게 만들 수 있다는 것이다.

# 40 요약

At the University of Iowa, students were briefly shown numbers that they had to memorize. Then they were offered the choice of either a fruit salad or a chocolate cake. When the number the students memorized was seven digits long, 63% of them chose the cake. When the number they were asked to remember had just two digits, however, 59% opted for the fruit salad. Our reflective brains know that the fruit salad is better for our health, but our reflexive brains desire that soft, fattening chocolate cake. If the reflective brain is busy figuring something else out — like trying to remember a seven-digit number — then impulse can easily win. On the other hand, if we're not thinking too hard about something else (with only a minor distraction like memorizing two digits), then the reflective system can deny the emotional impulse of the reflexive side.

→ According to the above experiment, the increased intellective load on the brain leads the reflexive side of the brain to become dominant.

Iowa 대학교에서, 학생들에게 그들이 암기해야 하는 숫자를 잠시 보여 주었다. 그리고 나서 그들에게 과일 샐러드나 초콜릿 케이크 중 하나를 선택하게 했다. 학생들이 외운 숫자가 일곱 자리일 때, 그들 중 63%가 케이크를 선택했다. 그러나 그들이 기억하도록 요청받은 숫자가 두 자리밖에 되지 않았을 때, 59%는 과일 샐러드를 선택했다. 우리의 숙고하는 뇌는 과일 샐러드가 우리의 건강에 더 좋다는 것을 알지만, 우리의 반사적인 뇌는 그 부드럽고 살이 찌는 초콜릿 케이크를 원한다. 만약 숙고하는 뇌가 일곱 자리 숫자를 기억하려고 애쓰는 일과 같은 다른 어떤 것을 해결하느라 바쁘다면, 충동이 쉽게 이길 수 있다. 다른 한편, 우리가 다른 것에 관해 너무 열심히 생각하고 있지 않다면(두 자리 숫자를 외우는 것과 같은 사소하게 주의를 산만하게 하는 일만 있을 때), 숙고하는 (뇌의) 계통은 반사적인 쪽의 감정적인 충동을 억제할 수 있다.
→ 위 실험에 따르면, 뇌에 가해지는 증가된 지적 부담은 뇌의 반사적인 부분이 우세해지게 한다.

# 41~42 제목, 어휘

Test scores are not a measure of self-worth; however, we often associate our sense of worthiness with our performance on an exam. Thoughts such as "If I don't pass this test, I'm a failure" are mental traps not rooted in truth. Failing a test is failing a test, nothing more. It is in no way descriptive of your value as a person. Believing that test performance is a reflection of your virtue places unreasonable pressure on your performance. Not passing the certification test only means that your certification status has been delayed. Maintaining a positive attitude is therefore important. If you have studied hard, reaffirm this mentally and believe that you will do well. If, on the other hand, you did not study as hard as you should have or wanted to, accept that as beyond your control for now and attend to the task of doing the best you can. If things do not go well this time, you know what needs to be done in preparation for the next exam. Talk to yourself in positive terms. Avoid rationalizing past or future test performance by placing the blame on secondary variables. Thoughts such as, "I didn't have enough time," or "I should have …," compound the stress of test-taking. Take control by affirming your value, self-worth, and dedication to meeting the test challenge head on. Repeat to yourself "I can and I will pass this exam."

시험 점수는 자부심의 척도가 아니지만, 우리는 흔히 우리의 자부심과 우리의 시험 성적을 연관시킨다. "이 시험에 합격하지 못하면 나는 실패자야."와 같은 생각은 사실에 뿌리를 두고 있지 않은 정신적 함정이다. 시험에 실패하는 것은 시험에 실패하는 것이지, 그 이상이 아니다. 그것은 결코 사람으로서의 여러분의 가치를 설명하지 않는다. 시험 성적이 여러분의 미덕을 반영하는 것이라고 믿는 것은 여러분의 수행에 부당한 압력을 가한다. 자격 시험을 통과하지 못한 것은 단지 여러분의 자격 지위가 지연되었다는 것을 의미할 따름이다. 그러므로 긍정적인 태도를 유지하는 것이 중요하다. 만약 여러분이 열심히 공부했다면, 마음속으로 이것을 재확인하고 좋은 성적이 나올 것이라고 믿으라. 다른 한편, 만약 여러분이 했어야 하거나 원하는 만큼 열심히 공부하지 않았다면, 지금으로서는 여러분이 어찌할 수 없는 것으로 그것을 받아들이고 여러분이 할 수 있는 최선의 것을 하는 과제에 주의를 기울이라. 만약 이번에 잘 되지 않는다면, 다음 시험 준비에서는 무엇을 해야 될지 알게 된다. 긍정적인 말로 자신에게 이야기하라. 부차적인 변수에 책임을 지움으로써 과거 또는 미래의 시험 성적을 합리화하는 것을 피하라. "나는 시간이 충분하지 않았어."라거나 "내가 그랬어야 했는데…"와 같은 생각은 시험을 보는 것의 스트레스를 완화시킨다(→ 악화시킨다). 자신의 가치, 자부심, 그리고 시험 과제에 정면으로 맞서는 것에 대한 헌신을 확인함으로써 통제권을 잡으라. "난 할 수 있고 이 시험에 합격할 거야."라고 자신에게 되풀이해 말하라.

## 43~45 순서, 지칭, 세부 내용

Once upon a time there lived a poor but cheerful shoemaker. He was so happy, he sang all day long. The children loved to stand around his window to listen to him. Next door to the shoemaker lived a rich man. He used to sit up all night to count his gold. In the morning, he went to bed, but he could not sleep because of the sound of the shoemaker's singing. One day, he thought of a way of stopping the singing. He wrote a letter to the shoemaker asking him to visit. The shoemaker came at once, and to his surprise the rich man gave him a bag of gold. When he got home again, the shoemaker opened the bag. He had never seen so much gold before! When he sat down at his bench and began, carefully, to count it, the children watched through the window. There was so much there that the shoemaker was afraid to let it out of his sight. So he took it to bed with him. But he could not sleep for worrying about it. Very early in the morning, he got up and brought his gold down from the bedroom. He had decided to hide it up the chimney instead. But he was still uneasy, and in a little while he dug a hole in the garden and buried his bag of gold in it. It was no use trying to work. He was too worried about the safety of his gold. And as for singing, he was too miserable to utter a note. He could not sleep, or work, or sing — and, worst of all, the children no longer came to see him. At last, the shoemaker felt so unhappy that he seized his bag of gold and ran next door to the rich man. "Please take back your gold," he said. "The worry of it is making me ill, and I have lost all of my friends. I would rather be a poor shoemaker, as I was before." And so the shoemaker was happy again and sang all day at his work.

옛날 옛적에 가난하지만 쾌활한 구두 만드는 사람이 살았다. 그는 너무 행복해서 하루 종일 노래를 불렀다. 아이들은 그의 창문에 둘러서서 그가 노래하는 것을 듣기 좋아했다. 구두 만드는 사람 옆집에는 부자가 살았다. 그는 자신의 금화를 세기 위해 밤을 새곤 했다. 아침에 그는 잠자리에 들었지만 구두 만드는 사람의 노랫소리 때문에 잠을 잘 수 없었다. 어느 날, 그는 그 노래를 멈추는 방법을 생각해냈다. 그는 구두 만드는 사람에게 방문해 달라고 요청하는 편지를 써 보냈다. 구두 만드는 사람은 즉시 왔고, 놀랍게도 부자는 그에게 금화가 든 가방을 주었다. 집에 다시 돌아왔을 때, 구두 만드는 사람은 그 가방을 열었다. 그는 그때까지 그렇게 많은 금화를 본 적이 없었다! 그가 의자에 앉아 조심스럽게 그것을 세기 시작했을 때, 아이들이 창문을 통해서 지켜보았다. 거기엔 금화가 너무 많아서 구두 만드는 사람은 그것을 자신에게 보이지 않는 곳에 두기가 겁났다. 그래서 그는 그것을 잠자리에 가져갔다. 그러나 그는 그것에 대한 걱정으로 잠을 잘 수 없었다. 매우 이른 아침에, 그는 일어나서 금화를 침실에서 가지고 내려왔다. 대신에 그는 그것을 굴뚝에 숨기기로 결정했다. 그러나 그는 여전히 불안했고, 잠시 후에 정원에 구멍을 파고 그 안에 금화가 든 가방을 묻었다. 일을 해보려고 해도 소용없었다. 그는 자신의 금화의 안전이 너무나 걱정되었다. 그리고 노래에 관해서라면, 그는 너무 불행해서 한 음도 낼 수 없었다. 그는 잠을 잘 수도, 일을 할 수도, 노래를 부를 수도 없었고, 최악은, 아이들이 더 이상 그를 보러 오지 않았다. 마침내, 구두 만드는 사람은 너무 불행해져서 그의 금화가 든 가방을 움켜쥐고 옆집 부자에게 달려갔다. "제발 당신의 금화를 다시 가져가세요."라고 그가 말했다. "그것에 대한 걱정이 저를 아프게 하고 있고, 저는 제 친구들을 모두 잃었어요. 저는 예전처럼 차라리 가난한 구두 만드는 사람이 되겠어요." 그래서 구두 만드는 사람은 다시 행복해졌고 일을 하면서 하루 종일 노래를 불렀다.

2021 고2 3월 모의고사          ❶ 회차 : :               점 / 250점

❶ voca    ❷ text    ❸ [ / ]    ❹ _____    ❺ quiz 1    ❻ quiz 2    ❼ quiz 3    ❽ quiz 4    ❾ quiz 5    ❿ quiz 6

## 18 목적

My name is Anthony Thompson and I am writing [ on / to ]¹⁾ behalf of the residents' association. Our [ recycled / recycling ]²⁾

program has been [ working / worked ]³⁾ well thanks to your participation. [ Therefore / However ]⁴⁾, a problem has recently [

occurred / been occurred ]⁵⁾ that needs your attention. [ Because / Because of ]⁶⁾ there is no [ given / giving ]⁷⁾ day for

recycling, residents are [ put / putting ]⁸⁾ their recycling out at any time. This makes the recycling area messy, [ that / which ]⁹⁾

requires extra labor and cost. To deal with(to부정사의 어떤 용법? _____)¹⁰⁾ this problem, the residents' association has

[ decided / been decided ]¹¹⁾ on a day to recycle. I would like to let you [ know / to know ]¹²⁾ that you can put out your

recycling on Wednesdays only. I am sure it will make our apartment complex look much more [ pleasant / pleasantly ]¹³⁾. Thank

you in advance for your cooperation.

제 이름은 Anthony Thompson이고 저는 입주민 조합을 대표하여 편지를 쓰고 있습니다. 우리의 재활용 프로그램은 여러분의 참여 덕분에 잘 운영되고 있습니다. 그런데 최근에 여러분의 관심이 필요한 문제가 생겼습니다. 재활용을 위해 정해진 날이 없어서 입주민들은 아무 때나 자신들의 재활용품을 내놓습니다. 이것이 재활용 구역을 어지럽혀서 추가 노동과 비용이 필요하게 합니다. 이 문제를 처리하기 위해서 입주민 조합은 재활용하는 날을 결정했습니다. 수요일에만 여러분의 재활용품을 내놓을 수 있다는 것을 알려드리고 싶습니다. 그것이 우리 아파트 단지를 훨씬 더 쾌적해 보이게 만들 것이라고 저는 확신합니다. 여러분의 협조에 미리 감사드립니다.

## 19 심경

It was a day I was due to give a presentation at work, not something I'd do often. As I stood up to begin, I froze. A chilly

'pins-and-needles' feeling crept over me, [ started / starting ]¹⁴⁾ in my hands. Time seemed to stand still as I [ struggled / was

struggled ]¹⁵⁾ to start speaking, and I felt a pressure around my throat, [ even though / as though ]¹⁶⁾ my voice [ trapped / was

trapped ]¹⁷⁾ and couldn't come out. Gazing(동명사? 현재분사? _____)¹⁸⁾ around at the blur of faces, I realized they

were all [ waiting / awaiting ]¹⁹⁾ for me to begin, but by now I knew I couldn't continue.

내가 직장에서 발표를 하기로 한 날이었고 내가 자주 하곤 했던 것이 아니었다. 시작하려고 일어섰을 때 나는 얼어붙었다. '핀과 바늘로 찌르는 듯한' 차가운 느낌이 손에서 시작해서 나를 엄습했다. 내가 말하기 시작하려고 애쓸 때 시간이 정지해 있는 것 같았고 나는 목 부근에서 압박감을 느꼈는데 마치 내 목소리가 갇혀서 빠져나올 수 없는 것 같았다. 흐릿한 형체의 얼굴들을 둘러보며 나는 그들이 모두 내가 시작하기를 기다리고 있다는 것을 깨달았지만 그때쯤 나는 내가 계속할 수 없다는 것을 알았다.

# 20 주장

No matter [ how / what ]20) your situation, whether you are an insider or an outsider, you need to become the voice [ that / what ]21) challenges yesterday's answers. [ Think / Thinking ]22) about the characteristics that make outsiders valuable to an organization. They are the people who have the perspective to see(to부정사의 어떤 용법? _____)23) problems that the insiders are too close to really notice. They are the ones who have the freedom to [ point / pointing ]24) out these problems and criticize them without risking their job or their career. Part of [ adapting / adopting ]25) an outsider mentality is [ forced / forcing ]26) yourself to look around your organization with this [ disassociated / disassociating ]27) , less emotional perspective. If you didn't know your coworkers and feel bonded to them by your shared experiences, [ what / how ]28) would you think of them? You may not have the job security or confidence to speak your mind to management, but you can make these "outsider" assessments of your organization on your own and use [ what / that ]29) you determine to advance your career.

여러분의 상황이 어떠하든, 여러분이 내부자이건 외부자이건, 여러분은 어제의 정답에 이의를 제기하는 목소리가 될 필요가 있다. 외부자를 조직에게 가치 있게 만드는 특성들에 관해 생각해 보라. 그들은 내부자가 너무 가까이 있어서 정말 알아차릴 수 없는 문제들을 볼 수 있는 관점을 가진 사람들이다. 그들은 자신의 일자리나 자신의 경력을 위태롭게 하지 않고 이런 문제들을 지적하고 그것들을 비판할 수 있는 자유를 가진 사람들이다. 외부자의 사고방식을 채택하는 것의 일부는 이렇게 분리된, 덜 감정적인 관점으로 여러분의 조직을 스스로 둘러보게 하는 것이다. 여러분이 자신의 동료를 모르고 여러분의 공유된 경험에 의해 그들에게 결속되어 있다고 느끼지 않는다면 여러분은 그들에 관해 어떻게 생각하겠는가? 여러분이 자신의 생각을 경영진에게 말할 직업 안정성이나 자신감을 갖고 있지 않을지도 모르지만 여러분은 자신의 조직에 관해 이런 '외부자의' 평가를 독자적으로 할 수 있고 여러분이 판정한 것을 자신의 경력을 발전시키기 위해 이용할 수 있다.

---

# 21 의미

The known fact of contingencies, [ with / without ]30) knowing precisely [ what / that ]31) those contingencies will be, [ show / shows ]32) that disaster preparation is not the same thing as disaster rehearsal. No matter [ how / what ]33) many mock disasters are staged [ in accordance / according ]34) to prior plans, the real disaster will never mirror any one of them.(무엇을 가리키는가? _____)35) Disaster-preparation planning is more like training for a marathon [ as / than ]36) training for a high-jump competition or a sprinting event. Marathon runners do not practice by running the full course of twenty-six miles; rather, they get into shape by running shorter distances and [ building / build ]37) up their endurance with cross-training. If they [ are / have ]38) prepared successfully, then they are in optimal condition to [ run / running ]39) the marathon over its predetermined course and length, assuming(동명사? 현재분사? _____)40) a range of weather conditions, predicted or not. This is normal marathon preparation.

비상사태에 관해 이미 알려진 사실은, 그 비상사태가 어떤 것이 될 것인지 정확히 아는 것이 없이, 재난 대비가 재난 예행연습과 똑같은 것이 아니라는 것을 보여 준다. 아무리 많은 모의 재난이 사전 계획에 따라 조직되더라도 실제 재난은 그런 것들 중 어느 하나라도 그대로 반영하지 않을 것이다. 재난 대비 계획 세우기는 높이뛰기 시합이나 단거리 달리기 경주를 위해 훈련하는 것이라기보다는 마라톤을 위해 훈련하는 것과 더 비슷하다. 마라톤 선수들은 26마일 전체 코스를 달리는 것으로 연습하는 것이 아니라 오히려 더 짧은 거리를 달리고 여러 가지 운동을 조합하여 행하는 훈련법으로 자신의 지구력을 강화함으로써 몸 상태를 좋게 만든다. 만약 그들이 성공적으로 준비했다면 그들은 마라톤의 미리 정해진 코스와 길이에 걸쳐 예상되었든 아니든 다양한 기상 조건을 가정하면서 마라톤을 달릴 수 있는 최적의 상태에 있다. 이것이 보통의 마라톤 준비이다.

# 22 요지

Fears of damaging ecosystems are based on the sound conservationist [ principle / principal ]⁴¹⁾ [ that / which ]⁴²⁾ we should aim to [ minimizing / minimize ]⁴³⁾ the disruption we cause, but there is a risk that(어떤 that? _____)⁴⁴⁾ this principle may be confused with the old idea of a 'balance of nature.' This supposes a perfect order of nature that will seek to maintain itself and that we should not change. It is a romantic, not to say idyllic, notion, but deeply misleading [ because / because of ]⁴⁵⁾ it supposes a static condition. Ecosystems are dynamic, and [ although / as though ]⁴⁶⁾ some may endure, apparently unchanged, for periods [ that / what ]⁴⁷⁾ are long in comparison with the human lifespan, they must and do change eventually. Species come and go, climates change, plant and animal communities [ adapt / adopt ]⁴⁸⁾ to [ altered / altering ]⁴⁹⁾ circumstances, and when [ examined / examining ]⁵⁰⁾ in fine detail such [ adoption / adaptation ]⁵¹⁾ and consequent change can be seen to be [ taking / taken ]⁵²⁾ place constantly. The 'balance of nature' is a myth. Our planet is dynamic, and so are the arrangements by which its inhabitants live together.

생태계를 손상하는 것에 대한 두려움은 우리가 초래하는 (환경) 파괴를 최소화하는 것을 목표로 해야 한다는 건전한 환경 보호주의자 원칙을 바탕으로 하지만, 이 원칙이 '자연의 균형'이라는 오래된 생각과 혼동될지도 모른다는 위험이 있다. 이것은 그 자체를 유지하려고 노력하고 우리가 바꾸어서는 안 되는 완벽한 자연의 질서를 전제로 한다. 그것은 목가적이라고까지는 할 수 없어도 낭만적인 개념이지만 정적인 상태를 전제로 하기 때문에 매우 잘못된 인식을 준다. 생태계는 역동적이고, 일부는 겉보기에는 변하지 않는 채로 인간의 수명과 비교해 보면 오랜 기간 동안 지속될지 모르지만, 그것은 결국 변할 것임에 틀림없고 정말 변한다. 생물 종(種)들은 생겼다 사라지고 기후는 변하며 동식물 군집은 달라진 환경에 적응하고 미세하게 자세히 검토하면 그런 적응과 결과적인 변화는 항상 일어나고 있는 것으로 보일 수 있다. '자연의 균형'은 잘못된 통념이다. 지구는 역동적이고 지구의 서식자들이 함께 사는 모습[생활 방식]도 그러하다.

---

# 23 주제

[ Before / After ]⁵³⁾ the modern scientific era, creativity was [ attributed / attributing ]⁵⁴⁾ to a superhuman force; all novel ideas [ originated / were originated ]⁵⁵⁾ with the gods. After all, how could a person create something [ that / what ]⁵⁶⁾ did not exist before the divine act of creation? In fact, the Latin meaning of the verb "inspire" is "to breathe into," [ reflects / reflecting ]⁵⁷⁾ the belief [ that / which ]⁵⁸⁾ creative inspiration was similar to the moment in creation [ when / which ]⁵⁹⁾ God first breathed life into man. Plato argued that the poet [ possessed / was possessed ]⁶⁰⁾ by divine inspiration, and Plotin [ written / wrote ]⁶¹⁾ that art could only be beautiful if it descended from God. The artist's job was not to imitate nature but rather to reveal(to부정사의 어떤 용법? _____)⁶²⁾ the sacred and transcendent qualities of nature. Art could only be a pale imitation of the perfection of the world of ideas. Greek artists did not blindly imitate what they saw in reality; [ thus / instead ]⁶³⁾ they tried to represent the pure, true forms underlying reality, resulting [ in / from ]⁶⁴⁾ a sort of compromise between abstraction and accuracy.

근대의 과학적인 시대 이전에 창의성은 초인적인 힘에 기인한 것으로 여겼는데 모든 새로운 생각은 신에게서 유래했다. 결국 신의 창조 행위 이전에 존재하지 않았던 것을 어떻게 인간이 만들 수 있었겠는가? 사실, '영감을 주다'라는 동사의 라틴어의 의미는 '숨결을 불어넣다'이고 창의적 영감은 신이 처음에 인간에게 생명을 불어 넣었을 때 창조의 순간과 비슷했다는 믿음을 반영한다. Plato는 시인은 신이 내린 영감에 사로잡혔다고 주장했고 Plotin은 예술은 그것이 신으로부터 내려온 경우에만 아름다울 수 있다고 썼다. 예술가의 일은 자연을 모방하는 것이라기보다는 오히려 자연의 신성하고 초월적인 특성을 드러내는 것이었다. 예술은 관념[이데아]의 세계의 완벽함을 어설프게 흉내 낸 것에 불과한 것일 수 있다. 그리스의 예술들은 그들이 현실에서 본 것을 맹목적으로 모방하지 않았고 그 대신 현실의 근저에 있는 순수하고 진정한 형태를 나타내려고 애썼는데 그 결과 추상과 정확성 간의 일종의 타협을 발생시켰다.

# 24 제목

Some beginning researchers mistakenly believe that(어떤 that? _____)65) a good hypothesis is one that is [ guaranteed / guaranteeing ]66) to be right (e.g., alcohol will slow down reaction time). [ However / Therefore ]67) , if we already know your hypothesis is true before you test it, [ testing / test ]68) your hypothesis won't tell us anything new. Remember, research is supposed to [ produce / producing ]69) new knowledge. To get new knowledge, you, as a researcher-explorer, need to leave the safety of the shore ([ established / establishing ]70) facts) and venture into [ uncharted / uncharting ]71) waters (as Einstein said, "If we knew [ what / that ]72) we were doing, it would not [ call / be called ]73) research, would it?"). If your predictions about [ what / which ]74) will [ happen / be happened ]75) in these uncharted waters [ is / are ]76) wrong, that's okay: Scientists are [ allowing / allowed ]77) to make mistakes (as Bates said, "Research is the process of going up alleys to see if they are blind"). Indeed, scientists often learn more from predictions [ that / what ]78) do not turn out than from those that do.

일부 처음 시작하는 연구자들은 좋은 가설은 옳다는 것이 보장된 것이라고 잘못 믿는다(예를 들면, '알코올은 반응 시간을 둔화시킬 것이다.'). 하지만 여러분의 가설을 여러분이 검사해 보기 전에 그것이 사실이라고 이미 우리가 알고 있다면 여러분의 가설을 검사하는 것은 우리에게 아무런 새로운 것도 말해 주지 않을 것이다. 연구란 '새로운' 지식을 생산해야 한다는 것을 기억하라. 새로운 지식을 얻기 위해서 연구자이자 탐험가로서 여러분은 해변의 안전함(기정 사실)을 떠나 미개척 영역으로 과감히 들어가 볼 필요가 있다(아인슈타인이 말했듯이, "우리가 무엇을 하고 있는지 안다면 그것은 연구라고 불리지 않을 것이다, 그렇지?"). 이런 미개척 영역에서 무엇이 일어날 것인지에 관한 여러분의 예측이 틀린다면 그것은 괜찮다. 과학자는 실수를 저지르도록 허용되어 있다(Bates가 말했듯이, "연구는 막다른 길인지 보려고 골목길을 올라가 보는 과정이다."). 정말로 과학자는 흔히 결과를 내는 예측들보다는 결과를 내지 않는 예측들로부터 더 많이 배운다.

---

# 29 어법

While [ reflected / reflecting ]79) on the needs of organizations, leaders, and families today, we realize [ what / that ]80) one of the unique characteristics is inclusivity. Why? [ Because / Because of ]81) inclusivity supports what everyone ultimately [ wants / want ]82) from their relationships: collaboration. Yet the majority of leaders, organizations, and families are still using the language of the old paradigm in which one person — typically the oldest, most educated, and/or wealthiest — [ make / makes ]83) all the decisions, and their decisions rule with little discussion or inclusion of others, resulting [ in / from ]84) exclusivity. Today, this person could be a director, CEO, or other senior leader of an organization. There is no need for others to present(to부정사의 어떤 용법? _____)85) their ideas [ because / because of ]86) they are considered [ inadequate / inadequately ]87). Yet research shows that exclusivity in problem solving, even with a genius, [ is / being ]88) not as effective as inclusivity, where everyone's ideas are heard and a solution is developed through collaboration.

오늘날 조직, 지도자, 그리고 가족의 요구에 관해 곰곰이 생각할 때 우리는 독특한 특성 중 하나가 포용성이라는 것을 깨닫는다. 왜 그런가? 포용성은 모든 사람이 자신의 관계에서 궁극적으로 원하는 것인 협력을 뒷받침하기 때문이다. 그러나 대다수의 지도자, 조직, 그리고 가족은 여전히 오래된 패러다임의 언어를 사용하고 있고, 거기서는 한 사람이, 보통 가장 연장자, 가장 교육을 많이 받은 사람, 그리고 / 또는 가장 부유한 사람인데, 모든 결정을 내리고 토론이나 다른 사람을 포함시키는 것이 거의 없이 그들의 결정이 지배하고 결과적으로 배타성을 초래한다. 오늘날 이 사람은 어떤 조직의 관리자, 최고 경영자, 또는 다른 상급 지도자일 수 있다. 다른 사람들이 자신의 생각을 제시할 필요가 없는데 왜냐하면 그것은 부적절한 것으로 여겨지기 때문이다. 그러나 연구에 따르면 문제 해결에 있어서 배타성은, 심지어 천재와 함께하는 것이더라도, 포용성만큼 효과적이지 않은데, 포용성이 있는 경우에는 모든 사람의 생각을 듣게 되고 해결책은 협력을 통해 발전된다.

# 30 어휘

The objective point of view is illustrated by John Ford's "philosophy of camera." Ford considered the camera to be a window and the audience to be outside the window viewing the people and events within. We are asked to watch the actions [ even if / as if ]89) they were taking place at a distance, and we are not asked to participate. The objective point of view [ employing / employs ]90) a static camera as [ many / much ]91) as possible in order to produce(to부정사의 어떤 용법? _____ )92) this window effect, and it concentrates on the actors and the action without drawing attention to the camera. The objective camera suggests an emotional distance between camera and subject; the camera seems [ simple / simply ]93) to be recording, as [ straightforward / straightforwardly ]94) as possible, the characters and actions of the story. For the most part, the director uses natural, normal types of camera positioning and camera angles. The objective camera does not comment on or interpret the action [ and / but ]95) merely records it, letting(동명사? 현재분사? _____ )96) it unfold. We see the action from the viewpoint of an impersonal observer. If the camera moves, it [ is done / does ]97) so unnoticeably, [ called / calling ]98) as little attention to itself as possible.

객관적인 관점은 John Ford의 '카메라의 철학'에 의해 설명된다. Ford는 카메라를 창문이라고 생각했고 관객은 창문 안에 있는 사람과 사건을 바라보면서 창문 밖에 있다고 생각했다. 우리는 사건들이 멀리서 일어나고 있는 것처럼 그것들을 바라보도록 요청받고, 참여하도록 요청받지 않는다. 객관적인 관점은 이런 창문 효과를 만들기 위해 정적인 카메라를 가능한 한 많이 이용하고, 그것은 카메라에 관심을 끄는 것 없이 배우와 사건에 집중한다. 객관적인 카메라는 카메라와 대상 간의 감정적인 거리를 보여 주는데, 카메라는 이야기의 등장인물과 사건을 가능한 한 있는 그대로 그저 기록하고 있는 것으로 보인다. 대부분의 경우, 감독은 자연스럽고 일반적인 종류의 카메라 위치 선정과 카메라 각도를 사용한다. 객관적인 카메라는 사건에 관해 논평하거나 해석하지 않고 그것이 전개되게 하면서 그저 그것을 기록한다. 우리는 냉담한 관찰자의 관점에서 사건을 본다. 만약 카메라가 움직인다면 그것은 눈에 띄지 않게, 가능한 한 자신[카메라]에게 거의 관심을 불러일으키지 않으면서, 그렇게 한다.

---

# 31 빈칸

Even the most [ respectable / respective ]99) of all musical institutions, the symphony orchestra, [ carries / carrying ]100) inside its DNA the legacy of the hunt. The various instruments in the orchestra can be traced back to these primitive origins — their earliest forms were made either from the animal (horn, hide, gut, bone) or the weapons employed in bringing the animal under control (stick, bow). Are we wrong to hear this history in the music itself, in the formidable aggression and awe-[ inspired / inspiring ]101)sfd assertiveness of those monumental symphonies [ that / what ]102) [ remain / is remained ]103) the core repertoire of the world's leading orchestras? [ Listening / Listen ]104) to Beethoven, Brahms, Mahler, Bruckner, Berlioz, Tchaikovsky, Shostakovich, and other great composers, I can easily summon up images of bands of men [ starting / started ]105) to chase animals, using(동명사? 현재분사? _____ )106) sound as a source and symbol of dominance, an expression of the will to predatory power.

심지어 모든 음악 단체 중 가장 훌륭한 단체인 교향악단도 자신의 DNA 안에 사냥의 유산을 지니고 있다. 교향악단에 있는 다양한 악기들은 다음의 원시적인 기원으로 거슬러 올라갈 수 있는데, 그것들의 초기 형태는 동물(뿔, 가죽, 내장, 뼈) 또는 동물을 진압하기 위해 사용된 무기(막대, 활)로 만들어졌다. 음악 그 자체에서, 세계의 주요한 교향악단의 핵심 레퍼토리로 남아 있는 기념비적인 교향곡들의 강력한 공격성과 경외감을 자아내는 당당함에서 이러한 역사를 듣는다면 우리가 틀린 것인가? 베토벤, 브람스, 말러, 브루크너, 베를리오즈, 차이코프스키, 쇼스타코비치 및 다른 위대한 작곡가들의 음악을 들으며, 나는 소리를 지배의 원천이자 상징으로, 공격적인 힘에 대한 의지의 표현으로 사용하면서 동물을 쫓기 시작하는 사람들 무리의 이미지를 쉽게 떠올릴 수 있다.

# 32 빈칸

Our brains have [ evolved / been evolved ]107) to remember unexpected events [ because / because of ]108) basic survival depends on the ability to perceive causes and predict effects. If the brain predicts one event and experiences another, the unusualness will be especially [ interested / interesting ]109) and will be [ encoded / encoding ]110) accordingly. Neurologist and classroom teacher Judith Willis has [ claimed / been claimed ]111) that surprise in the classroom is one of the [ least / most ]112) effective ways of teaching with brain stimulation in mind. If students are [ exposed / exposing ]113) to new experiences via demonstrations or through the unexpected enthusiasm of their teachers or peers, they will be much more likely to connect with the information [ what / that ]114) follows. Willis has [ written / been written ]115) that encouraging(동명사? 현재분사? _____)116) active discovery in the classroom allows students [ interacting / to interact ]117) with new information, [ moves / moving ]118) it(어떤 it? _____)119) beyond working memory to be processed in the frontal lobe, [ that / which ]120) is devoted to advanced cognitive functioning. Preference for novelty sets us up for learning by directing attention, [ provides / providing ]121) stimulation to developing perceptual systems, and feeding curious and exploratory behavior.

우리의 뇌는 예상치 못한 사건들을 기억하도록 진화해 왔는데, 왜냐하면 기본적인 생존이 원인을 인식하고 결과를 예측하는 능력에 달려 있기 때문이다. 만약 뇌가 어떤 사건을 예측하고 (그것과) 다른 사건을 경험한다면, 그 특이함은 특히 흥미로울 것이고 그에 따라 (뇌 속의 정보로) 입력될 것이다. 신경학자이자 학급 교사인 Judith Willis는 교실에서의 놀라움은 뇌 자극을 염두에 두고 가르치는 가장 효과적인 방법 중 하나라고 주장했다. 학생들이 실연, 혹은 교사나 또래 친구의 예상치 못한 열의를 통해 새로운 경험에 노출되면, 그들은 뒤따르는 정보와 연결될 가능성이 훨씬 더 클 것이다. Willis는 교실에서의 능동적인 발견을 장려하는 것이 학생들로 하여금 새로운 정보와 상호 작용하게 해 주어서, 그것(새로운 정보)이 작동 기억을 넘어 고도의 인지 기능을 전담하는 (대뇌의) 전두엽에서 처리되도록 한다고 기술했다. 새로움에 대한 선호는, 주의를 이끌고, 지각 체계를 발전시키는 데 자극을 제공하며, 호기심 많고 탐구적인 행동을 충족함으로써 우리를 학습하도록 준비시킨다.

# 33 빈칸

Psychological research has [ shown / been shown ]122) that people naturally divide up cognitive labor, often without thinking about it. Imagine you're cooking(동명사? 현재분사? _____)123) up a special dinner with a friend. You're a great cook, but your friend is the wine expert, an amateur sommelier. A neighbor drops by and starts [ telling / told ]124) you both about the terrific new wines [ being / having been ]125) sold at the liquor store just down the street. There are many new wines, so there's a lot to remember. How [ hard / hardly ]126) are you going to try to remember [ that / what ]127) the neighbor has to say about which wines to buy? Why bother when the information would be better [ retained / retaining ]128) by the wine expert [ sitting / seating ]129) next to you? If your friend wasn't around, you might try harder. After all, it would be good to know [ what / that ]130) a good wine would be for the evening's festivities. But your friend, the wine expert, is likely to [ remember / remembering ]131) the information without even trying.

심리학 연구에 따르면, 사람들은 자연스럽게 인지 노동을 나누는데, 흔히 그것에 대해서 별 생각 없이 그렇게 한다. 여러분이 친구와 함께 특별한 저녁식사를 요리하고 있다고 상상해 보라. 여러분은 요리를 잘하지만, 친구는 아마추어 소믈리에라고 할 수 있는 와인 전문가이다. 이웃이 들르더니 여러분 두 사람에게 거리를 따라가면 바로 있는 주류 가게에서 파는 기막히게 좋은 새로운 와인에 대해 말하기 시작한다. 많은 새로운 와인이 있어서 기억해야 할 것이 많다. 어떤 와인을 사야 하는지에 관해 이웃이 할 말을 기억하기 위해 여러분은 얼마나 열심히 노력할까? 여러분 옆에 앉아 있는 와인 전문가가 그 정보를 더 잘 기억하고 있는데 무엇 하러 그러겠는가? 여러분의 친구가 곁에 없다면 더 열심히 애쓸지도 모른다. 어쨌든 저녁 만찬을 위해 뭐가 좋은 와인이 될지 아는 것은 좋은 일일 것이다. 하지만, 와인 전문가인 여러분의 친구는 애쓰지도 않고 그 정보를 기억하기가 쉽다.

# 34 빈칸

Even companies that sell physical products to [ make / making ]132) profit [ is / are ]133) forced by their boards and investors to reconsider their underlying motives and to collect as [ much / many ]134) data as possible from consumers. Supermarkets no longer make all their money selling their produce and [ manufactured / manufactiring ]135) goods. They give you loyalty cards with [ which / what ]136) they track your purchasing behaviors [ precisely / concisely ]137). Then supermarkets sell this purchasing behavior to marketing analytics companies. The marketing analytics companies perform machine learning procedures, [ sliced / slicing ]138) the data in new ways, and resell behavioral data back to(부정사? 전치사? _____)139) product manufacturers as marketing insights. When data and machine learning become currencies of value in a capitalist system, then every company's natural tendency is to [ maximize / maximizing ]140) its ability to conduct surveillance on its own customers [ because / because of ]141) the customers are themselves the new value-creation devices.

수익을 내기 위해 물적 제품을 판매하는 기업조차도 이사회와 투자자에 의해 어쩔 수 없이 자신의 근원적인 동기를 재고하게 되고 고객에게서 가능한 한 많은 정보를 수집하게 된다. 슈퍼마켓은 더 이상 자신의 농산물과 제조된 물품을 판매해서 자신의 모든 돈을 버는 것이 아니다. 그들은 여러분의 구매 행동을 정밀하게 추적하게 해 주는 고객 우대 카드를 여러분에게 준다. 그러고 나서 슈퍼마켓은 이 구매 행위를 마케팅 분석 기업에 판매한다. 마케팅 분석 기업은 기계 학습 절차를 수행하고 그 정보를 새로운 방식으로 쪼개서 행동 정보를 제품 제조 기업에 통찰력 있는 마케팅 정보로 다시 되판다. 정보와 기계 학습이 자본주의 체제에서 가치 있는 통화가 될 때, 고객 자체가 새로운 가치 창출 장치이기 때문에 모든 기업의 자연스러운 경향은 자신의 고객을 관찰하는 능력을 최대화하는 것이다.

# 35 무관

Academics, politicians, marketers and others have in the past [ debated / was debated ]142) whether or not it is ethically correct to [ marketing / market ]143) products and services directly to young consumers. This is also a dilemma for psychologists who have questioned whether they ought to help advertisers [ manipulate / manipulating ]144) children into purchasing more products they have seen [ advertising / advertised ]145). Advertisers have admitted to [ take / taking ]146) advantage of the fact that it is easy to make(to부정사의 어떤 용법? _____)147) children [ feel / to feel ]148) that they are losers if they do not own the 'right' products. [ Clever / Cleverly ]149) advertising [ informs / inform ]150) children that they will be viewed by their peers in an unfavorable way if they do not have the products [ that / what ]151) are advertised, [ thereby / whereas ]152) playing on their emotional vulnerabilities. The constant feelings of inadequateness created by advertising have [ suggested / been suggested ]153) to contribute to children becoming [ fixating / fixated ]154) with instant gratification and beliefs [ that / which ]155) material possessions are important.

지금까지 대학 교수, 정치인, 마케팅 담당자, 그리고 그 외의 사람들은 제품과 서비스를 어린 소비자들에게 직접 판촉하는 것이 윤리적으로 옳은지 그렇지 않은지를 논쟁해 왔다. 이것은 또한, 광고주들이 아이들을 조종해서 광고되는 것을 그들이 본 더 많은 제품을 구매하게 하는 것을 도와야 하는지 의문을 제기하는 심리학자들에게도 딜레마이다. 광고주들은 아이들이 그 '적절한' 제품을 소유하고 있지 않으면 자신이 패배자라고 느끼게 만드는 것이 쉽다는 사실을 이용한 것을 인정했다. 영리한 광고는 아이들에게 만약 그들이 광고되는 제품을 가지고 있지 않으면 자신의 또래 친구들에게 부정적으로 보일 것이라고 알려 주고, 그로 인해 아이들의 정서적인 취약성을 이용한다. 광고가 만들어 내는, 끊임없이 부적절하다고 느끼는 감정은, 아이들이 즉각적인 만족감과 물질적 소유물이 중요하다는 믿음에 집착하게 되는 데 기여한다고 언급되어 왔다.

# 36 순서

Once we recognize the false-cause issue, we see it(무엇을 가리키는가? _____)156) everywhere. For example, a recent long-term study of University of Toronto medical students [ included / concluded ]157) that medical school class presidents lived an average of 2.4 years less than other medical school graduates. At first glance, this seemed to imply that being(동명사? 현재분사? _____)158) a medical school class president is bad for you. Does this mean that you should avoid being medical school class president at all costs? Probably not. Just [ because / because of ]159) being class president is correlated with shorter life expectancy does not mean [ that / what ]160) it causes shorter life expectancy. In fact, it seems likely that(어떤 that? _____)161) the sort of person who becomes medical school class president is, [ on / in ]162) average, extremely hard-working, serious, and ambitious. Perhaps this extra stress, and the corresponding lack of social and relaxation time—rather than being class president per se— [ contribute / contributes ]163) to lower life expectancy. If so, the real lesson of the study is [ that / which ]164) we should all relax a little and not let our work [ take / to take ]165) over our lives.

일단 잘못 파악한 원인 문제를 우리가 인식하면, 우리는 그것을 어디에서나 보게 된다. 예를 들어, 토론토 대학의 의대생들에 대한 최근의 장기간의 연구는 의대 학년 대표들이 다른 의대 졸업생들보다 평균 2.4년 더 적게 살았다는 결론을 내렸다. 처음 봐서는, 이것은 의대 학년 대표인 것이 여러분에게 해롭다는 것을 의미하는 것처럼 보였다. 이것은 여러분이 무슨 수를 써서라도 의대 학년 대표가 되는 것을 피해야 한다는 것을 의미하는가? 아마도 그렇지는 않을 것이다. 단지 학년 대표인 것이 더 짧은 평균 수명과 서로 관련된다고 해서 그것이 더 짧은 평균 수명을 '유발한다'는 의미는 아니다. 사실, 아마도 의대 학년 대표가 되는 그런 부류의 사람은 평균적으로 몹시 열심히 공부하고, 진지하며, 야망이 있는 것 같다. 의대 학년 대표인 것 그 자체라기보다 아마도 이러한 가중된 스트레스와 그에 상응하는 사교와 휴식 시간의 부족이 더 짧은 평균 수명의 원인인 것 같다. 만약 그렇다면, 이 연구의 진정한 교훈은 우리 모두가 약간의 휴식을 취해야 하고 우리의 일이 우리의 삶을 장악하게 해서는 안 된다는 것이다.

# 37 순서

We commonly argue about the fairness of taxation—whether this or that tax will [ fall / fell ]166) more heavily on the rich or the poor. But the expressive dimension of taxation goes beyond debates about fairness, to the moral judgements societies make about [ that / which ]167) activities are [ worth / worthy ]168) of honor and recognition, and [ which / that ]169) ones should be discouraged. Sometimes, these judgements are explicit. Taxes on tobacco, alcohol, and casinos [ call / are called ]170) "sin taxes" because they seek to discourage activities [ considered / are considered ]171) harmful or undesirable. Such taxes express society's disapproval of these activities by [ rising / raising ]172) the cost of [ engaging / being engaged ]173) in them. Proposals to(부정사? 전치사? _____)174) tax sugary sodas (to combat obesity) or carbon emissions (to address climate change) [ likewise / otherwise ]175) seek to change norms and [ shape / shaping ]176) behavior. Not all taxes have this aim. We do not tax income to express disapproval of paid employment or to discourage people from engaging in it.(무엇을 가리키는가? _____)177) Nor is a general sales tax [ intended / was intended ]178) as a deterrent to buying things. These are simply ways of [ rising / raising ]179) revenue.

우리는 흔히 과세의 공정성, 즉 이런 저런 세금이 부자들에게 더 과중하게 부과될 것인지 아니면 가난한 사람들에게 그럴 것인지에 관해 논한다. 그러나 과세의 표현적 차원은 공정성에 대한 논쟁을 넘어, 어떤 활동이 명예와 인정을 받을 가치가 있고 어떤 활동이 억제되어야 하는지에 대해 사회가 내리는 도덕적 판단에까지 이른다. 때때로 이러한 판단은 명백하다. 담배, 술, 그리고 카지노에 대한 세금은 해롭거나 바람직하지 않은 것으로 간주되는 활동들을 억제하려고 하기 때문에 '죄악세'라고 불린다. 그런 세금은 이러한 활동을 하는 데 드는 비용을 증가시킴으로써 그것에 대한 사회의 반대를 표현한다. 마찬가지로 (비만에 맞서기 위해) 설탕이 든 탄산음료에 세금을 부과하는 제안이나 (기후 변화에 대처하기 위해) 탄소 배출에 세금을 부과하는 제안은 규범을 바꾸고 행동을 형성하려 한다. 모든 세금이 이런 목적을 가진 것은 아니다. 우리는 유급 고용에 대한 반대를 표명하거나 사람들이 그것을 하는 것을 막기 위해 소득에 세금을 부과하는 것은 아니다. 일반 판매세 역시 물건을 사는 것의 억제책으로서 의도된 것이 아니다. 이것들은 단순히 세입을 올리는 방법이다.

# 38 삽입

Most beliefs — but not all — are open to tests of verification. This means [ that / which ]180) beliefs can be tested to see [ if / that ]181) they are correct or false. Beliefs can be [ verified / verifying ]182) or falsified with objective criteria external to the person. There are people who believe the Earth is flat and not a sphere. Because we have objective evidence that(어떤 that? _____)183) the Earth is in fact a sphere, the flat Earth belief can [ show / be shown ]184) to be false. Also, the belief that(어떤 that? _____)185) it will rain tomorrow can be tested for truth by [ waiting / awaiting ]186) until tomorrow and seeing whether it rains or not. [ However / Indeed ]187), some types of beliefs cannot be tested for truth [ because / unless ]188) we cannot get external evidence in our lifetimes (such as a belief [ which / that ]189) the Earth will stop [ spinning / to spin ]190) on its axis by the year 9999 or that there is life on a planet 100-million light-years away). [ Besides / Consequently ]191), meta-physical beliefs (such as the existence and nature of a god) present [ considerable / considerate ]192) challenges in generating evidence [ that / which ]193) everyone is willing to use as a truth criterion.

전부는 아니지만 대부분의 믿음은 검증 시험을 받을 수 있다. 이것은 믿음이 옳거나 그른지를 확인하기 위해 시험될 수 있다는 것을 의미한다. 믿음은 그 사람의 외부에 있는 객관적인 기준을 통해 진실임이 입증되거나 거짓임이 입증될 수 있다. 지구가 평평하고 구가 아니라고 믿는 사람들이 있다. 우리는 지구가 사실은 구라는 객관적인 증거를 가지고 있기 때문에, 지구가 평평하다는 믿음은 거짓임이 증명될 수 있다. 또한, 내일 비가 올 것이라는 믿음은 내일까지 기다려 비가 오는지 안 오는지 봄으로써 진실인지 확인될 수 있다. 하지만, (9999년이 되면 지구가 자전하는 것을 멈출 것이라는 믿음이나 1억 광년 떨어진 행성에 생명체가 있다는 것 같은) 어떤 종류의 믿음은 우리가 일생 동안 외부 증거를 얻을 수 없기 때문에 진실인지 확인될 수 없다. 또한, (신의 존재와 본질과 같은) 형이상학적 믿음은 모든 사람이 진리 기준으로 기꺼이 사용할 증거를 만드는 데 있어서 상당한 난제가 된다.

# 39 삽입

Everyone automatically categorizes and generalizes all the time. Unconsciously. It is not a question of being(동명사? 현재분사? _____)194) prejudiced or enlightened. Categories are absolutely necessary [ of / for ]195) us to [ function / be functioned ]196). They give structure to our thoughts. Imagine if we saw every item and every scenario as truly unique — we would not even have a language to describe the world around us. But the necessary and useful instinct to generalize(to부정사의 어떤 용법? _____)197) can distort our world view. It can make us mistakenly [ group / to group ]198) together things, or people, or countries [ where / that ]199) are actually very different. It can make us [ assume / to assume ]200) everything or everyone in one category is similar. And, maybe, most [ unfortunate / unfortunately ]201) of all, it can make us [ jump / to jump ]202) to conclusions about a whole category based on a few, or even just one, unusual example.

모든 사람들은 항상 자동적으로 분류하고 일반화한다. 무의식적으로 (그렇게 한다). 그것은 편견을 갖고 있다거나 계몽되어 있다는 것의 문제가 아니다. 범주는 우리가 (정상적으로) 활동하는 데 반드시 필요하다. 그것들은 우리의 사고에 체계를 준다. 만일 우리가 모든 품목과 모든 있을 법한 상황을 정말로 유일무이한 것으로 본다고 상상해 보라. 그러면 우리는 우리 주변의 세계를 설명할 언어조차 갖지 못할 것이다. 그러나 필요하고 유용한 일반화하려는 본능은 우리의 세계관을 왜곡할 수 있다. 그것은 우리가 실제로는 아주 다른 사물들이나, 사람들, 혹은 나라들을 하나로 잘못 묶게 만들 수 있다. 그것은 우리가 하나의 범주 안에 있는 모든 것이나 모든 사람이 비슷하다고 가정하게 만들 수 있다. 그리고 어쩌면 모든 것 중에서 가장 유감스러운 것은, 그것이 우리로 하여금 몇 가지, 또는 심지어 고작 하나의 특이한 사례를 바탕으로 전체 범주에 대해 성급하게 결론을 내리게 만들 수 있다는 것이다.

# 40 요약

At the University of Iowa, students were briefly [ shown / showing ]203) numbers that(어떤 that? _____)204) they had to memorize. Then they [ offered / were offered ]205) the choice of either a fruit salad or a chocolate cake. When the number the students memorized was seven digits long, 63% of them chose the cake. When the number they [ asked / were asked ]206) to remember had just two digits, [ however / furthermore ]207) , 59% opted [ in / for ]208) the fruit salad. Our [ reflective / reflexive ]209) brains know that the fruit salad is better for our health, but our [ reflective / reflexive ]210) brains desire that soft, fattening chocolate cake. If the [ reflective / reflexive ]211) brain is busy [ figuring / to figure ]212) something else out — like trying to remember a seven-digit number — then impulse can easily win. [ Besides / On the other hand ]213), if we're not thinking too hard about something else (with only a minor distraction like memorizing two digits), then the [ reflective / reflexive ]214) system can deny the emotional impulse of the [ reflective / reflexive ]215) side.

→ [ According / In accordance ]216) to the above experiment, the increased intellective load on the brain [ leads / leading ]217) the [ reflective / reflexive ]218) side of the brain to become dominant.

Iowa 대학교에서, 학생들에게 그들이 암기해야 하는 숫자를 잠시 보여 주었다. 그리고 나서 그들에게 과일 샐러드나 초콜릿 케이크 중 하나를 선택하게 했다. 학생들이 외운 숫자가 일곱 자리일 때, 그들 중 63%가 케이크를 선택했다. 그러나 그들이 기억하도록 요청받은 숫자가 두 자리밖에 되지 않았을 때, 59%는 과일 샐러드를 선택했다. 우리의 숙고하는 뇌는 과일 샐러드가 우리의 건강에 더 좋다는 것을 알지만, 우리의 반사적인 뇌는 그 부드럽고 살이 찌는 초콜릿 케이크를 원한다. 만약 숙고하는 뇌가 일곱 자리 숫자를 기억하려고 애쓰는 일과 같은 다른 어떤 것을 해결하느라 바쁘다면, 충동이 쉽게 이길 수 있다. 다른 한편, 우리가 다른 것에 관해 너무 열심히 생각하고 있지 않다면(두 자리 숫자를 외우는 것과 같은 사소하게 주의를 산만하게 하는 일만 있을 때), 숙고하는 (뇌의) 계통은 반사적인 쪽의 감정적인 충동을 억제할 수 있다.
→ 위 실험에 따르면, 뇌에 가해지는 증가된 지적 부담은 뇌의 반사적인 부분이 우세해지게 한다.

# 41~42 제목, 어휘

Test scores are not a measure of self-worth; [ however / hence ]219), we often associate our sense of worthiness with our performance on an exam. Thoughts such as "If I don't pass this test, I'm a failure" are mental traps not [ rooting / rooted ]220) in truth. Failing a test is failing a test, nothing more. It(무엇을 가리키는가? _____)221) is in no way descriptive of your value as a person. [ Believe / Believing ]222) that test performance is a reflection of your virtue places unreasonable pressure on your performance. Not passing the certification test only means that your certification [ status / statue ]223) has [ delayed / been delayed ]224). [ Maintain / Maintaining ]225) a positive attitude is therefore important. If you have studied hard, reaffirm this mentally and believe that you will do well. If, on the other hand, you did not study as [ hard / hardly ]226) as you should have or wanted to, [ accept / accepting ]227) that as beyond your control for now and attend [ x / to ]228) the task of doing the best you can. If things do not go well this time, you know what needs to [ do / be done ]229) in preparation for the next exam. Talk to yourself in positive terms. Avoid [ to rationalize / rationalizing ]230) past or future test performance by placing the blame on secondary variables. Thoughts such as, "I didn't have enough time," or "I should have ...," [ compound / compounds ]231) the stress of test-taking. Take control by affirming your value, self-worth, and dedication to [ meeting / meet ]232) the test challenge head on. Repeat to yourself "I can and I will pass this exam."

시험 점수는 자부심의 척도가 아니지만, 우리는 흔히 우리의 자부심과 우리의 시험 성적을 연관시킨다. "이 시험에 합격하지 못하면 나는 실패자야."와 같은 생각은 사실에 뿌리를 두고 있지 않은 정신적 함정이다. 시험에 실패하는 것은 시험에 실패하는 것이지, 그 이상이 아니다. 그것은 결코 사람으로서의 여러분의 가치를 설명하지 않는다. 시험 성적이 여러분의 미덕을 반영하는 것이라고 믿는 것은 여러분의 수행에 부당한 압력을 가한다. 자격 시험을 통과하지 못한 것은 단지 여러분의 자격 지위가 지연되었다는 것을 의미할 따름이다. 그러므로 긍정적인 태도를 유지하는 것이 중요하다. 만약 여러분이 열심히 공부했다면, 마음속으로 이것을 재확인하고 좋은 성적이 나올 것이라고 믿으라. 다른 한편, 만약 여러분이 했어야 하거나 원하는 만큼 열심히 공부하지 않았다면, 지금으로서는 여러분이 어찌할 수 없는 것으로 그것을 받아들이고 여러분이 할 수 있는 최선의 것을 하는 과제에 주의를 기울이라. 만약 이번에 잘 되지 않는다면, 다음 시험 준비에서는 무엇을 해야 될지 알게 된다. 긍정적인 말로 자신에게 이야기하라. 부차적인 변수에 책임을 지움으로써 과거 또는 미래의 시험 성적을 합리화하는 것을 피하라. "나는 시간이 충분하지 않았어."라거나 "내가 그랬어야 했는데…"와 같은 생각은 시험을 보는 것의 스트레스를 완화시킨다(→ 악화시킨다). 자신의 가치, 자부심, 그리고 시험 과제에 정면으로 맞서는 것에 대한 헌신을 확인함으로써 통제권을 잡으라. "난 할 수 있고 이 시험에 합격할 거야."라고 자신에게 되풀이해 말하라.

# 43~45 순서, 지칭, 세부 내용

Once upon a time there lived a poor but cheerful shoemaker. He was so happy, he sang all day long. The children loved to stand around his window to listen to him. Next door to the shoemaker lived a rich man. He [ used / was used ]233) to [ sit / seat ]234) up all night to count his gold. In the morning, he went to bed, but he could not sleep [ because / because of ]235) the sound of the shoemaker's singing. One day, he thought of a way of stopping(동명사? 현재분사? _____)236) the singing. He wrote a letter to the shoemaker asking him [ visiting / to visit ]237). The shoemaker came at once, and to his surprise the rich man gave him a bag of gold. When he got home again, the shoemaker opened the bag. He [ has / had ]238) never seen so [ much / many ]239) gold before! When he sat down at his bench and began, carefully, to count it,(무엇을 가리키는가? _____)240) the children watched through the window. There was so much there [ that / which ]241) the shoemaker was afraid to let it out of his sight. So he took it to bed with him. But he could not sleep for worrying about it. Very early in the morning, he got up and brought his gold down from the bedroom. He had decided [ hiding / to hide ]242) it up the chimney instead. [ But / Therefore ]243) he was still uneasy, and in a little while he dug a hole in the garden and buried his bag of gold in it. It was no use [ trying / to try ]244) to work. He was too [ worried / worrying ]245) about the safety of his gold. And as for singing, he was too miserable [ to utter / uttering ]246) a note. He could not sleep, or work, or sing — and, worst of all, the children no longer came to see him. At last, the shoemaker felt [ so / too ]247) unhappy [ which / that ]248) he [ seized / ceased ]249) his bag of gold and ran next door to the rich man. "Please take back your gold," he said. "The worry of it is making me ill, and I have lost all of my friends. I would rather be a poor shoemaker, as I [ was / did ]250) before." And so the shoemaker was happy again and sang all day at his work.

옛날 옛적에 가난하지만 쾌활한 구두 만드는 사람이 살았다. 그는 너무 행복해서 하루 종일 노래를 불렀다. 아이들은 그의 창문에 둘러서서 그가 노래하는 것을 듣기 좋아했다. 구두 만드는 사람 옆집에는 부자가 살았다. 그는 자신의 금화를 세기 위해 밤을 새곤 했다. 아침에 그는 잠자리에 들었지만 구두 만드는 사람의 노랫소리 때문에 잠을 잘 수 없었다. 어느 날, 그는 그 노래를 멈추는 방법을 생각해냈다. 그는 구두 만드는 사람에게 방문해 달라고 요청하는 편지를 써 보냈다. 구두 만드는 사람은 즉시 왔고, 놀랍게도 부자는 그에게 금화가 든 가방을 주었다. 집에 다시 돌아왔을 때, 구두 만드는 사람은 그 가방을 열었다. 그는 그때까지 그렇게 많은 금화를 본 적이 없었다! 그가 의자에 앉아 조심스럽게 그것을 세기 시작했을 때, 아이들이 창문을 통해서 지켜보았다. 거기엔 금화가 너무 많아서 구두 만드는 사람은 그것을 자신에게 보이지 않는 곳에 두기가 겁났다. 그래서 그는 그것을 잠자리에 가져갔다. 그러나 그는 그것에 대한 걱정으로 잠을 잘 수 없었다. 매우 이른 아침에, 그는 일어나서 금화를 침실에서 가지고 내려왔다. 대신에 그는 그것을 굴뚝에 숨기기로 결정했다. 그러나 그는 여전히 불안했고, 잠시 후에 정원에 구멍을 파고 그 안에 금화가 든 가방을 묻었다. 일을 해보려고 해도 소용없었다. 그는 자신의 금화의 안전이 너무나 걱정되었다. 그리고 노래에 관해서라면, 그는 너무 불행해서 한 음도 낼 수 없었다. 그는 잠을 잘 수도, 일을 할 수도, 노래를 부를 수도 없었고, 최악은, 아이들이 더 이상 그를 보러 오지 않았다. 마침내, 구두 만드는 사람은 너무 불행해져서 그의 금화가 든 가방을 움켜쥐고 옆집 부자에게 달려갔다. "제발 당신의 금화를 다시 가져가세요."라고 그가 말했다. "그것에 대한 걱정이 저를 아프게 하고 있고, 저는 제 친구들을 모두 잃었어요. 저는 예전처럼 차라리 가난한 구두 만드는 사람이 되겠어요." 그래서 구두 만드는 사람은 다시 행복해졌고 일을 하면서 하루 종일 노래를 불렀다.

# 18 목적

My name is Anthony Thompson and I am writing [ on / to ]¹⁾ behalf of the residents' association. Our [ recycled / recycling ]²⁾ program has been [ working / worked ]³⁾ well thanks to your participation. [ Therefore / However ]⁴⁾, a problem has recently [ occurred / been occurred ]⁵⁾ that needs your attention. [ Because / Because of ]⁶⁾ there is no [ given / giving ]⁷⁾ day for recycling, residents are [ put / putting ]⁸⁾ their recycling out at any time. This makes the recycling area messy, [ that / which ]⁹⁾ requires extra labor and cost. To deal with(to부정사의 어떤 용법? _____)¹⁰⁾ this problem, the residents' association has [ decided / been decided ]¹¹⁾ on a day to recycle. I would like to let you [ know / to know ]¹²⁾ that you can put out your recycling on Wednesdays only. I am sure it will make our apartment complex look much more [ pleasant / pleasantly ]¹³⁾. Thank you in advance for your cooperation.

# 19 심경

It was a day I was due to give a presentation at work, not something I'd do often. As I stood up to begin, I froze. A chilly 'pins-and-needles' feeling crept over me, [ started / starting ]¹⁴⁾ in my hands. Time seemed to stand still as I [ struggled / was struggled ]¹⁵⁾ to start speaking, and I felt a pressure around my throat, [ even though / as though ]¹⁶⁾ my voice [ trapped / was trapped ]¹⁷⁾ and couldn't come out. Gazing(동명사? 현재분사? _____)¹⁸⁾ around at the blur of faces, I realized they were all [ waiting / awaiting ]¹⁹⁾ for me to begin, but by now I knew I couldn't continue.

# 20 주장

No matter [ how / what ]²⁰⁾ your situation, whether you are an insider or an outsider, you need to become the voice [ that / what ]²¹⁾ challenges yesterday's answers. [ Think / Thinking ]²²⁾ about the characteristics that make outsiders valuable to an organization. They are the people who have the perspective to see(to부정사의 어떤 용법? _____)²³⁾ problems that the insiders are too close to really notice. They are the ones who have the freedom to [ point / pointing ]²⁴⁾ out these problems and criticize them without risking their job or their career. Part of [ adapting / adopting ]²⁵⁾ an outsider mentality is [ forced / forcing ]²⁶⁾ yourself to look around your organization with this [ disassociated / disassociating ]²⁷⁾, less emotional perspective. If you didn't know your coworkers and feel bonded to them by your shared experiences, [ what / how ]²⁸⁾ would you think of them? You may not have the job security or confidence to speak your mind to management, but you can make these "outsider" assessments of your organization on your own and use [ what / that ]²⁹⁾ you determine to advance your career.

# 21 의미

The known fact of contingencies, [ with / without ]30) knowing precisely [ what / that ]31) those contingencies will be, [ show / shows ]32) that disaster preparation is not the same thing as disaster rehearsal. No matter [ how / what ]33) many mock disasters are staged [ in accordance / according ]34) to prior plans, the real disaster will never mirror any one of them.(무엇을 가리키는가? _____)35) Disaster-preparation planning is more like training for a marathon [ as / than ]36) training for a high-jump competition or a sprinting event. Marathon runners do not practice by running the full course of twenty-six miles; rather, they get into shape by running shorter distances and [ building / build ]37) up their endurance with cross-training. If they [ are / have ]38) prepared successfully, then they are in optimal condition to [ run / running ]39) the marathon over its predetermined course and length, assuming(동명사? 현재분사? _____)40) a range of weather conditions, predicted or not. This is normal marathon preparation.

# 22 요지

Fears of damaging ecosystems are based on the sound conservationist [ principle / principal ]41) [ that / which ]42) we should aim to [ minimizing / minimize ]43) the disruption we cause, but there is a risk that(어떤 that? _____)44) this principle may be confused with the old idea of a 'balance of nature.' This supposes a perfect order of nature that will seek to maintain itself and that we should not change. It is a romantic, not to say idyllic, notion, but deeply misleading [ because / because of ]45) it supposes a static condition. Ecosystems are dynamic, and [ although / as though ]46) some may endure, apparently unchanged, for periods [ that / what ]47) are long in comparison with the human lifespan, they must and do change eventually. Species come and go, climates change, plant and animal communities [ adapt / adopt ]48) to [ altered / altering ]49) circumstances, and when [ examined / examining ]50) in fine detail such [ adoption / adaptation ]51) and consequent change can be seen to be [ taking / taken ]52) place constantly. The 'balance of nature' is a myth. Our planet is dynamic, and so are the arrangements by which its inhabitants live together.

# 23 주제

[ Before / After ]53) the modern scientific era, creativity was [ attributed / attributing ]54) to a superhuman force; all novel ideas [ originated / were originated ]55) with the gods. After all, how could a person create something [ that / what ]56) did not exist before the divine act of creation? In fact, the Latin meaning of the verb "inspire" is "to breathe into," [ reflects / reflecting ]57) the belief [ that / which ]58) creative inspiration was similar to the moment in creation [ when / which ]59) God first breathed life into man. Plato argued that the poet [ possessed / was possessed ]60) by divine inspiration, and Plotin [ written / wrote ]61) that art could only be beautiful if it descended from God. The artist's job was not to imitate nature but rather to reveal(to부정사의 어떤 용법? _____)62) the sacred and transcendent qualities of nature. Art could only be a pale imitation of the perfection of the world of ideas. Greek artists did not blindly imitate what they saw in reality; [ thus / instead ]63) they tried to represent the pure, true forms underlying reality, resulting [ in / from ]64) a sort of compromise between abstraction and accuracy.

# 24 제목

Some beginning researchers mistakenly believe that(어떤 that? _____)65) a good hypothesis is one that is [ guaranteed / guaranteeing ]66) to be right (e.g., alcohol will slow down reaction time). [ However / Therefore ]67) , if we already know your hypothesis is true before you test it, [ testing / test ]68) your hypothesis won't tell us anything new. Remember, research is supposed to [ produce / producing ]69) new knowledge. To get new knowledge, you, as a researcher-explorer, need to leave the safety of the shore ([ established / establishing ]70) facts) and venture into [ uncharted / uncharting ]71) waters (as Einstein said, "If we knew [ what / that ]72) we were doing, it would not [ call / be called ]73) research, would it?"). If your predictions about [ what / which ]74) will [ happen / be happened ]75) in these uncharted waters [ is / are ]76) wrong, that's okay: Scientists are [ allowing / allowed ]77) to make mistakes (as Bates said, "Research is the process of going up alleys to see if they are blind"). Indeed, scientists often learn more from predictions [ that / what ]78) do not turn out than from those that do.

# 29 어법

While [ reflected / reflecting ]79) on the needs of organizations, leaders, and families today, we realize [ what / that ]80) one of the unique characteristics is inclusivity. Why? [ Because / Because of ]81) inclusivity supports what everyone ultimately [ wants / want ]82) from their relationships: collaboration. Yet the majority of leaders, organizations, and families are still using the language of the old paradigm in which one person — typically the oldest, most educated, and/or wealthiest — [ make / makes ]83) all the decisions, and their decisions rule with little discussion or inclusion of others, resulting [ in / from ]84) exclusivity. Today, this person could be a director, CEO, or other senior leader of an organization. There is no need for others to present(to부정사의 어떤 용법? _____)85) their ideas [ because / because of ]86) they are considered [ inadequate / inadequately ]87). Yet research shows that exclusivity in problem solving, even with a genius, [ is / being ]88) not as effective as inclusivity, where everyone's ideas are heard and a solution is developed through collaboration.

# 30 어휘

The objective point of view is illustrated by John Ford's "philosophy of camera." Ford considered the camera to be a window and the audience to be outside the window viewing the people and events within. We are asked to watch the actions [ even if / as if ]89) they were taking place at a distance, and we are not asked to participate. The objective point of view [ employing / employs ]90) a static camera as [ many / much ]91) as possible in order to produce(to부정사의 어떤 용법? _____)92) this window effect, and it concentrates on the actors and the action without drawing attention to the camera. The objective camera suggests an emotional distance between camera and subject; the camera seems [ simple / simply ]93) to be recording, as [ straightforward / straightforwardly ]94) as possible, the characters and actions of the story. For the most part, the director uses natural, normal types of camera positioning and camera angles. The objective camera does not comment on or interpret the action [ and / but ]95) merely records it, letting(동명사? 현재분사? _____)96) it unfold. We see the action from the viewpoint of an impersonal observer. If the camera moves, it [ is done / does ]97) so unnoticeably, [ called / calling ]98) as little attention to itself as possible.

## 31 빈칸

Even the most [ respectable / respective ]99) of all musical institutions, the symphony orchestra, [ carries / carrying ]100) inside its DNA the legacy of the hunt. The various instruments in the orchestra can be traced back to these primitive origins — their earliest forms were made either from the animal (horn, hide, gut, bone) or the weapons employed in bringing the animal under control (stick, bow). Are we wrong to hear this history in the music itself, in the formidable aggression and awe-[ inspired / inspiring ]101)sfd assertiveness of those monumental symphonies [ that / what ]102) [ remain / is remained ]103) the core repertoire of the world's leading orchestras? [ Listening / Listen ]104) to Beethoven, Brahms, Mahler, Bruckner, Berlioz, Tchaikovsky, Shostakovich, and other great composers, I can easily summon up images of bands of men [ starting / started ]105) to chase animals, using(동명사? 현재분사? _____)106) sound as a source and symbol of dominance, an expression of the will to predatory power.

## 32 빈칸

Our brains have [ evolved / been evolved ]107) to remember unexpected events [ because / because of ]108) basic survival depends on the ability to perceive causes and predict effects. If the brain predicts one event and experiences another, the unusualness will be especially [ interested / interesting ]109) and will be [ encoded / encoding ]110) accordingly. Neurologist and classroom teacher Judith Willis has [ claimed / been claimed ]111) that surprise in the classroom is one of the [ least / most ]112) effective ways of teaching with brain stimulation in mind. If students are [ exposed / exposing ]113) to new experiences via demonstrations or through the unexpected enthusiasm of their teachers or peers, they will be much more likely to connect with the information [ what / that ]114) follows. Willis has [ written / been written ]115) that encouraging(동명사? 현재분사? _____)116) active discovery in the classroom allows students [ interacting / to interact ]117) with new information, [ moves / moving ]118) it(어떤 it? _____)119) beyond working memory to be processed in the frontal lobe, [ that / which ]120) is devoted to advanced cognitive functioning. Preference for novelty sets us up for learning by directing attention, [ provides / providing ]121) stimulation to developing perceptual systems, and feeding curious and exploratory behavior.

## 33 빈칸

Psychological research has [ shown / been shown ]122) that people naturally divide up cognitive labor, often without thinking about it. Imagine you're cooking(동명사? 현재분사? _____)123) up a special dinner with a friend. You're a great cook, but your friend is the wine expert, an amateur sommelier. A neighbor drops by and starts [ telling / told ]124) you both about the terrific new wines [ being / having been ]125) sold at the liquor store just down the street. There are many new wines, so there's a lot to remember. How [ hard / hardly ]126) are you going to try to remember [ that / what ]127) the neighbor has to say about which wines to buy? Why bother when the information would be better [ retained / retaining ]128) by the wine expert [ sitting / seating ]129) next to you? If your friend wasn't around, you might try harder. After all, it would be good to know [ what / that ]130) a good wine would be for the evening's festivities. But your friend, the wine expert, is likely to [ remember / remembering ]131) the information without even trying.

## 34 빈칸

Even companies that sell physical products to [ make / making ]132) profit [ is / are ]133) forced by their boards and investors to reconsider their underlying motives and to collect as [ much / many ]134) data as possible from consumers. Supermarkets no longer make all their money selling their produce and [ manufactured / manufactiring ]135) goods. They give you loyalty cards with [ which / what ]136) they track your purchasing behaviors [ precisely / concisely ]137). Then supermarkets sell this purchasing behavior to marketing analytics companies. The marketing analytics companies perform machine learning procedures, [ sliced / slicing ]138) the data in new ways, and resell behavioral data back to(부정사? 전치사? _____)139) product manufacturers as marketing insights. When data and machine learning become currencies of value in a capitalist system, then every company's natural tendency is to [ maximize / maximizing ]140) its ability to conduct surveillance on its own customers [ because / because of ]141) the customers are themselves the new value-creation devices.

## 35 무관

Academics, politicians, marketers and others have in the past [ debated / was debated ]142) whether or not it is ethically correct to [ marketing / market ]143) products and services directly to young consumers. This is also a dilemma for psychologists who have questioned whether they ought to help advertisers [ manipulate / manipulating ]144) children into purchasing more products they have seen [ advertising / advertised ]145). Advertisers have admitted to [ take / taking ]146) advantage of the fact that it is easy to make(to부정사의 어떤 용법? _____)147) children [ feel / to feel ]148) that they are losers if they do not own the 'right' products. [ Clever / Cleverly ]149) advertising [ informs / inform ]150) children that they will be viewed by their peers in an unfavorable way if they do not have the products [ that / what ]151) are advertised, [ thereby / whereas ]152) playing on their emotional vulnerabilities. The constant feelings of inadequateness created by advertising have [ suggested / been suggested ]153) to contribute to children becoming [ fixating / fixated ]154) with instant gratification and beliefs [ that / which ]155) material possessions are important.

## 36 순서

Once we recognize the false-cause issue, we see it(무엇을 가리키는가? _____)156) everywhere. For example, a recent long-term study of University of Toronto medical students [ included / concluded ]157) that medical school class presidents lived an average of 2.4 years less than other medical school graduates. At first glance, this seemed to imply that being(동명사? 현재분사? _____)158) a medical school class president is bad for you. Does this mean that you should avoid being medical school class president at all costs? Probably not. Just [ because / because of ]159) being class president is correlated with shorter life expectancy does not mean [ that / what ]160) it causes shorter life expectancy. In fact, it seems likely that(어떤 that? _____)161) the sort of person who becomes medical school class president is, [ on / in ]162) average, extremely hard-working, serious, and ambitious. Perhaps this extra stress, and the corresponding lack of social and relaxation time—rather than being class president per se— [ contribute / contributes ]163) to lower life expectancy. If so, the real lesson of the study is [ that / which ]164) we should all relax a little and not let our work [ take / to take ]165) over our lives.

# 37 순서

We commonly argue about the fairness of taxation—whether this or that tax will [ fall / fell ]166) more heavily on the rich or the poor. But the expressive dimension of taxation goes beyond debates about fairness, to the moral judgements societies make about [ that / which ]167) activities are [ worth / worthy ]168) of honor and recognition, and [ which / that ]169) ones should be discouraged. Sometimes, these judgements are explicit. Taxes on tobacco, alcohol, and casinos [ call / are called ]170) "sin taxes" because they seek to discourage activities [ considered / are considered ]171) harmful or undesirable. Such taxes express society's disapproval of these activities by [ rising / raising ]172) the cost of [ engaging / being engaged ]173) in them. Proposals to(부정사? 전치사? _____)174) tax sugary sodas (to combat obesity) or carbon emissions (to address climate change) [ likewise / otherwise ]175) seek to change norms and [ shape / shaping ]176) behavior. Not all taxes have this aim. We do not tax income to express disapproval of paid employment or to discourage people from engaging in it.(무엇을 가리키는가? _____)177) Nor is a general sales tax [ intended / was intended ]178) as a deterrent to buying things. These are simply ways of [ rising / raising ]179) revenue.

# 38 삽입

Most beliefs—but not all—are open to tests of verification. This means [ that / which ]180) beliefs can be tested to see [ if / that ]181) they are correct or false. Beliefs can be [ verified / verifying ]182) or falsified with objective criteria external to the person. There are people who believe the Earth is flat and not a sphere. Because we have objective evidence that(어떤 that? _____)183) the Earth is in fact a sphere, the flat Earth belief can [ show / be shown ]184) to be false. Also, the belief that(어떤 that? _____)185) it will rain tomorrow can be tested for truth by [ waiting / awaiting ]186) until tomorrow and seeing whether it rains or not. [ However / Indeed ]187), some types of beliefs cannot be tested for truth [ because / unless ]188) we cannot get external evidence in our lifetimes (such as a belief [ which / that ]189) the Earth will stop [ spinning / to spin ]190) on its axis by the year 9999 or that there is life on a planet 100-million light-years away). [ Besides / Consequently ]191), meta-physical beliefs (such as the existence and nature of a god) present [ considerable / considerate ]192) challenges in generating evidence [ that / which ]193) everyone is willing to use as a truth criterion.

# 39 삽입

Everyone automatically categorizes and generalizes all the time. Unconsciously. It is not a question of being(동명사? 현재분사? _____)194) prejudiced or enlightened. Categories are absolutely necessary [ of / for ]195) us to [ function / be functioned ]196). They give structure to our thoughts. Imagine if we saw every item and every scenario as truly unique—we would not even have a language to describe the world around us. But the necessary and useful instinct to generalize(to부정사의 어떤 용법? _____)197) can distort our world view. It can make us mistakenly [ group / to group ]198) together things, or people, or countries [ where / that ]199) are actually very different. It can make us [ assume / to assume ]200) everything or everyone in one category is similar. And, maybe, most [ unfortunate / unfortunately ]201) of all, it can make us [ jump / to jump ]202) to conclusions about a whole category based on a few, or even just one, unusual example.

# 40 요약

At the University of Iowa, students were briefly [ shown / showing ]203) numbers that(어떤 that? _____)204) they had to memorize. Then they [ offered / were offered ]205) the choice of either a fruit salad or a chocolate cake. When the number the students memorized was seven digits long, 63% of them chose the cake. When the number they [ asked / were asked ]206) to remember had just two digits, [ however / furthermore ]207), 59% opted [ in / for ]208) the fruit salad. Our [ reflective / reflexive ]209) brains know that the fruit salad is better for our health, but our [ reflective / reflexive ]210) brains desire that soft, fattening chocolate cake. If the [ reflective / reflexive ]211) brain is busy [ figuring / to figure ]212) something else out—like trying to remember a seven-digit number—then impulse can easily win. [ Besides / On the other hand ]213), if we're not thinking too hard about something else (with only a minor distraction like memorizing two digits), then the [ reflective / reflexive ]214) system can deny the emotional impulse of the [ reflective / reflexive ]215) side.

→ [ According / In accordance ]216) to the above experiment, the increased intellective load on the brain [ leads / leading ]217) the [ reflective / reflexive ]218) side of the brain to become dominant.

# 41~42 제목, 어휘

Test scores are not a measure of self-worth; [ however / hence ]219), we often associate our sense of worthiness with our performance on an exam. Thoughts such as "If I don't pass this test, I'm a failure" are mental traps not [ rooting / rooted ]220) in truth. Failing a test is failing a test, nothing more. It(무엇을 가리키는가? _____)221) is in no way descriptive of your value as a person. [ Believe / Believing ]222) that test performance is a reflection of your virtue places unreasonable pressure on your performance. Not passing the certification test only means that your certification [ status / statue ]223) has [ delayed / been delayed ]224). [ Maintain / Maintaining ]225) a positive attitude is therefore important. If you have studied hard, reaffirm this mentally and believe that you will do well. If, on the other hand, you did not study as [ hard / hardly ]226) as you should have or wanted to, [ accept / accepting ]227) that as beyond your control for now and attend [ x / to ]228) the task of doing the best you can. If things do not go well this time, you know what needs to [ do / be done ]229) in preparation for the next exam. Talk to yourself in positive terms. Avoid [ to rationalize / rationalizing ]230) past or future test performance by placing the blame on secondary variables. Thoughts such as, "I didn't have enough time," or "I should have ...," [ compound / compounds ]231) the stress of test-taking. Take control by affirming your value, self-worth, and dedication to [ meeting / meet ]232) the test challenge head on. Repeat to yourself "I can and I will pass this exam."

# 43~45 순서, 지칭, 세부 내용

Once upon a time there lived a poor but cheerful shoemaker. He was so happy, he sang all day long. The children loved to stand around his window to listen to him. Next door to the shoemaker lived a rich man. He [ used / was used ]233) to [ sit / seat ]234) up all night to count his gold. In the morning, he went to bed, but he could not sleep [ because / because of ]235) the sound of the shoemaker's singing. One day, he thought of a way of stopping(동명사? 현재분사? _____)236) the singing. He wrote a letter to the shoemaker asking him [ visiting / to visit ]237). The shoemaker came at once, and to his surprise the rich man gave him a bag of gold. When he got home again, the shoemaker opened the bag. He [ has / had ]238) never seen so [ much / many ]239) gold before! When he sat down at his bench and began, carefully, to count it,(무엇을 가리키는가? _____)240) the children watched through the window. There was so much there [ that / which ]241) the shoemaker was afraid to let it out of his sight. So he took it to bed with him. But he could not sleep for worrying about it. Very early in the morning, he got up and brought his gold down from the bedroom. He had decided [ hiding / to hide ]242) it up the chimney instead. [ But / Therefore ]243) he was still uneasy, and in a little while he dug a hole in the garden and buried his bag of gold in it. It was no use [ trying / to try ]244) to work. He was too [ worried / worrying ]245) about the safety of his gold. And as for singing, he was too miserable [ to utter / uttering ]246) a note. He could not sleep, or work, or sing — and, worst of all, the children no longer came to see him. At last, the shoemaker felt [ so / too ]247) unhappy [ which / that ]248) he [ seized / ceased ]249) his bag of gold and ran next door to the rich man. "Please take back your gold," he said. "The worry of it is making me ill, and I have lost all of my friends. I would rather be a poor shoemaker, as I [ was / did ]250) before." And so the shoemaker was happy again and sang all day at his work.

# 18 목적

My name is Anthony Thompson and I am writing on b_____1) of the residents' a_____2). Our r_____3) program has been working well thanks to your p_____4). However, a problem has r_____5) occurred that needs your attention. Because there is no g_____6) day for recycling, residents are putting their recycling out at any time. This makes the recycling area m_____7), which requires extra labor and cost. To d_____8) with this problem, the residents' association has decided on a day to recycle. I would like to let you know that you can put out your recycling on Wednesdays only. I am sure it will make our apartment complex look m_____9) more p_____10). Thank you in a_____11) for your cooperation.

제 이름은 Anthony Thompson이고 저는 입주민 조합을 대표하여 편지를 쓰고 있습니다. 우리의 재활용 프로그램은 여러분의 참여 덕분에 잘 운영되고 있습니다. 그런데 최근에 여러분의 관심이 필요한 문제가 생겼습니다. 재활용을 위해 정해진 날이 없어서 입주민들은 아무 때나 자신들의 재활용품을 내놓습니다. 이것이 재활용 구역을 어지럽혀서 추가 노동과 비용이 필요하게 합니다. 이 문제를 처리하기 위해서 입주민 조합은 재활용하는 날을 결정했습니다. 수요일에만 여러분의 재활용품을 내놓을 수 있다는 것을 알려드리고 싶습니다. 그것이 우리 아파트 단지를 훨씬 더 쾌적해 보이게 만들 것이라고 저는 확신합니다. 여러분의 협조에 미리 감사드립니다.

# 19 심경

It was a day I was d_____12) to give a presentation at work, not something I'd do often. As I stood up to begin, I froze. A chilly 'pins-and-needles' feeling c_____13) over me, starting in my hands. Time s_____14) to stand still as I s_____15) to start speaking, and I felt a p_____16) around my throat, as though my voice was t_____17) and couldn't come out. G_____18) around at the blur of faces, I realized they were all waiting for me to begin, but by now I knew I couldn't continue.

내가 직장에서 발표를 하기로 한 날이었고 내가 자주 하곤 했던 것이 아니었다. 시작하려고 일어섰을 때 나는 얼어붙었다. '핀과 바늘로 찌르는 듯한' 차가운 느낌이 손에서 시작해서 나를 엄습했다. 내가 말하기 시작하려고 애쓸 때 시간이 정지해 있는 것 같았고 나는 목 부근에서 압박감을 느꼈는데 마치 내 목소리가 갇혀서 빠져나올 수 없는 것 같았다. 흐릿한 형체의 얼굴들을 둘러보며 나는 그들이 모두 내가 시작하기를 기다리고 있다는 것을 깨달았지만 그때쯤 나는 내가 계속할 수 없다는 것을 알았다.

## 20 주장

No matter what your situation, whether you are an insider or an outsider, you need to become the voice that c_____19) yesterday's answers. Think about the c_____20) that make outsiders valuable to an organization. They are the people who have the p_____21) to see problems that the insiders are too close to really notice. They are the ones who have the freedom to point out these problems and criticize them without risking their job or their career. Part of a_____22) an outsider m_____23) is forcing yourself to look around your organization with this d_____24), less emotional p_____25). If you didn't know your coworkers and feel b_____26) to them by your shared experiences, what would you think of them? You may not have the job security or confidence to speak your mind to management, but you can make these "outsider" a_____27) of your organization on your own and use what you d_____28) to advance your career.

여러분의 상황이 어떠하든, 여러분이 내부자이건 외부자이건, 여러분은 어제의 정답에 이의를 제기하는 목소리가 될 필요가 있다. 외부자를 조직에게 가치 있게 만드는 특성들에 관해 생각해 보라. 그들은 내부자가 너무 가까이 있어서 정말 알아차릴 수 없는 문제들을 볼 수 있는 관점을 가진 사람들이다. 그들은 자신의 일자리나 자신의 경력을 위태롭게 하지 않고 이런 문제들을 지적하고 그것들을 비판할 수 있는 자유를 가진 사람들이다. 외부자의 사고방식을 채택하는 것의 일부는 이렇게 분리된, 덜 감정적인 관점으로 여러분의 조직을 스스로 둘러보게 하는 것이다. 여러분이 자신의 동료를 모르고 여러분의 공유된 경험에 의해 그들에게 결속되어 있다고 느끼지 않는다면 여러분은 그들에 관해 어떻게 생각하겠는가? 여러분이 자신의 생각을 경영진에게 말할 직업 안정성이나 자신감을 갖고 있지 않을지도 모르지만 여러분은 자신의 조직에 관해 이런 '외부자의' 평가를 독자적으로 할 수 있고 여러분이 판정한 것을 자신의 경력을 발전시키기 위해 이용할 수 있다.

## 21 의미

The known fact of c_____29), without knowing p_____30) what those c_____31) will be, shows that disaster preparation is not the same thing as disaster rehearsal. No matter h_____32) many mock disasters are s_____33) according to prior plans, the real disaster will never m_____34) any one of them. Disaster-preparation planning is more like training for a marathon than training for a high-jump competition or a sprinting event. Marathon runners do not practice by running the full course of twenty-six miles; rather, they get into s_____35) by running shorter distances and building up their e_____36) with cross-training. If they have prepared successfully, then they are in o_____37) condition to run the marathon over its p_____38) course and length, a_____39) a range of weather conditions, predicted or not. This is normal marathon preparation.

비상사태에 관해 이미 알려진 사실은, 그 비상사태가 어떤 것이 될 것인지 정확히 아는 것이 없이, 재난 대비가 재난 예행연습과 똑같은 것이 아니라는 것을 보여 준다. 아무리 많은 모의 재난이 사전 계획에 따라 조직되더라도 실제 재난은 그런 것들 중 어느 하나라도 그대로 반영하지 않을 것이다. 재난 대비 계획 세우기는 높이뛰기 시합이나 단거리 달리기 경주를 위해 훈련하는 것이라기보다는 마라톤을 위해 훈련하는 것과 더 비슷하다. 마라톤 선수들은 26마일 전체 코스를 달리는 것으로 연습하는 것이 아니라 오히려 더 짧은 거리를 달리고 여러 가지 운동을 조합하여 행하는 훈련법으로 자신의 지구력을 강화함으로써 몸 상태를 좋게 만든다. 만약 그들이 성공적으로 준비했다면 그들은 마라톤의 미리 정해진 코스와 길이에 걸쳐 예상되었든 아니든 다양한 기상 조건을 가정하면서 마라톤을 달릴 수 있는 최적의 상태에 있다. 이것이 보통의 마라톤 준비이다.

## 22 요지

Fears of damaging ecosystems are b_____40) on the sound c_____41) principle that we should a_____42) to minimize the d_____43) we cause, but there is a risk that this principle may be confused with the old idea of a 'balance of nature.' This supposes a perfect order of nature that will s_____44) to m_____45) itself and that we should not change. It is a romantic, not to say i_____46), notion, but deeply misleading because it supposes a s_____47) condition. Ecosystems are d_____48), and although some may e_____49), apparently unchanged, for periods that are long in c_____50) with the human lifespan, they must and do change eventually. Species come and go, climates change, plant and animal communities a_____51) to a_____52) circumstances, and when examined in f_____53) detail such a_____54) and consequent change can be seen to be taking place c_____55). The 'balance of nature' is a myth. Our planet is dynamic, and so are the arrangements by which its inhabitants live together.

생태계를 손상하는 것에 대한 두려움은 우리가 초래하는 (환경) 파괴를 최소화하는 것을 목표로 해야 한다는 건전한 환경 보호주의자 원칙을 바탕으로 하지만, 이 원칙이 '자연의 균형'이라는 오래된 생각과 혼동될지도 모른다는 위험이 있다. 이것은 그 자체를 유지하려고 노력하고 우리가 바꾸어서는 안 되는 완벽한 자연의 질서를 전제로 한다. 그것은 목적적이라고까지는 할 수 없어도 낭만적인 개념이지만 정적인 상태를 전제로 하기 때문에 매우 잘못된 인식을 준다. 생태계는 역동적이고, 일부는 겉보기에는 변하지 않는 채로 인간의 수명과 비교해 보면 오랜 기간 동안 지속될지 모르지만, 그것은 결국 변할 것임에 틀림없고 정말 변한다. 생물 종(種)들은 생겼다 사라지고 기후는 변하며 동식물 군집은 달라진 환경에 적응하고 미세하게 자세히 검토하면 그런 적응과 결과적인 변화는 항상 일어나고 있는 것으로 보일 수 있다. '자연의 균형'은 잘못된 통념이다. 지구는 역동적이고 지구의 서식자들이 함께 사는 모습[생활 방식]도 그러하다.

## 23 주제

Before the modern scientific e_____56), creativity was a_____57) to a s_____58) force; all n_____59) ideas originated with the gods. After all, how could a person create something that did not exist before the d_____60) act of creation? In fact, the Latin meaning of the verb "inspire" is "to breathe into," r_____61) the belief that creative inspiration was similar to the moment in creation when God first breathed life into man. Plato argued that the poet was p_____62) by divine inspiration, and Plotin wrote that art could only be beautiful if it descended from God. The artist's job was not to i_____63) nature but rather to reveal the s_____64) and t_____65) qualities of nature. Art could only be a p_____66) imitation of the perfection of the world of ideas. Greek artists did not b_____67) imitate what they saw in reality; instead they tried to represent the pure, true forms u_____68) reality, resulting in a sort of c_____69) between a_____70) and a_____71).

근대의 과학적인 시대 이전에 창의성은 초인적인 힘에 기인한 것으로 여겼는데 모든 새로운 생각은 신에게서 유래했다. 결국 신의 창조 행위 이전에 존재하지 않았던 것을 어떻게 인간이 만들 수 있었겠는가? 사실, '영감을 주다'라는 동사의 라틴어의 의미는 '숨결을 불어넣다'이고 창의적 영감은 신이 처음에 인간에게 생명을 불어 넣었을 때 창조의 순간과 비슷했다는 믿음을 반영한다. Plato는 시인은 신이 내린 영감에 사로잡혔다고 주장했고 Plotin은 예술은 그것이 신으로부터 내려온 경우에만 아름다울 수 있다고 썼다. 예술가의 일은 자연을 모방하는 것이라기보다는 오히려 자연의 신성하고 초월적인 특성을 드러내는 것이었다. 예술은 관념[이데아]의 세계의 완벽함을 어설프게 흉내 낸 것에 불과한 것일 수 있다. 그리스의 예술가들은 그들이 현실에서 본 것을 맹목적으로 모방하지 않았고 그 대신 현실의 근저에 있는 순수하고 진정한 형태를 나타내려고 애썼는데 그 결과 추상과 정확성 간의 일종의 타협을 발생시켰다.

# 24 제목

Some beginning researchers mistakenly believe that a good h_____72) is one that is g_____73) to be right (e.g., alcohol will slow down reaction time). However, if we already know your hypothesis is true before you test it, testing your hypothesis won't tell us anything new. Remember, research _____ _____ _____74) produce new knowledge. To get new knowledge, you, as a researcher-explorer, need to leave the safety of the shore (established facts) and v_____75) into u_____76) waters (as Einstein said, "If we knew what we were doing, it would not be called research, would it?"). If your p_____77) about what will happen in these u_____78) waters are wrong, that's okay: Scientists are a_____79) to make mistakes (as Bates said, "Research is the process of going up a_____80) to see if they are blind"). Indeed, scientists often learn more from p_____81) that do not t_____82) out than from those that do.

일부 처음 시작하는 연구자들은 좋은 가설은 옳다는 것이 보장된 것이라고 잘못 믿는다(예를 들면, '알코올은 반응 시간을 둔화시킬 것이다.'). 하지만 여러분의 가설을 여러분이 검사해 보기 전에 그것이 사실이라고 이미 우리가 알고 있다면 여러분의 가설을 검사하는 것은 우리에게 아무런 새로운 것도 말해 주지 않을 것이다. 연구란 '새로운' 지식을 생산해야 한다는 것을 기억하라. 새로운 지식을 얻기 위해서 연구자이자 탐험가로서 여러분은 해변의 안전함(기정 사실)을 떠나 미개척 영역으로 과감히 들어가 볼 필요가 있다(아인슈타인이 말했듯이, "우리가 무엇을 하고 있는지 안다면 그것은 연구라고 불리지 않을 것이다, 그렇지?"). 이런 미개척 영역에서 무엇이 일어날 것인지에 관한 여러분의 예측이 틀린다면 그것은 괜찮다. 과학자는 실수를 저지르도록 허용되어 있다(Bates가 말했듯이, "연구는 막다른 길인지 보려고 골목길을 올라가 보는 과정이다."). 정말로 과학자는 흔히 결과를 내는 예측들보다는 결과를 내지 않는 예측들로부터 더 많이 배운다.

# 29 어법

While r_____83) on the needs of organizations, leaders, and families today, we r_____84) that one of the unique characteristics is i_____85). Why? Because i_____86) supports what everyone ultimately wants from their relationships: c_____87). Yet the m_____88) of leaders, organizations, and families are still using the language of the old paradigm in which one person—typically the oldest, most educated, and/or wealthiest—makes all the decisions, and their decisions rule with little d_____89) or i_____90) of others, resulting in e_____91). Today, this person could be a director, CEO, or other senior leader of an organization. There is no need for others to p_____92) their ideas because they are considered i_____93). Yet research shows that e_____94) in problem solving, even with a genius, is not as effective as i_____95), where everyone's ideas are heard and a solution is developed through c_____96).

오늘날 조직, 지도자, 그리고 가족의 요구에 관해 곰곰이 생각할 때 우리는 독특한 특성 중 하나가 포용성이라는 것을 깨닫는다. 왜 그런가? 포용성은 모든 사람이 자신의 관계에서 궁극적으로 원하는 것인 협력을 뒷받침하기 때문이다. 그러나 대다수의 지도자, 조직, 그리고 가족은 여전히 오래된 패러다임의 언어를 사용하고 있고, 거기서는 한 사람이, 보통 가장 연장자, 가장 교육을 많이 받은 사람, 그리고 / 또는 가장 부유한 사람인데, 모든 결정을 내리고 토론이나 다른 사람을 포함시키는 것이 거의 없이 그들의 결정이 지배하고 결과적으로 배타성을 초래한다. 오늘날 이 사람은 어떤 조직의 관리자, 최고 경영자, 또는 다른 상급 지도자일 수 있다. 다른 사람들이 자신의 생각을 제시할 필요가 없는데 왜냐하면 그것은 부적절한 것으로 여겨지기 때문이다. 그러나 연구에 따르면 문제 해결에 있어서 배타성은, 심지어 천재와 함께하는 것이더라도, 포용성만큼 효과적이지 않은데, 포용성이 있는 경우에는 모든 사람의 생각을 듣게 되고 해결책은 협력을 통해 발전된다.

## 30 어휘

The o_____97) point of view is i_____98) by John Ford's "philosophy of camera." Ford considered the camera to be a window and the audience to be outside the window viewing the people and events within. We are asked to watch the actions as if they were t_____99) place at a distance, and we are not asked to p_____100). The o_____101) point of view employs a s_____102) camera as much as possible in o_____103) to produce this window effect, and it c_____104) on the actors and the action without d_____105) attention to the camera. The objective camera suggests an e_____106) distance between camera and subject; the camera seems simply to be recording, as s_____107) as possible, the characters and actions of the story. For the most part, the director uses natural, normal types of camera positioning and camera angles. The o_____108) camera does not c_____109) on or i_____110) the action but m_____111) records it, letting it u_____112). We see the action from the viewpoint of an i_____113) observer. If the camera moves, it does so u_____114), calling as little attention to itself as possible.

객관적인 관점은 John Ford의 '카메라의 철학'에 의해 설명된다. Ford는 카메라를 창문이라고 생각했고 관객은 창문 안에 있는 사람과 사건을 바라보면서 창문 밖에 있다고 생각했다. 우리는 사건들이 멀리서 일어나고 있는 것처럼 그것들을 바라보도록 요청받고, 참여하도록 요청받지 않는다. 객관적인 관점은 이런 창문 효과를 만들기 위해 정적인 카메라를 가능한 한 많이 이용하고, 그것은 카메라에 관심을 끄는 것 없이 배우와 사건에 집중한다. 객관적인 카메라는 카메라와 대상 간의 감정적인 거리를 보여 주는데, 카메라는 이야기의 등장인물과 사건을 가능한 한 있는 그대로 그저 기록하고 있는 것으로 보인다. 대부분의 경우, 감독은 자연스럽고 일반적인 종류의 카메라 위치 선정과 카메라 각도를 사용한다. 객관적인 카메라는 사건에 관해 논평하거나 해석하지 않고 그것이 전개되게 하면서 그저 그것을 기록한다. 우리는 냉담한 관찰자의 관점에서 사건을 본다. 만약 카메라가 움직인다면 그것은 눈에 띄지 않게, 가능한 한 자신[카메라]에게 거의 관심을 불러일으키지 않으면서, 그렇게 한다.

## 31 빈칸

Even the most r_____115) of all musical institutions, the symphony orchestra, carries inside its DNA the l_____116) of the hunt. The various instruments in the orchestra can be t_____117) back to these p_____118) origins—their earliest forms were made either from the animal (horn, hide, gut, bone) or the weapons employed in bringing the animal under control (stick, bow). Are we wrong to hear this history in the music itself, in the f_____119) a_____120) and awe-inspiring a_____121) of those monumental symphonies that remain the core repertoire of the world's leading orchestras? Listening to Beethoven, Brahms, Mahler, Bruckner, Berlioz, Tchaikovsky, Shostakovich, and other great composers, I can easily s_____122) up images of b_____123) of men starting to chase animals, using sound as a source and symbol of d_____124), an expression of the will to p_____125) power.

심지어 모든 음악 단체 중 가장 훌륭한 단체인 교향악단도 자신의 DNA 안에 사냥의 유산을 지니고 있다. 교향악단에 있는 다양한 악기들은 다음의 원시적인 기원으로 거슬러 올라갈 수 있는데, 그것들의 초기 형태는 동물(뿔, 가죽, 내장, 뼈) 또는 동물을 진압하기 위해 사용된 무기(막대, 활)로 만들어졌다. 음악 그 자체에서, 세계의 주요한 교향악단의 핵심 레퍼토리로 남아 있는 기념비적인 교향곡들의 강력한 공격성과 경외감을 자아내는 당당함에서 이러한 역사를 듣는다면 우리가 틀린 것인가? 베토벤, 브람스, 말러, 브루크너, 베를리오즈, 차이코프스키, 쇼스타코비치 및 다른 위대한 작곡가들의 음악을 들으며, 나는 소리를 지배의 원천이자 상징으로, 공격적인 힘에 대한 의지의 표현으로 사용하면서 동물을 쫓기 시작하는 사람들 무리의 이미지를 쉽게 떠올릴 수 있다.

# 32 빈칸

Our brains have e_____126) to remember u_____127) events because basic survival depends on the ability to p_____128) causes and predict effects. If the brain predicts one event and experiences another, the u_____129) will be especially interesting and will be encoded a_____130). Neurologist and classroom teacher Judith Willis has c_____131) that surprise in the classroom is one of the most effective ways of teaching with brain s_____132) in mind. If students are e_____133) to new experiences via demonstrations or through the u_____134) e_____135) of their teachers or peers, they will be m_____136) more l_____137) to connect with the information that follows. Willis has written that encouraging active discovery in the classroom allows students to i_____138) with new information, moving it b_____139) working memory to be p_____140) in the frontal lobe, which is d_____141) to advanced c_____142) functioning. Preference for n_____143) sets us up for learning by directing attention, providing s_____144) to developing p_____145) systems, and f_____146) curious and exploratory behavior.

우리의 뇌는 예상치 못한 사건들을 기억하도록 진화해 왔는데, 왜냐하면 기본적인 생존이 원인을 인식하고 결과를 예측하는 능력에 달려 있기 때문이다. 만약 뇌가 어떤 사건을 예측하고 (그것과) 다른 사건을 경험한다면, 그 특이함은 특히 흥미로울 것이고 그에 따라 (뇌 속의 정보로) 입력될 것이다. 신경학자이자 학급 교사인 Judith Willis는 교실에서의 놀라움은 뇌 자극을 염두에 두고 가르치는 가장 효과적인 방법 중 하나라고 주장했다. 학생들이 실연, 혹은 교사나 또래 친구의 예상치 못한 열의를 통해 새로운 경험에 노출되면, 그들은 뒤따르는 정보와 연결될 가능성이 훨씬 더 클 것이다. Willis는 교실에서의 능동적인 발견을 장려하는 것이 학생으로 하여금 새로운 정보와 상호 작용하게 해 주어서, 그것(새로운 정보)이 작동 기억을 넘어 고도의 인지 기능을 전담하는 (대뇌의) 전두엽에서 처리되도록 한다고 기술했다. 새로움에 대한 선호는, 주의를 이끌고, 지각 체계를 발전시키는 데 자극을 제공하며, 호기심 많고 탐구적인 행동을 충족함으로써 우리를 학습하도록 준비시킨다.

# 33 빈칸

P_____147) research has shown that people naturally d_____148) up c_____149) labor, often without thinking about it. Imagine you're cooking up a special dinner with a friend. You're a great cook, but your friend is the wine expert, an amateur s_____150). A neighbor d_____151) by and starts telling you both about the terrific new wines being sold at the l_____152) store just down the street. There are many new wines, so there's a lot to remember. How hard are you going to try to remember what the neighbor has to say about which wines to buy? Why b_____153) when the information would be better r_____154) by the wine expert sitting next to you? If your friend wasn't around, you might try harder. After all, it would be good to know what a good wine would be for the evening's f_____155) But your friend, the wine expert, is likely to remember the information without even t_____156).

심리학 연구에 따르면, 사람들은 자연스럽게 인지 노동을 나누는데, 흔히 그것에 대해서 별 생각 없이 그렇게 한다. 여러분이 친구와 함께 특별한 저녁식사를 요리하고 있다고 상상해 보라. 여러분은 요리를 잘하지만, 친구는 아마추어 소믈리에라고 할 수 있는 와인 전문가이다. 이웃이 들르더니 여러분 두 사람에게 거리를 따라가면 바로 있는 주류 가게에서 파는 기막히게 좋은 새로운 와인에 대해 말하기 시작한다. 많은 새로운 와인이 있어서 기억해야 할 것이 많다. 어떤 와인을 사야 하는지에 관해 이웃이 할 말을 기억하기 위해 여러분은 얼마나 열심히 노력할까? 여러분 옆에 앉아 있는 와인 전문가가 그 정보를 더 잘 기억하고 있는데 무엇 하러 그러겠는가? 여러분의 친구가 곁에 없다면 더 열심히 애쓸지도 모른다. 어쨌든 저녁 만찬을 위해 뭐가 좋은 와인이 될지 아는 것은 좋은 일일 것이다. 하지만, 와인 전문가인 여러분의 친구는 애쓰지도 않고 그 정보를 기억하기가 쉽다.

## 34 빈칸

Even companies that sell p_____157) products to make p_____158) are f_____159) by their boards and investors to r_____160) their u_____161) m_____162) and to collect as much data as possible from consumers. Supermarkets no l_____163) make all their money selling their produce and manufactured goods. They give you loyalty cards with which they t_____164) your purchasing behaviors p_____165). Then supermarkets sell this purchasing behavior to marketing a_____166) companies. The marketing analytics companies perform m_____167) l_____168) procedures, s_____169) the data in new ways, and resell behavioral data back to product manufacturers as marketing i_____170). When data and machine learning become c_____171) of value in a c_____172) system, then every company's natural t_____173) is to m_____174) its ability to conduct s_____175) on its own customers because the customers are themselves the new value-creation devices.

수익을 내기 위해 물적 제품을 판매하는 기업조차도 이사회와 투자자에 의해 어쩔 수 없이 자신의 근원적인 동기를 재고하게 되고 고객에게서 가능한 한 많은 정보를 수집하게 된다. 슈퍼마켓은 더 이상 자신의 농산물과 제조된 물품을 판매해서 자신의 모든 돈을 버는 것이 아니다. 그들은 여러분의 구매 행동을 정밀하게 추적하게 해 주는 고객 우대 카드를 여러분에게 준다. 그리고 나서 슈퍼마켓은 이 구매 행위를 마케팅 분석 기업에 판매한다. 마케팅 분석 기업은 기계 학습 절차를 수행하고 그 정보를 새로운 방식으로 쪼개서 행동 정보를 제품 제조 기업에 통찰력 있는 마케팅 정보로 다시 되판다. 정보와 기계 학습이 자본주의 체제에서 가치 있는 통화가 될 때, 고객 자체가 새로운 가치 창출 장치이기 때문에 모든 기업의 자연스러운 경향은 자신의 고객을 관찰하는 능력을 최대화하는 것이다.

## 35 무관

Academics, politicians, marketers and others have in the past d_____176) whether or not it is e_____177) correct to market products and services directly to young consumers. This is also a d_____178) for psychologists who have questioned whether they o_____179) to help advertisers m_____180) children into purchasing more products they have seen advertised. Advertisers have a_____181) to taking advantage of the fact that it is easy to make children feel that they are losers if they do not o_____182) the 'right' products. Clever advertising i_____183) children that they will be viewed by their peers in an u_____184) way if they do not have the products that are advertised, t_____185) playing on their emotional v_____186). The c_____187) feelings of i_____188) created by advertising have been suggested to contribute to children becoming f_____189) with instant g_____190) and beliefs that material p_____191) are important.

지금까지 대학 교수, 정치인, 마케팅 담당자, 그리고 그 외의 사람들은 제품과 서비스를 어린 소비자들에게 직접 판촉하는 것이 윤리적으로 옳은지 그렇지 않은지를 논쟁해 왔다. 이것은 또한, 광고주들이 아이들을 조종해서 광고되는 것을 그들이 본 더 많은 제품을 구매하게 하는 것을 도와야 하는지 의문을 제기하는 심리학자들에게도 딜레마이다. 광고주들은 아이들이 그 '적절한' 제품을 소유하고 있지 않으면 자신이 패배자라고 느끼게 만드는 것이 쉽다는 사실을 이용한 것을 인정했다. 영리한 광고는 아이들에게 만약 그들이 광고되는 제품을 가지고 있지 않으면 자신의 또래 친구들에게 부정적으로 보일 것이라고 알려 주고, 그로 인해 아이들의 정서적인 취약성을 이용한다. 광고가 만들어 내는, 끊임없이 부적절하다고 느끼는 감정은, 아이들이 즉각적인 만족감과 물질적 소유물이 중요하다는 믿음에 집착하게 되는 데 기여한다고 언급되어 왔다.

# 36 순서

Once we r_____192) the false-cause issue, we see it everywhere. For example, a recent long-term study of University of Toronto medical students c_____193) that medical school class presidents lived an average of 2.4 years less than other medical school graduates. At first glance, this s_____194) to i_____195) that being a medical school class president is bad for you. Does this mean that you should avoid being medical school class president at all costs? Probably not. Just because being class president is c_____196) with shorter life expectancy does not mean that it causes shorter life expectancy. In fact, it s_____197) likely that the sort of person who becomes medical school class president is, on average, extremely hard-working, serious, and a_____198). Perhaps this extra stress, and the corresponding l_____199) of social and relaxation time — rather than being class president p_____200) s_____201) — c_____202) to lower life expectancy. If so, the real lesson of the study is that we should all r_____203) a little and not let our work t_____204) over our lives.

일단 잘못 파악한 원인 문제를 우리가 인식하면, 우리는 그것을 어디에서나 보게 된다. 예를 들어, 토론토 대학의 의대생들에 대한 최근의 장기간의 연구는 의대 학년 대표들이 다른 의대 졸업생들보다 평균 2.4년 더 적게 살았다는 결론을 내렸다. 처음 봐서는, 이것은 의대 학년 대표인 것이 여러분에게 해롭다는 것을 의미하는 것처럼 보였다. 이것은 여러분이 무슨 수를 써서라도 의대 학년 대표가 되는 것을 피해야 한다는 것을 의미하는가? 아마도 그렇지는 않을 것이다. 단지 학년 대표인 것이 더 짧은 평균 수명과 서로 관련된다고 해서 그것이 더 짧은 평균 수명을 '유발한다'는 의미는 아니다. 사실, 아마도 의대 학년 대표가 되는 그런 부류의 사람은 평균적으로 몹시 열심히 공부하고, 진지하며, 야망이 있는 것 같다. 의대 학년 대표인 것 그 자체라기보다 아마도 이러한 가중된 스트레스와 그에 상응하는 사교와 휴식 시간의 부족이 더 짧은 평균 수명의 원인인 것 같다. 만약 그렇다면, 이 연구의 진정한 교훈은 우리 모두가 약간의 휴식을 취해야 하고 우리의 일이 우리의 삶을 장악하게 해서는 안 된다는 것이다.

---

# 37 순서

We commonly argue about the f_____205) of t_____206) — whether this or that tax will f_____207) more heavily on the rich or the poor. But the e_____208) dimension of t_____209) goes b_____210) d_____211) about fairness, to the moral judgements societies make about which activities are worthy of honor and r_____212), and which ones should be d_____213). Sometimes, these judgements are e_____214). Taxes on tobacco, alcohol, and casinos are called "sin taxes" because they s_____215) to discourage activities considered h_____216) or u_____217). Such taxes express society's disapproval of these activities by r_____218) the cost of e_____219) in them. Proposals to tax sugary sodas (to combat obesity) or carbon emissions (to address climate change) likewise seek to change n_____220) and shape behavior. Not all taxes have this a_____221). We do not tax income to express d_____222) of paid employment or to discourage people from engaging in it. N_____223) is a general sales tax intended as a d_____224) to buying things. These are simply ways of raising r_____225).

우리는 흔히 과세의 공정성, 즉 이런 저런 세금이 부자들에게 더 과중하게 부과될 것인지 아니면 가난한 사람들에게 그럴 것인지에 관해 논한다. 그러나 과세의 표현적 차원은 공정성에 대한 논쟁을 넘어, 어떤 활동이 명예와 인정을 받을 가치가 있고 어떤 활동이 억제되어야 하는지에 대해 사회가 내리는 도덕적 판단에까지 이른다. 때때로 이러한 판단은 명백하다. 담배, 술, 그리고 카지노에 대한 세금은 해롭거나 바람직하지 않은 것으로 간주되는 활동들을 억제하려고 하기 때문에 '죄악세'라고 불린다. 그런 세금은 이러한 활동을 하는 데 드는 비용을 증가시킴으로써 그것에 대한 사회의 반대를 표현한다. 마찬가지로 (비만에 맞서기 위해) 설탕이 든 탄산음료에 세금을 부과하는 제안이나 (기후 변화에 대처하기 위해) 탄소 배출에 세금을 부과하는 제안은 규범을 바꾸고 행동을 형성하려 한다. 모든 세금이 이런 목적을 가진 것은 아니다. 우리는 유급 고용에 대한 반대를 표명하거나 사람들이 그것을 하는 것을 막기 위해 소득에 세금을 부과하는 것은 아니다. 일반 판매세 역시 물건을 사는 것의 억제책으로서 의도된 것이 아니다. 이것들은 단순히 세입을 올리는 방법이다.

# 38 삽입

Most beliefs—but not all—are open to tests of v_____226). This means that beliefs can be tested to see if they are correct or false. Beliefs can be v_____227) or f_____228) with objective c_____229) e_____230) to the person. There are people who believe the Earth is flat and not a sphere. Because we have objective evidence that the Earth is in fact a sphere, the flat Earth belief can be shown to be false. Also, the belief that it will rain tomorrow can be tested for truth by waiting until tomorrow and seeing whether it rains or not. However, some types of beliefs cannot be tested for truth because we cannot get e_____231) e_____232) in our lifetimes (such as a belief that the Earth will stop spinning on its axis by the year 9999 or that there is life on a planet 100-million light-years away). Also, meta-physical beliefs (such as the e_____233) and nature of a god) present c_____234) challenges in generating evidence that everyone is w_____235) to use as a truth c_____236).

전부는 아니지만 대부분의 믿음은 검증 시험을 받을 수 있다. 이것은 믿음이 옳거나 그른지를 확인하기 위해 시험될 수 있다는 것을 의미한다. 믿음은 그 사람의 외부에 있는 객관적인 기준을 통해 진실임이 입증되거나 거짓임이 입증될 수 있다. 지구가 평평하고 구가 아니라고 믿는 사람들이 있다. 우리는 지구가 사실은 구라는 객관적인 증거를 가지고 있기 때문에, 지구가 평평하다는 믿음은 거짓임이 증명될 수 있다. 또한, 내일 비가 올 것이라는 믿음은 내일까지 기다려 비가 오는지 안 오는지 봄으로써 진실인지 확인될 수 있다. 하지만, (9999년이 되면 지구가 자전하는 것을 멈출 것이라는 믿음이나 1억 광년 떨어진 행성에 생명체가 있다는 것 같은) 어떤 종류의 믿음은 우리가 일생 동안 외부 증거를 얻을 수 없기 때문에 진실인지 확인될 수 없다. 또한, (신의 존재와 본질과 같은) 형이상학적 믿음은 모든 사람이 진리 기준으로 기꺼이 사용할 증거를 만드는 데 있어서 상당한 난제가 된다.

# 39 삽입

Everyone automatically c_____237) and g_____238) all the time. Unconsciously. It is not a question of being p_____239) or e_____240). Categories are absolutely necessary for us to function. They give structure to our thoughts. Imagine if we saw every item and every scenario as truly u_____241) — we would not even have a language to d_____242) the world around us. But the necessary and useful i_____243) to generalize can d_____244) our world view. It can make us m_____245) group together things, or people, or countries that are actually very different. It can make us a_____246) everything or everyone in one category is similar. And, maybe, most u_____247) of all, it can make us j_____248) to conclusions about a whole category b_____249) on a few, or even just one, u_____250) example.

모든 사람들은 항상 자동적으로 분류하고 일반화한다. 무의식적으로 (그렇게 한다). 그것은 편견을 갖고 있다거나 계몽되어 있다는 것의 문제가 아니다. 범주는 우리가 (정상적으로) 활동하는 데 반드시 필요하다. 그것들은 우리의 사고에 체계를 준다. 만일 우리가 모든 품목과 모든 있을 법한 상황을 정말로 유일무이한 것으로 본다고 상상해 보라. 그러면 우리는 우리 주변의 세계를 설명할 언어조차 갖지 못할 것이다. 그러나 필요하고 유용한 일반화하려는 본능은 우리의 세계관을 왜곡할 수 있다. 그것은 우리가 실제로는 아주 다른 사물들이나, 사람들, 혹은 나라들을 하나로 잘못 묶게 만들 수 있다. 그것은 우리가 하나의 범주 안에 있는 모든 것이나 모든 사람이 비슷하다고 가정하게 만들 수 있다. 그리고 어쩌면 모든 것 중에서 가장 유감스러운 것은, 그것이 우리로 하여금 몇 가지, 또는 심지어 고작 하나의 특이한 사례를 바탕으로 전체 범주에 대해 성급하게 결론을 내리게 만들 수 있다는 것이다.

# 40 요약

At the University of Iowa, students were b_____251) shown numbers that they had to m_____252). Then they were o_____253) the choice of either a fruit salad or a chocolate cake. When the number the students memorized was seven digits long, 63% of them chose the cake. When the number they were asked to remember had just two digits, however, 59% o_____254) for the fruit salad. Our r_____255) brains know that the fruit salad is better for our health, but our r_____256) brains d_____257) that soft, fattening chocolate cake. If the reflective brain is busy f_____258) something else out — like trying to remember a seven-digit number — then i_____259) can easily win. On the other hand, if we're not thinking too hard about something else (with only a minor d_____260) like memorizing two digits), then the reflective system can d_____261) the emotional impulse of the reflexive side.

→ According to the above experiment, the increased i_____262) l_____263) on the brain leads the reflexive side of the brain to become d_____264).

Iowa 대학교에서, 학생들에게 그들이 암기해야 하는 숫자를 잠시 보여 주었다. 그러고 나서 그들에게 과일 샐러드나 초콜릿 케이크 중 하나를 선택하게 했다. 학생들이 외운 숫자가 일곱 자리일 때, 그들 중 63%가 케이크를 선택했다. 그러나 그들이 기억하도록 요청받은 숫자가 두 자리밖에 되지 않았을 때, 59%는 과일 샐러드를 선택했다. 우리의 숙고하는 뇌는 과일 샐러드가 우리의 건강에 더 좋다는 것을 알지만, 우리의 반사적인 뇌는 그 부드럽고 살이 찌는 초콜릿 케이크를 원한다. 만약 숙고하는 뇌가 일곱 자리 숫자를 기억하려고 애쓰는 일과 같은 다른 어떤 것을 해결하느라 바쁘다면, 충동이 쉽게 이길 수 있다. 다른 한편, 우리가 다른 것에 관해 너무 열심히 생각하고 있지 않다면(두 자리 숫자를 외우는 것과 같은 사소하게 주의를 산만하게 하는 일만 있을 때), 숙고하는 (뇌의) 계통은 반사적인 쪽의 감정적인 충동을 억제할 수 있다.
→ 위 실험에 따르면, 뇌에 가해지는 증가된 지적 부담은 뇌의 반사적인 부분이 우세해지게 한다.

## 41~42 제목, 어휘

Test scores are not a m_____265) of self-worth; however, we often a_____266) our sense of w_____267) with our performance on an exam. Thoughts such as "If I don't pass this test, I'm a failure" are mental traps not r_____268) in truth. Failing a test is failing a test, nothing more. It is in no way d_____269) of your v_____270) as a person. Believing that test performance is a r_____ _271) of your v_____272) places u_____273) pressure on your performance. Not passing the certification test only means that your certification status has been delayed. M_____274) a positive attitude is t_____275) important. If you have studied hard, r_____276) this mentally and believe that you will do well. If, on the other hand, you did not study as hard as you should have or wanted to, accept that as b_____277) your control for now and a_____278) to the task of doing the best you can. If things do not go well this time, you know what needs to be done _____ _____ _____279) the next exam. Talk to yourself in positive terms. Avoid r_____280) past or future test performance by placing the blame on secondary variables. Thoughts such as, "I didn't have enough time," or "I should have ...," c_____281) the stress of test-taking. Take control by a_____282) your value, self-worth, and d_____283) to meeting the test challenge head on. Repeat to yourself "I can and I will pass this exam."

시험 점수는 자부심의 척도가 아니지만, 우리는 흔히 우리의 자부심과 우리의 시험 성적을 연관시킨다. "이 시험에 합격하지 못하면 나는 실패자야."와 같은 생각은 사실에 뿌리를 두고 있지 않은 정신적 함정이다. 시험에 실패하는 것은 시험에 실패하는 것이지, 그 이상이 아니다. 그것은 결코 사람으로서의 여러분의 가치를 설명하지 않는다. 시험 성적이 여러분의 미덕을 반영하는 것이라고 믿는 것은 여러분의 수행에 부당한 압력을 가한다. 자격 시험을 통과하지 못한 것은 단지 여러분의 자격 지위가 지연되었다는 것을 의미할 따름이다. 그러므로 긍정적인 태도를 유지하는 것이 중요하다. 만약 여러분이 열심히 공부했다면, 마음속으로 이것을 재확인하고 좋은 성적이 나올 것이라고 믿으라. 다른 한편, 만약 여러분이 했어야 하거나 원하는 만큼 열심히 공부하지 않았다면, 지금으로서는 여러분이 어찌할 수 없는 것으로 그것을 받아들이고 여러분이 할 수 있는 최선의 것을 하는 과제에 주의를 기울이라. 만약 이번에 잘 되지 않는다면, 다음 시험 준비에서는 무엇을 해야 될지 알게 된다. 긍정적인 말로 자신에게 이야기하라. 부차적인 변수에 책임을 지움으로써 과거 또는 미래의 시험 성적을 합리화하는 것을 피하라. "나는 시간이 충분하지 않았어."라거나 "내가 그랬어야 했는데…"와 같은 생각은 시험을 보는 것의 스트레스를 완화시킨다(→ 악화시킨다). 자신의 가치, 자부심, 그리고 시험 과제에 정면으로 맞서는 것에 대한 헌신을 확인함으로써 통제권을 잡으라. "난 할 수 있고 이 시험에 합격할 거야."라고 자신에게 되풀이해 말하라.

# 43~45 순서, 지칭, 세부 내용

Once upon a time there lived a p_____284) but c_____285) shoemaker. He was so happy, he sang all day long. The children loved to stand around his window to listen to him. Next door to the shoemaker lived a rich man. He _____ _____286) sit up all night to count his gold. In the morning, he went to bed, but he could not sleep because of the sound of the shoemaker's singing. One day, he thought of a way of stopping the singing. He wrote a letter to the shoemaker asking him to visit. The shoemaker came at o_____287), and to his surprise the rich man gave him a bag of gold. When he got home again, the shoemaker opened the bag. He had never seen so much gold before! When he sat down at his bench and began, carefully, to count it, the children watched through the window. There was _____288) much there that the shoemaker was a_____289) to let it o_____290) of his s_____291). So he took it to bed with him. But he could not sleep for w_____292) about it. Very early in the morning, he got up and brought his gold down from the bedroom. He had d_____293) to hide it up the c_____294) instead. But he was still u_____295), and in a little while he d_____296) a hole in the garden and buried his bag of gold in it. It was no use trying to work. He was too worried about the safety of his gold. And as for singing, he was too m_____297) to u_____298) a note. He could not sleep, or work, or sing—and, worst of all, the children no longer came to see him. At last, the shoemaker felt so unhappy that he s_____299) his bag of gold and ran next door to the rich man. "Please take back your gold," he said. "The worry of it is making me i_____300), and I have lost all of my friends. I would rather be a poor shoemaker, as I was before." And so the shoemaker was happy again and sang all day at his work.

옛날 옛적에 가난하지만 쾌활한 구두 만드는 사람이 살았다. 그는 너무 행복해서 하루 종일 노래를 불렀다. 아이들은 그의 창문에 둘러서서 그가 노래하는 것을 듣기 좋아했다. 구두 만드는 사람 옆집에는 부자가 살았다. 그는 자신의 금화를 세기 위해 밤을 새곤 했다. 아침에 그는 잠자리에 들었지만 구두 만드는 사람의 노랫소리 때문에 잠을 잘 수 없었다. 어느 날, 그는 그 노래를 멈추는 방법을 생각해냈다. 그는 구두 만드는 사람에게 방문해 달라고 요청하는 편지를 써 보냈다. 구두 만드는 사람은 즉시 왔고, 놀랍게도 부자는 그에게 금화가 든 가방을 주었다. 집에 다시 돌아왔을 때, 구두 만드는 사람은 그 가방을 열었다. 그는 그때까지 그렇게 많은 금화를 본 적이 없었다! 그가 의자에 앉아 조심스럽게 그것을 세기 시작했을 때, 아이들이 창문을 통해서 지켜보았다. 거기엔 금화가 너무 많아서 구두 만드는 사람은 그것을 자신에게 보이지 않는 곳에 두기가 겁났다. 그래서 그는 그것을 잠자리에 가져갔다. 그러나 그는 그것에 대한 걱정으로 잠을 잘 수 없었다. 매우 이른 아침에, 그는 일어나서 금화를 침실에서 가지고 내려왔다. 대신에 그는 그것을 굴뚝에 숨기기로 결정했다. 그러나 그는 여전히 불안했고, 잠시 후에 정원에 구멍을 파고 그 안에 금화가 든 가방을 묻었다. 일을 해보려고 해도 소용없었다. 그는 자신의 금화의 안전이 너무나 걱정되었다. 그리고 노래에 관해서라면, 그는 너무 불행해서 한 음도 낼 수 없었다. 그는 잠을 잘 수도, 일을 할 수도, 노래를 부를 수도 없었고, 최악은, 아이들이 더 이상 그를 보러 오지 않았다. 마침내, 구두 만드는 사람은 너무 불행해져서 그의 금화가 든 가방을 움켜쥐고 옆집 부자에게 달려갔다. "제발 당신의 금화를 다시 가져가세요."라고 그가 말했다. "그것에 대한 걱정이 저를 아프게 하고 있고, 저는 제 친구들을 모두 잃었어요. 저는 예전처럼 차라리 가난한 구두 만드는 사람이 되겠어요." 그래서 구두 만드는 사람은 다시 행복해졌고 일을 하면서 하루 종일 노래를 불렀다.

# 2021 고2 3월 모의고사 ❷ 회차 : : 점 / 300점

❶ voca  ❷ text  ❸ [ / ]  ④ _____  ❺ quiz 1  ❻ quiz 2  ❼ quiz 3  ❽ quiz 4  ❾ quiz 5  ❿ quiz 6

## 18 목적

My name is Anthony Thompson and I am writing on b_____1) of the residents' a_____2). Our r_____3) program has been working well thanks to your p_____4). However, a problem has r_____5) occurred that needs your attention. Because there is no g_____6) day for recycling, residents are putting their recycling out at any time. This makes the recycling area m_____7), which requires extra labor and cost. To d_____8) with this problem, the residents' association has decided on a day to recycle. I would like to let you know that you can put out your recycling on Wednesdays only. I am sure it will make our apartment complex look m_____9) more p_____10). Thank you in a_____11) for your cooperation.

## 19 심경

It was a day I was d_____12) to give a presentation at work, not something I'd do often. As I stood up to begin, I froze. A chilly 'pins-and-needles' feeling c_____13) over me, starting in my hands. Time s_____14) to stand still as I s_____15) to start speaking, and I felt a p_____16) around my throat, as though my voice was t_____17) and couldn't come out. G_____18) around at the blur of faces, I realized they were all waiting for me to begin, but by now I knew I couldn't continue.

## 20 주장

No matter what your situation, whether you are an insider or an outsider, you need to become the voice that c_____19) yesterday's answers. Think about the c_____20) that make outsiders valuable to an organization. They are the people who have the p_____21) to see problems that the insiders are too close to really notice. They are the ones who have the freedom to point out these problems and criticize them without risking their job or their career. Part of a_____22) an outsider m_____23) is forcing yourself to look around your organization with this d_____24), less emotional p_____25). If you didn't know your coworkers and feel b_____26) to them by your shared experiences, what would you think of them? You may not have the job security or confidence to speak your mind to management, but you can make these "outsider" a_____27) of your organization on your own and use what you d_____28) to advance your career.

# 21 의미

The known fact of c_____29), without knowing p_____30) what those c_____31) will be, shows that disaster preparation is not the same thing as disaster rehearsal. No matter h_____32) many mock disasters are s_____33) according to prior plans, the real disaster will never m_____34) any one of them. Disaster-preparation planning is more like training for a marathon than training for a high-jump competition or a sprinting event. Marathon runners do not practice by running the full course of twenty-six miles; rather, they get into s_____35) by running shorter distances and building up their e_____36) with cross-training. If they have prepared successfully, then they are in o_____37) condition to run the marathon over its p_____38) course and length, a_____39) a range of weather conditions, predicted or not. This is normal marathon preparation.

# 22 요지

Fears of damaging ecosystems are b_____40) on the sound c_____41) principle that we should a_____42) to minimize the d_____43) we cause, but there is a risk that this principle may be confused with the old idea of a 'balance of nature.' This supposes a perfect order of nature that will s_____44) to m_____45) itself and that we should not change. It is a romantic, not to say i_____46), notion, but deeply misleading because it supposes a s_____47) condition. Ecosystems are d_____48), and although some may e_____49), apparently unchanged, for periods that are long in c_____50) with the human lifespan, they must and do change eventually. Species come and go, climates change, plant and animal communities a_____51) to a_____52) circumstances, and when examined in f_____53) detail such a_____54) and consequent change can be seen to be taking place c_____55). The 'balance of nature' is a myth. Our planet is dynamic, and so are the arrangements by which its inhabitants live together.

# 23 주제

Before the modern scientific e_____56), creativity was a_____57) to a s_____58) force; all n_____59) ideas originated with the gods. After all, how could a person create something that did not exist before the d_____60) act of creation? In fact, the Latin meaning of the verb "inspire" is "to breathe into," r_____61) the belief that creative inspiration was similar to the moment in creation when God first breathed life into man. Plato argued that the poet was p_____62) by divine inspiration, and Plotin wrote that art could only be beautiful if it descended from God. The artist's job was not to i_____63) nature but rather to reveal the s_____64) and t_____65) qualities of nature. Art could only be a p_____66) imitation of the perfection of the world of ideas. Greek artists did not b_____67) imitate what they saw in reality; instead they tried to represent the pure, true forms u_____68) reality, resulting in a sort of c_____69) between a_____70) and a_____71).

## 24 제목

Some beginning researchers mistakenly believe that a good h_____72) is one that is g_____73) to be right (e.g., alcohol will slow down reaction time). However, if we already know your hypothesis is true before you test it, testing your hypothesis won't tell us anything new. Remember, research _____ _____ _____74) produce new knowledge. To get new knowledge, you, as a researcher-explorer, need to leave the safety of the shore (established facts) and v_____75) into u_____76) waters (as Einstein said, "If we knew what we were doing, it would not be called research, would it?"). If your p_____77) about what will happen in these u_____78) waters are wrong, that's okay: Scientists are a_____79) to make mistakes (as Bates said, "Research is the process of going up a_____80) to see if they are blind"). Indeed, scientists often learn more from p_____81) that do not t_____82) out than from those that do.

## 29 어법

While r_____83) on the needs of organizations, leaders, and families today, we r_____84) that one of the unique characteristics is i_____85). Why? Because i_____86) supports what everyone ultimately wants from their relationships: c_____87). Yet the m_____88) of leaders, organizations, and families are still using the language of the old paradigm in which one person — typically the oldest, most educated, and/or wealthiest — makes all the decisions, and their decisions rule with little d_____89) or i_____90) of others, resulting in e_____91). Today, this person could be a director, CEO, or other senior leader of an organization. There is no need for others to p_____92) their ideas because they are considered i_____93). Yet research shows that e_____94) in problem solving, even with a genius, is not as effective as i_____95), where everyone's ideas are heard and a solution is developed through c_____96).

## 30 어휘

The o_____97) point of view is i_____98) by John Ford's "philosophy of camera." Ford considered the camera to be a window and the audience to be outside the window viewing the people and events within. We are asked to watch the actions as if they were t_____99) place at a distance, and we are not asked to p_____100). The o_____101) point of view employs a s_____102) camera as much as possible in o_____103) to produce this window effect, and it c_____104) on the actors and the action without d_____105) attention to the camera. The objective camera suggests an e_____106) distance between camera and subject; the camera seems simply to be recording, as s_____107) as possible, the characters and actions of the story. For the most part, the director uses natural, normal types of camera positioning and camera angles. The o_____108) camera does not c_____109) on or i_____110) the action but m_____111) records it, letting it u_____112). We see the action from the viewpoint of an i_____113) observer. If the camera moves, it does so u_____114), calling as little attention to itself as possible.

## 31 빈칸

Even the most r_____115) of all musical institutions, the symphony orchestra, carries inside its DNA the l_____116) of the hunt. The various instruments in the orchestra can be t_____117) back to these p_____118) origins — their earliest forms were made either from the animal (horn, hide, gut, bone) or the weapons employed in bringing the animal under control (stick, bow). Are we wrong to hear this history in the music itself, in the f_____119) a_____120) and awe-inspiring a_____121) of those monumental symphonies that remain the core repertoire of the world's leading orchestras? Listening to Beethoven, Brahms, Mahler, Bruckner, Berlioz, Tchaikovsky, Shostakovich, and other great composers, I can easily s_____122) up images of b_____123) of men starting to chase animals, using sound as a source and symbol of d_____124), an expression of the will to p_____125) power.

## 32 빈칸

Our brains have e_____126) to remember u_____127) events because basic survival depends on the ability to p_____128) causes and predict effects. If the brain predicts one event and experiences another, the u_____129) will be especially interesting and will be encoded a_____130). Neurologist and classroom teacher Judith Willis has c_____131) that surprise in the classroom is one of the most effective ways of teaching with brain s_____132) in mind. If students are e_____133) to new experiences via demonstrations or through the u_____134) e_____135) of their teachers or peers, they will be m_____136) more l_____137) to connect with the information that follows. Willis has written that encouraging active discovery in the classroom allows students to i_____138) with new information, moving it b_____139) working memory to be p_____140) in the frontal lobe, which is d_____141) to advanced c_____142) functioning. Preference for n_____143) sets us up for learning by directing attention, providing s_____144) to developing p_____145) systems, and f_____146) curious and exploratory behavior.

## 33 빈칸

P_____147) research has shown that people naturally d_____148) up c_____149) labor, often without thinking about it. Imagine you're cooking up a special dinner with a friend. You're a great cook, but your friend is the wine expert, an amateur s_____150). A neighbor d_____151) by and starts telling you both about the terrific new wines being sold at the l_____152) store just down the street. There are many new wines, so there's a lot to remember. How hard are you going to try to remember what the neighbor has to say about which wines to buy? Why b_____153) when the information would be better r_____154) by the wine expert sitting next to you? If your friend wasn't around, you might try harder. After all, it would be good to know what a good wine would be for the evening's f_____155) But your friend, the wine expert, is likely to remember the information without even t_____156).

## 34 빈칸

Even companies that sell p_____157) products to make p_____158) are f_____159) by their boards and investors to r_____160) their u_____161) m_____162) and to collect as much data as possible from consumers. Supermarkets no l_____163) make all their money selling their produce and manufactured goods. They give you loyalty cards with which they t_____164) your purchasing behaviors p_____165). Then supermarkets sell this purchasing behavior to marketing a_____166) companies. The marketing analytics companies perform m_____167) l_____168) procedures, s_____169) the data in new ways, and resell behavioral data back to product manufacturers as marketing i_____170). When data and machine learning become c_____171) of value in a c_____172) system, then every company's natural t_____173) is to m_____174) its ability to conduct s_____175) on its own customers because the customers are themselves the new value-creation devices.

## 35 무관

Academics, politicians, marketers and others have in the past d_____176) whether or not it is e_____177) correct to market products and services directly to young consumers. This is also a d_____178) for psychologists who have questioned whether they o_____179) to help advertisers m_____180) children into purchasing more products they have seen advertised. Advertisers have a_____181) to taking advantage of the fact that it is easy to make children feel that they are losers if they do not o_____182) the 'right' products. Clever advertising i_____183) children that they will be viewed by their peers in an u_____184) way if they do not have the products that are advertised, t_____185) playing on their emotional v_____186). The c_____187) feelings of i_____188) created by advertising have been suggested to contribute to children becoming f_____189) with instant g_____190) and beliefs that material p_____191) are important.

## 36 순서

Once we r_____192) the false-cause issue, we see it everywhere. For example, a recent long-term study of University of Toronto medical students c_____193) that medical school class presidents lived an average of 2.4 years less than other medical school graduates. At first glance, this s_____194) to i_____195) that being a medical school class president is bad for you. Does this mean that you should avoid being medical school class president at all costs? Probably not. Just because being class president is c_____196) with shorter life expectancy does not mean that it causes shorter life expectancy. In fact, it s_____197) likely that the sort of person who becomes medical school class president is, on average, extremely hard-working, serious, and a_____198). Perhaps this extra stress, and the corresponding l_____199) of social and relaxation time—rather than being class president p_____200) s_____201)—c_____202) to lower life expectancy. If so, the real lesson of the study is that we should all r_____203) a little and not let our work t_____204) over our lives.

# 37 순서

We commonly argue about the f_____205) of t_____206) — whether this or that tax will f_____207) more heavily on the rich or the poor. But the e_____208) dimension of t_____209) goes b_____210) d_____211) about fairness, to the moral judgements societies make about which activities are worthy of honor and r_____212), and which ones should be d_____213). Sometimes, these judgements are e_____214). Taxes on tobacco, alcohol, and casinos are called "sin taxes" because they s_____215) to discourage activities considered h_____216) or u_____217). Such taxes express society's disapproval of these activities by r_____218) the cost of e_____219) in them. Proposals to tax sugary sodas (to combat obesity) or carbon emissions (to address climate change) likewise seek to change n_____220) and shape behavior. Not all taxes have this a_____221). We do not tax income to express d_____222) of paid employment or to discourage people from engaging in it. N_____223) is a general sales tax intended as a d_____224) to buying things. These are simply ways of raising r_____225).

# 38 삽입

Most beliefs — but not all — are open to tests of v_____226). This means that beliefs can be tested to see if they are correct or false. Beliefs can be v_____227) or f_____228) with objective c_____229) e_____230) to the person. There are people who believe the Earth is flat and not a sphere. Because we have objective evidence that the Earth is in fact a sphere, the flat Earth belief can be shown to be false. Also, the belief that it will rain tomorrow can be tested for truth by waiting until tomorrow and seeing whether it rains or not. However, some types of beliefs cannot be tested for truth because we cannot get e_____231) e_____232) in our lifetimes (such as a belief that the Earth will stop spinning on its axis by the year 9999 or that there is life on a planet 100-million light-years away). Also, meta-physical beliefs (such as the e_____233) and nature of a god) present c_____234) challenges in generating evidence that everyone is w_____235) to use as a truth c_____236).

# 39 삽입

Everyone automatically c_____237) and g_____238) all the time. Unconsciously. It is not a question of being p_____239) or e_____240). Categories are absolutely necessary for us to function. They give structure to our thoughts. Imagine if we saw every item and every scenario as truly u_____241) — we would not even have a language to d_____242) the world around us. But the necessary and useful i_____243) to generalize can d_____244) our world view. It can make us m_____245) group together things, or people, or countries that are actually very different. It can make us a_____246) everything or everyone in one category is similar. And, maybe, most u_____247) of all, it can make us j_____248) to conclusions about a whole category b_____249) on a few, or even just one, u_____250) example.

# 40 요약

At the University of Iowa, students were b_____251) shown numbers that they had to m_____252). Then they were o_____253) the choice of either a fruit salad or a chocolate cake. When the number the students memorized was seven digits long, 63% of them chose the cake. When the number they were asked to remember had just two digits, however, 59% o_____254) for the fruit salad. Our r_____255) brains know that the fruit salad is better for our health, but our r_____256) brains d_____257) that soft, fattening chocolate cake. If the reflective brain is busy f_____258) something else out — like trying to remember a seven-digit number — then i_____259) can easily win. On the other hand, if we're not thinking too hard about something else (with only a minor d_____260) like memorizing two digits), then the reflective system can d_____261) the emotional impulse of the reflexive side.

→ According to the above experiment, the increased i_____262) l_____263) on the brain leads the reflexive side of the brain to become d_____264).

# 41~42 제목, 어휘

Test scores are not a m_____265) of self-worth; however, we often a_____266) our sense of w_____267) with our performance on an exam. Thoughts such as "If I don't pass this test, I'm a failure" are mental traps not r_____268) in truth. Failing a test is failing a test, nothing more. It is in no way d_____269) of your v_____270) as a person. Believing that test performance is a r_____271) of your v_____272) places u_____273) pressure on your performance. Not passing the certification test only means that your certification status has been delayed. M_____274) a positive attitude is t_____275) important. If you have studied hard, r_____276) this mentally and believe that you will do well. If, on the other hand, you did not study as hard as you should have or wanted to, accept that as b_____277) your control for now and a_____278) to the task of doing the best you can. If things do not go well this time, you know what needs to be done _____ _____ _____279) the next exam. Talk to yourself in positive terms. Avoid r_____280) past or future test performance by placing the blame on secondary variables. Thoughts such as, "I didn't have enough time," or "I should have ...," c_____281) the stress of test-taking. Take control by a_____282) your value, self-worth, and d_____283) to meeting the test challenge head on. Repeat to yourself "I can and I will pass this exam."

# 43~45 순서, 지칭, 세부 내용

Once upon a time there lived a p_____284) but c_____285) shoemaker. He was so happy, he sang all day long. The children loved to stand around his window to listen to him. Next door to the shoemaker lived a rich man. He _____ _____286) sit up all night to count his gold. In the morning, he went to bed, but he could not sleep because of the sound of the shoemaker's singing. One day, he thought of a way of stopping the singing. He wrote a letter to the shoemaker asking him to visit. The shoemaker came at o_____287), and to his surprise the rich man gave him a bag of gold. When he got home again, the shoemaker opened the bag. He had never seen so much gold before! When he sat down at his bench and began, carefully, to count it, the children watched through the window. There was _____288) much there that the shoemaker was a_____289) to let it o_____290) of his s_____291). So he took it to bed with him. But he could not sleep for w_____292) about it. Very early in the morning, he got up and brought his gold down from the bedroom. He had d_____293) to hide it up the c_____294) instead. But he was still u_____295), and in a little while he d_____296) a hole in the garden and buried his bag of gold in it. It was no use trying to work. He was too worried about the safety of his gold. And as for singing, he was too m_____297) to u_____298) a note. He could not sleep, or work, or sing—and, worst of all, the children no longer came to see him. At last, the shoemaker felt so unhappy that he s_____299) his bag of gold and ran next door to the rich man. "Please take back your gold," he said. "The worry of it is making me i_____300), and I have lost all of my friends. I would rather be a poor shoemaker, as I was before." And so the shoemaker was happy again and sang all day at his work.

# 2021 고2 3월 모의고사

❶ voca  ❷ text  ❸ [ / ]  ❹ ___  ❺ quiz 1  ❻ quiz 2  ❼ quiz 3  ❽ quiz 4  ❾ quiz 5  ❿ quiz 6

**\*다음 주어진 글에 이어질 순서를 적으시오.**

## 18 1)

My name is Anthony Thompson and I am writing on behalf of the residents' association.

(A) Because there is no given day for recycling, residents are putting their recycling out at any time. This makes the recycling area messy, which requires extra labor and cost.

(B) I am sure it will make our apartment complex look much more pleasant. Thank you in advance for your cooperation.

(C) To deal with this problem, the residents' association has decided on a day to recycle. I would like to let you know that you can put out your recycling on Wednesdays only.

(D) Our recycling program has been working well thanks to your participation. However, a problem has recently occurred that needs your attention.

## 19 2)

It was a day I was due to give a presentation at work, not something I'd do often.

(A) Time seemed to stand still as I struggled to start speaking, and I felt a pressure around my throat, as though my voice was trapped and couldn't come out.

(B) A chilly 'pins-and-needles' feeling crept over me, starting in my hands.

(C) Gazing around at the blur of faces, I realized they were all waiting for me to begin, but by now I knew I couldn't continue.

(D) As I stood up to begin, I froze.

## 20 3)

No matter what your situation, whether you are an insider or an outsider, you need to become the voice that challenges yesterday's answers.

(A) If you didn't know your coworkers and feel bonded to them by your shared experiences, what would you think of them? You may not have the job security or confidence to speak your mind to management, but you can make these "outsider" assessments of your organization on your own and use what you determine to advance your career.

(B) They are the ones who have the freedom to point out these problems and criticize them without risking their job or their career. Part of adopting an outsider mentality is forcing yourself to look around your organization with this disassociated, less emotional perspective.

(C) Think about the characteristics that make outsiders valuable to an organization. They are the people who have the perspective to see problems that the insiders are too close to really notice.

## 21 4)

The known fact of contingencies, without knowing precisely what those contingencies will be, shows that disaster preparation is not the same thing as disaster rehearsal.

(A) Marathon runners do not practice by running the full course of twenty-six miles; rather, they get into shape by running shorter distances and building up their endurance with cross-training. If they have prepared successfully, then they are in optimal condition to run the marathon over its predetermined course and length, assuming a range of weather conditions, predicted or not.

(B) This is normal marathon preparation.

(C) No matter how many mock disasters are staged according to prior plans, the real disaster will never mirror any one of them. Disaster-preparation planning is more like training for a marathon than training for a high-jump competition or a sprinting event.

## 22 5)

Fears of damaging ecosystems are based on the sound conservationist principle that we should aim to minimize the disruption we cause, but there is a risk that this principle may be confused with the old idea of a 'balance of nature'.

(A) This supposes a perfect order of nature that will seek to maintain itself and that we should not change. It is a romantic, not to say idyllic, notion, but deeply misleading because it supposes a static condition.

(B) Ecosystems are dynamic, and although some may endure, apparently unchanged, for periods that are long in comparison with the human lifespan, they must and do change eventually. Species come and go, climates

change, plant and animal communities adapt to altered circumstances, and when examined in fine detail such adaptation and consequent change can be seen to be taking place constantly.

(C) The 'balance of nature' is a myth. Our planet is dynamic, and so are the arrangements by which its inhabitants live together.

## 23 6)

Before the modern scientific era, creativity was attributed to a superhuman force; all novel ideas originated with the gods.

(A) Greek artists did not blindly imitate what they saw in reality; instead they tried to represent the pure, true forms underlying reality, resulting in a sort of compromise between abstraction and accuracy.

(B) Art could only be a pale imitation of the perfection of the world of ideas.

(C) After all, how could a person create something that did not exist before the divine act of creation? In fact, the Latin meaning of the verb "inspire" is "to breathe into", reflecting the belief that creative inspiration was similar to the moment in creation when God first breathed life into man.

(D) Plato argued that the poet was possessed by divine inspiration, and Plotin wrote that art could only be beautiful if it descended from God. The artist's job was not to imitate nature but rather to reveal the sacred and transcendent qualities of nature.

## 24 7)

Some beginning researchers mistakenly believe that a good hypothesis is one that is guaranteed to be right (e.g., alcohol will slow down reaction time).

(A) If your predictions about what will happen in these uncharted waters are wrong, that's okay: Scientists are allowed to make mistakes (as Bates said, "Research is the process of going up alleys to see if they are blind").

(B) Indeed, scientists often learn more from predictions that do not turn out than from those that do.

(C) To get new knowledge, you, as a researcher-explorer, need to leave the safety of the shore (established facts) and venture into uncharted waters (as Einstein said, "If we knew what we were doing, it would not be called research, would it"?).

(D) However, if we already know your hypothesis is true before you test it, testing your hypothesis won't tell us anything new. Remember, research is supposed to produce new knowledge.

## 29 8)

While reflecting on the needs of organizations, leaders, and families today, we realize that one of the unique characteristics is inclusivity.

(A) Yet research shows that exclusivity in problem solving, even with a genius, is not as effective as inclusivity, where everyone's ideas are heard and a solution is developed through collaboration.

(B) There is no need for others to present their ideas because they are considered inadequate.

(C) Yet the majority of leaders, organizations, and families are still using the language of the old paradigm in which one person—typically the oldest, most educated, and/or wealthiest—makes all the decisions, and their decisions rule with little discussion or inclusion of others, resulting in exclusivity. Today, this person could be a director, CEO, or other senior leader of an organization.

(D) Why? Because inclusivity supports what everyone ultimately wants from their relationships: collaboration.

## 30 9)

The objective point of view is illustrated by John Ford's "philosophy of camera".

(A) The objective point of view employs a static camera as much as possible in order to produce this window effect, and it concentrates on the actors and the action without drawing attention to the camera.

(B) Ford considered the camera to be a window and the audience to be outside the window viewing the people and events within. We are asked to watch the actions as if they were taking place at a distance, and we are not asked to participate.

(C) For the most part, the director uses natural, normal types of camera positioning and camera angles. The objective camera does not comment on or interpret the action but merely records it, letting it unfold. We see the action from the viewpoint of an impersonal observer. If the camera moves, it does so unnoticeably, calling as little attention to itself as possible.

(D) The objective camera suggests an emotional distance between camera and subject; the camera seems simply to be recording, as straightforwardly as possible, the characters and actions of the story.

## 31 10)

Even the most respectable of all musical institutions, the symphony orchestra, carries inside its DNA the legacy of the hunt.

(A) The various instruments in the orchestra can be traced back to these primitive origins—their earliest forms were made either from the animal (horn, hide, gut, bone) or the weapons employed in bringing the animal under control (stick, bow).

(B) Listening to Beethoven, Brahms, Mahler, Bruckner, Berlioz, Tchaikovsky, Shostakovich, and other great composers, I can easily summon up images of bands of men starting to chase animals, using sound as a source and symbol of dominance, an expression of the will to predatory power.

(C) Are we wrong to hear this history in the music itself, in the formidable aggression and awe-inspiring assertiveness of those monumental symphonies that remain the core repertoire of the world's leading orchestras?

## 32 11)

Our brains have evolved to remember unexpected events because basic survival depends on the ability to perceive causes and predict effects.

(A) If the brain predicts one event and experiences another, the unusualness will be especially interesting and will be encoded accordingly. Neurologist and classroom teacher Judith Willis has claimed that surprise in the classroom is one of the most effective ways of teaching with brain stimulation in mind.

(B) Preference for novelty sets us up for learning by directing attention, providing stimulation to developing perceptual systems, and feeding curious and exploratory behavior.

(C) If students are exposed to new experiences via demonstrations or through the unexpected enthusiasm of their teachers or peers, they will be much more likely to connect with the information that follows. Willis has written that encouraging active discovery in the classroom allows students to interact with new information, moving it beyond working memory to be processed in the frontal lobe, which is devoted to advanced cognitive functioning.

## 33 12)

Psychological research has shown that people naturally divide up cognitive labor, often without thinking about it.

(A) If your friend wasn't around, you might try harder. After all, it would be good to know what a good wine would be for the evening's festivities.

(B) But your friend, the wine expert, is likely to remember the information without even trying.

(C) How hard are you going to try to remember what the neighbor has to say about which wines to buy? Why bother when the information would be better retained by the wine expert sitting next to you?

(D) Imagine you're cooking up a special dinner with a friend. You're a great cook, but your friend is the wine expert, an amateur sommelier. A neighbor drops by and starts telling you both about the terrific new wines being sold at the liquor store just down the street. There are many new wines, so there's a lot to remember.

## 34 13)

Even companies that sell physical products to make profit are forced by their boards and investors to reconsider their underlying motives and to collect as much data as possible from consumers.

(A) Then supermarkets sell this purchasing behavior to marketing analytics companies. The marketing analytics companies perform machine learning procedures, slicing the data in new ways, and resell behavioral data back to product manufacturers as marketing insights.

(B) Supermarkets no longer make all their money selling their produce and manufactured goods. They give you loyalty cards with which they track your purchasing behaviors precisely.

(C) When data and machine learning become currencies of value in a capitalist system, then every company's natural tendency is to maximize its ability to conduct surveillance on its own customers because the customers are themselves the new value-creation devices.

## 35 14)

Academics, politicians, marketers and others have in the past debated whether or not it is ethically correct to market products and services directly to young consumers.

(A) The constant feelings of inadequateness created by advertising have been suggested to contribute to children becoming fixated with instant gratification and beliefs that material possessions are important.

(B) Clever advertising informs children that they will be viewed by their peers in an unfavorable way if they do not have the products that are advertised, thereby playing on their emotional vulnerabilities.

(C) This is also a dilemma for psychologists who have questioned whether they ought to help advertisers manipulate children into purchasing more products they have seen advertised. Advertisers have admitted to taking advantage of the fact that it is easy to make children feel that they are losers if they do not own the 'right' products.

## 36 15)

Once we recognize the false-cause issue, we see it everywhere.

(A) For example, a recent long-term study of University of Toronto medical students concluded that medical school class presidents lived an average of 2.4 years less than other medical school graduates.

(B) At first glance, this seemed to imply that being a medical school class president is bad for you. Does this mean that you should avoid being medical school class president at all costs? Probably not. Just because being class president is correlated with shorter life expectancy does not mean that it causes shorter life expectancy.

(C) If so, the real lesson of the study is that we should all relax a little and not let our work take over our lives.

(D) In fact, it seems likely that the sort of person who becomes medical school class president is, on average, extremely hard-working, serious, and ambitious. Perhaps this extra stress, and the corresponding lack of social and relaxation time—rather than being class president per se—contributes to lower life expectancy.

## 37 16)

We commonly argue about the fairness of taxation— whether this or that tax will fall more heavily on the rich or the poor.

(A) Such taxes express society's disapproval of these activities by raising the cost of engaging in them. Proposals to tax sugary sodas (to combat obesity) or carbon emissions (to address climate change) likewise seek to change norms and shape behavior. Not all taxes have this aim.

(B) We do not tax income to express disapproval of paid employment or to discourage people from engaging in it. Nor is a general sales tax intended as a deterrent to buying things.  These are simply ways of raising revenue.

(C) But the expressive dimension of taxation goes beyond debates about fairness, to the moral judgements societies make about which activities are worthy of honor and recognition, and which ones should be discouraged. Sometimes, these judgements are explicit. Taxes on tobacco, alcohol, and casinos are called "sin taxes" because they seek to discourage activities considered harmful or undesirable.

## 38 17)

Most beliefs—but not all—are open to tests of verification.

(A) Also, the belief that it will rain tomorrow can be tested for truth by waiting until tomorrow and seeing whether it rains or not. However, some types of beliefs cannot be tested for truth because we cannot get external evidence in our lifetimes (such as a belief that the Earth will stop spinning on its axis by the year 9999 or that there is life on a planet 100-million light-years away).

(B) Also, meta-physical beliefs (such as the existence and nature of a god) present considerable challenges in generating evidence that everyone is willing to use as a truth criterion.

(C) There are people who believe the Earth is flat and not a sphere. Because we have objective evidence that the Earth is in fact a sphere, the flat Earth belief can be shown to be false.

(D) This means that beliefs can be tested to see if they are correct or false. Beliefs can be verified or falsified with objective criteria external to the person.

## 39 18)

Everyone automatically categorizes and generalizes all the time.

(A) They give structure to our thoughts. Imagine if we saw every item and every scenario as truly unique—we would not even have a language to describe the world around us.

(B) But the necessary and useful instinct to generalize can distort our world view. It can make us mistakenly group together things, or people, or countries that are actually very different.

(C) Unconsciously. It is not a question of being prejudiced or enlightened. Categories are absolutely necessary for us to function.

(D) It can make us assume everything or everyone in one category is similar.  And, maybe, most unfortunate of all, it can make us jump to conclusions about a whole category based on a few, or even just one, unusual example.

## 40 19)

At the University of Iowa, students were briefly shown numbers that they had to memorize.

(A) When the number they were asked to remember had just two digits, however, 59% opted for the fruit salad. Our reflective brains know that the fruit salad is better for our health, but our reflexive brains desire that soft, fattening chocolate cake.

(B) Then they were offered the choice of either a fruit salad or a chocolate cake. When the number the students memorized was seven digits long, 63% of them chose the cake.

(C) If the reflective brain is busy figuring something else out—like trying to remember a seven-digit number—then impulse can easily win. On the other hand, if we're not thinking too hard about something else (with only a minor distraction like memorizing two digits), then the reflective system can deny the emotional impulse of the reflexive side.

## 41~42 20)

Test scores are not a measure of self-worth; however, we often associate our sense of worthiness with our performance on an exam.

(A) Thoughts such as "If I don't pass this test, I'm a failure" are mental traps not rooted in truth. Failing a test is failing a test, nothing more. It is in no way descriptive of your value as a person. Believing that test performance is a reflection of your virtue places unreasonable pressure on your performance.

(B) Avoid rationalizing past or future test performance by placing the blame on secondary variables. Thoughts such as, "I didn't have enough time", or "I should have ...", compound the stress of test-taking. Take control by affirming your value, self-worth, and dedication to meeting the test challenge head on. Repeat to yourself "I can and I will pass this exam".

(C) Not passing the certification test only means that your certification status has been delayed. Maintaining a positive attitude is therefore important. If you have studied hard, reaffirm this mentally and believe that you will do well.

(D) If, on the other hand, you did not study as hard as you should have or wanted to, accept that as beyond your control for now and attend to the task of doing the best you can. If things do not go well this time, you know what needs to be done in preparation for the next exam. Talk to yourself in positive terms.

# 43~45 ₂₁₎

Once upon a time there lived a poor but cheerful shoemaker.

(A) He was so happy, he sang all day long. The children loved to stand around his window to listen to him. Next door to the shoemaker lived a rich man. He used to sit up all night to count his gold. In the morning, he went to bed, but he could not sleep because of the sound of the shoemaker's singing. One day, he thought of a way of stopping the singing. He wrote a letter to the shoemaker asking him to visit. The shoemaker came at once, and to his surprise the rich man gave him a bag of gold. When he got home again, the shoemaker opened the bag.

(B) He was too worried about the safety of his gold. And as for singing, he was too miserable to utter a note. He could not sleep, or work, or sing—and, worst of all, the children no longer came to see him. At last, the shoemaker felt so unhappy that he seized his bag of gold and ran next door to the rich man. "Please take back your gold", he said. "The worry of it is making me ill, and I have lost all of my friends. I would rather be a poor shoemaker, as I was before". And so the shoemaker was happy again and sang all day at his work.

(C) He had never seen so much gold before! When he sat down at his bench and began, carefully, to count it, the children watched through the window. There was so much there that the shoemaker was afraid to let it out of his sight. So he took it to bed with him. But he could not sleep for worrying about it. Very early in the morning, he got up and brought his gold down from the bedroom. He had decided to hide it up the chimney instead. But he was still uneasy, and in a little while he dug a hole in the garden and buried his bag of gold in it. It was no use trying to work.

**\*글의 흐름으로 보아, 주어진 문장이 들어가기에 가장 적절한 곳은?**

## 18 22)

This makes the recycling area messy, which requires extra labor and cost.

My name is Anthony Thompson and I am writing on behalf of the residents' association. Our recycling program has been working well thanks to your participation. ( ① ) However, a problem has recently occurred that needs your attention. ( ② ) Because there is no given day for recycling, residents are putting their recycling out at any time. ( ③ ) To deal with this problem, the residents' association has decided on a day to recycle. ( ④ ) I would like to let you know that you can put out your recycling on Wednesdays only. ( ⑤ ) I am sure it will make our apartment complex look much more pleasant. Thank you in advance for your cooperation.

## 19 23)

Gazing around at the blur of faces, I realized they were all waiting for me to begin.

It was a day I was due to give a presentation at work, not something I'd do often. ( ① ) As I stood up to begin, I froze. ( ② ) A chilly 'pins-and-needles' feeling crept over me, starting in my hands. ( ③ ) Time seemed to stand still as I struggled to start speaking. ( ④ ) And I felt a pressure around my throat, as though my voice was trapped and couldn't come out. ( ⑤ ) But by now I knew I couldn't continue.

## 20 24)

If you didn't know your coworkers and feel bonded to them by your shared experiences, what would you think of them?

No matter what your situation, whether you are an insider or an outsider, you need to become the voice that challenges yesterday's answers. ( ① ) Think about the characteristics that make outsiders valuable to an organization. ( ② ) They are the people who have the perspective to see problems that the insiders are too close to really notice. ( ③ ) They are the ones who have the freedom to point out these problems and criticize them without risking their job or their career. ( ④ ) Part of adopting an outsider mentality is forcing yourself to look around your organization with this disassociated, less emotional perspective. ( ⑤ ) You may not have the job security or confidence to speak your mind to management, but you can make these "outsider" assessments of your organization on your own and use what you determine to advance your career.

## 21 25)

> Marathon runners do not practice by running the full course of twenty-six miles.

The known fact of contingencies, without knowing precisely what those contingencies will be, shows that disaster preparation is not the same thing as disaster rehearsal. ( ① ) No matter how many mock disasters are staged according to prior plans, the real disaster will never mirror any one of them. ( ② ) Disaster-preparation planning is more like training for a marathon than training for a high-jump competition or a sprinting event. ( ③ ) Rather, they get into shape by running shorter distances and building up their endurance with cross-training. ( ④ ) If they have prepared successfully, then they are in optimal condition to run the marathon over its predetermined course and length, assuming a range of weather conditions, predicted or not. ( ⑤ ) This is normal marathon preparation.

## 22 26)

> This supposes a perfect order of nature that will seek to maintain itself and that we should not change.

Fears of damaging ecosystems are based on the sound conservationist principle that we should aim to minimize the disruption we cause, but there is a risk that this principle may be confused with the old idea of a 'balance of nature'. ( ① ) It is a romantic, not to say idyllic, notion, but deeply misleading because it supposes a static condition. ( ② ) Ecosystems are dynamic, and although some may endure, apparently unchanged, for periods that are long in comparison with the human lifespan, they must and do change eventually. ( ③ ) Species come and go, climates change, plant and animal communities adapt to altered circumstances, and when examined in fine detail such adaptation and consequent change can be seen to be taking place constantly. ( ④ ) The 'balance of nature' is a myth. ( ⑤ ) Our planet is dynamic, and so are the arrangements by which its inhabitants live together.

## 23 27)

> Art could only be a pale imitation of the perfection of the world of ideas.

Before the modern scientific era, creativity was attributed to a superhuman force; all novel ideas originated with the gods. ( ① ) After all, how could a person create something that did not exist before the divine act of creation? ( ② ) In fact, the Latin meaning of the verb "inspire" is "to breathe into", reflecting the belief that creative inspiration was similar to the moment in creation when God first breathed life into man. ( ③ ) Plato argued that the poet was possessed by divine inspiration, and Plotin wrote that art could only be beautiful if it descended from God. ( ④ ) The artist's job was not to imitate nature but rather to reveal the sacred and transcendent qualities of nature. ( ⑤ ) Greek artists did not blindly imitate what they saw in reality; instead they tried to represent the pure, true forms underlying reality, resulting in a sort of compromise between abstraction and accuracy.

## 24 <sub>28)</sub>

However, if we already know your hypothesis is true before you test it, testing your hypothesis won't tell us anything new.

Some beginning researchers mistakenly believe that a good hypothesis is one that is guaranteed to be right (e.g., alcohol will slow down reaction time). ( ① ) Remember, research is supposed to produce new knowledge. ( ② ) To get new knowledge, you, as a researcher-explorer, need to leave the safety of the shore (established facts) and venture into uncharted waters (as Einstein said, "If we knew what we were doing, it would not be called research, would it"?). ( ③ ) If your predictions about what will happen in these uncharted waters are wrong, that's okay. ( ④ ) Scientists are allowed to make mistakes (as Bates said, "Research is the process of going up alleys to see if they are blind"). ( ⑤ ) Indeed, scientists often learn more from predictions that do not turn out than from those that do.

## 29 <sub>29)</sub>

Yet the majority of leaders, organizations, and families are still using the language of the old paradigm in which one person—typically the oldest, most educated, andor wealthiest—makes all the decisions, and their decisions rule with little discussion or inclusion of others, resulting in exclusivity.

While reflecting on the needs of organizations, leaders, and families today, we realize that one of the unique characteristics is inclusivity. ( ① ) Why? Because inclusivity supports what everyone ultimately wants from their relationships: collaboration. ( ② ) Today, this person could be a director, CEO, or other senior leader of an organization. ( ③ ) There is no need for others to present their ideas because they are considered inadequate. ( ④ ) Yet research shows that exclusivity in problem solving, even with a genius, is not as effective as inclusivity. ( ⑤ ) And there, everyone's ideas are heard and a solution is developed through collaboration.

## 30 <sub>30)</sub>

The objective point of view employs a static camera as much as possible in order to produce this window effect, and it concentrates on the actors and the action without drawing attention to the camera.

The objective point of view is illustrated by John Ford's "philosophy of camera". ( ① ) Ford considered the camera to be a window and the audience to be outside the window viewing the people and events within. ( ② ) We are asked to watch the actions as if they were taking place at a distance, and we are not asked to participate. ( ③ ) The objective camera suggests an emotional distance between camera and subject; the camera seems simply to be recording, as straightforwardly as possible, the characters and actions of the story. ( ④ ) For the most part, the director uses natural, normal types of camera positioning and camera angles. ( ⑤ ) The objective camera does not comment on or interpret the action but merely records it, letting it unfold. We see the action from the viewpoint of an impersonal observer. If the camera moves, it does so unnoticeably, calling as little attention to itself as possible.

## 31 31)

Are we wrong to hear this history in the music itself, in the formidable aggression and awe-inspiring assertiveness of those monumental symphonies that remain the core repertoire of the world's leading orchestras?

Even the most respectable of all musical institutions, the symphony orchestra, carries inside its DNA the legacy of the hunt. (①) The various instruments in the orchestra can be traced back to these primitive origins. (②) Their earliest forms were made from the animal (horn, hide, gut, bone). (③) They were also made from the weapons employed in bringing the animal under control (stick, bow). (④) Listening to Beethoven, Brahms, Mahler, Bruckner, Berlioz, Tchaikovsky, Shostakovich, and other great composers, I can easily summon up images of bands of men starting to chase animals. (⑤) They are using sound as a source and symbol of dominance, an expression of the will to predatory power.

## 32 32)

If the brain predicts one event and experiences another, the unusualness will be especially interesting and will be encoded accordingly.

Our brains have evolved to remember unexpected events because basic survival depends on the ability to perceive causes and predict effects. (①) Neurologist and classroom teacher Judith Willis has claimed that surprise in the classroom is one of the most effective ways of teaching with brain stimulation in mind. (②) If students are exposed to new experiences via demonstrations or through the unexpected enthusiasm of their teachers or peers, they will be much more likely to connect with the information that follows. (③) Willis has written that encouraging active discovery in the classroom allows students to interact with new information, moving it beyond working memory to be processed in the frontal lobe. (④) And that is devoted to advanced cognitive functioning. (⑤) Preference for novelty sets us up for learning by directing attention, providing stimulation to developing perceptual systems, and feeding curious and exploratory behavior.

## 33 33)

Why bother when the information would be better retained by the wine expert sitting next to you?

Psychological research has shown that people naturally divide up cognitive labor, often without thinking about it. (①) Imagine you're cooking up a special dinner with a friend. You're a great cook, but your friend is the wine expert, an amateur sommelier. (②) A neighbor drops by and starts telling you both about the terrific new wines being sold at the liquor store just down the street. (③) There are many new wines, so there's a lot to remember. (④) How hard are you going to try to remember what the neighbor has to say about which wines to buy? (⑤) If your friend wasn't around, you might try harder. After all, it would be good to know what a good wine would be for the evening's festivities. But your friend, the wine expert, is likely to remember the information without even trying.

## 34 34)

They give you loyalty cards with which they track your purchasing behaviors precisely.

Even companies that sell physical products to make profit are forced by their boards and investors to reconsider their underlying motives and to collect as much data as possible from consumers. ( ① ) Supermarkets no longer make all their money selling their produce and manufactured goods. ( ② ) Then supermarkets sell this purchasing behavior to marketing analytics companies. ( ③ ) The marketing analytics companies perform machine learning procedures, slicing the data in new ways, and resell behavioral data back to product manufacturers as marketing insights. ( ④ ) When data and machine learning become currencies of value in a capitalist system. ( ⑤ ) Then every company's natural tendency is to maximize its ability to conduct surveillance on its own customers because the customers are themselves the new value-creation devices.

## 35 35)

This is also a dilemma for psychologists who have questioned whether they ought to help advertisers manipulate children into purchasing more products they have seen advertised.

Academics, politicians, marketers and others have in the past debated whether or not it is ethically correct to market products and services directly to young consumers. ( ① ) Advertisers have admitted to taking advantage of the fact that it is easy to make children feel that they are losers if they do not own the 'right' products. ( ② ) Clever advertising informs children that they will be viewed by their peers in an unfavorable way if they do not have the products that are advertised. ( ③ ) By informing them this, advertising plays on children's emotional vulnerabilities. ( ④ ) The constant feelings of inadequateness created by advertising have been suggested to contribute to children becoming fixated with instant gratification. ( ⑤ ) It might also form beliefs that material possessions are important.

## 36 36)

Perhaps this extra stress, and the corresponding lack of social and relaxation time—rather than being class president per se—contributes to lower life expectancy.

Once we recognize the false-cause issue, we see it everywhere. For example, a recent long-term study of University of Toronto medical students concluded that medical school class presidents lived an average of 2.4 years less than other medical school graduates. ( ① ) At first glance, this seemed to imply that being a medical school class president is bad for you. ( ② ) Does this mean that you should avoid being medical school class president at all costs? ( ③ ) Probably not. Just because being class president is correlated with shorter life expectancy does not mean that it causes shorter life expectancy. ( ④ ) In fact, it seems likely that the sort of person who becomes medical school class president is, on average, extremely hard-working, serious, and ambitious. ( ⑤ ) If so, the real lesson of the study is that we should all relax a little and not let our work take over our lives.

## 37 **37)**

> Such taxes express society's disapproval of these activities by raising the cost of engaging in them.

We commonly argue about the fairness of taxation— whether this or that tax will fall more heavily on the rich or the poor. (①) But the expressive dimension of taxation goes beyond debates about fairness, to the moral judgements societies make about which activities are worthy of honor and recognition, and which ones should be discouraged. (②) Sometimes, these judgements are explicit. (③) Taxes on tobacco, alcohol, and casinos are called "sin taxes" because they seek to discourage activities considered harmful or undesirable. (④) Proposals to tax sugary sodas (to combat obesity) or carbon emissions (to address climate change) likewise seek to change norms and shape behavior. (⑤) Not all taxes have this aim. We do not tax income to express disapproval of paid employment or to discourage people from engaging in it. Nor is a general sales tax intended as a deterrent to buying things. These are simply ways of raising revenue.

## 38 **38)**

> Also, the belief that it will rain tomorrow can be tested for truth by waiting until tomorrow and seeing whether it rains or not.

Most beliefs—but not all—are open to tests of verification. This means that beliefs can be tested to see if they are correct or false. (①) Beliefs can be verified or falsified with objective criteria external to the person. (②) There are people who believe the Earth is flat and not a sphere. (③) Because we have objective evidence that the Earth is in fact a sphere, the flat Earth belief can be shown to be false. (④) However, some types of beliefs cannot be tested for truth because we cannot get external evidence in our lifetimes (such as a belief that the Earth will stop spinning on its axis by the year 9999 or that there is life on a planet 100-million light-years away). (⑤) Also, meta-physical beliefs (such as the existence and nature of a god) present considerable challenges in generating evidence that everyone is willing to use as a truth criterion.

## 39 **39)**

> It can make us mistakenly group together things, or people, or countries that are actually very different.

Everyone automatically categorizes and generalizes all the time. Unconsciously. It is not a question of being prejudiced or enlightened. (①) Categories are absolutely necessary for us to function. (②) They give structure to our thoughts. (③) Imagine if we saw every item and every scenario as truly unique—we would not even have a language to describe the world around us. (④) But the necessary and useful instinct to generalize can distort our world view. (⑤) It can make us assume everything or everyone in one category is similar. And, maybe, most unfortunate of all, it can make us jump to conclusions about a whole category based on a few, or even just one, unusual example.

## 40 40)

Our reflective brains know that the fruit salad is better for our health, but our reflexive brains desire that soft, fattening chocolate cake.

At the University of Iowa, students were briefly shown numbers that they had to memorize. ( ① ) Then they were offered the choice of either a fruit salad or a chocolate cake. ( ② ) When the number the students memorized was seven digits long, 63% of them chose the cake. ( ③ ) When the number they were asked to remember had just two digits, however, 59% opted for the fruit salad. ( ④ ) If the reflective brain is busy figuring something else out—like trying to remember a seven-digit number—then impulse can easily win. ( ⑤ ) On the other hand, if we're not thinking too hard about something else (with only a minor distraction like memorizing two digits), then the reflective system can deny the emotional impulse of the reflexive side.

## 41~42 41)

If, on the other hand, you did not study as hard as you should have or wanted to, accept that as beyond your control for now and attend to the task of doing the best you can.

Test scores are not a measure of self-worth; however, we often associate our sense of worthiness with our performance on an exam. Thoughts such as "If I don't pass this test, I'm a failure" are mental traps not rooted in truth. Failing a test is failing a test, nothing more. It is in no way descriptive of your value as a person. ( ① ) Believing that test performance is a reflection of your virtue places unreasonable pressure on your performance. ( ② ) Not passing the certification test only means that your certification status has been delayed. ( ③ ) Maintaining a positive attitude is therefore important. ( ④ ) If you have studied hard, reaffirm this mentally and believe that you will do well. ( ⑤ ) If things do not go well this time, you know what needs to be done in preparation for the next exam. Talk to yourself in positive terms. Avoid rationalizing past or future test performance by placing the blame on secondary variables. Thoughts such as, "I didn't have enough time", or "I should have ...", compound the stress of test-taking. Take control by affirming your value, self-worth, and dedication to meeting the test challenge head on. Repeat to yourself "I can and I will pass this exam".

# 43~45 42)

> He had never seen so much gold before!

Once upon a time there lived a poor but cheerful shoemaker. He was so happy, he sang all day long. The children loved to stand around his window to listen to him. Next door to the shoemaker lived a rich man. He used to sit up all night to count his gold. In the morning, he went to bed, but he could not sleep because of the sound of the shoemaker's singing. One day, he thought of a way of stopping the singing. He wrote a letter to the shoemaker asking him to visit. ( ① ) The shoemaker came at once, and to his surprise the rich man gave him a bag of gold. When he got home again, the shoemaker opened the bag. ( ② ) When he sat down at his bench and began, carefully, to count it, the children watched through the window. ( ③ ) There was so much there that the shoemaker was afraid to let it out of his sight. ( ④ ) So he took it to bed with him. But he could not sleep for worrying about it. ( ⑤ ) Very early in the morning, he got up and brought his gold down from the bedroom. He had decided to hide it up the chimney instead. But he was still uneasy, and in a little while he dug a hole in the garden and buried his bag of gold in it. It was no use trying to work. He was too worried about the safety of his gold. And as for singing, he was too miserable to utter a note. He could not sleep, or work, or sing—and, worst of all, the children no longer came to see him. At last, the shoemaker felt so unhappy that he seized his bag of gold and ran next door to the rich man. "Please take back your gold", he said. "The worry of it is making me ill, and I have lost all of my friends. I would rather be a poor shoemaker, as I was before". And so the shoemaker was happy again and sang all day at his work.

# 2021 고2 3월 모의고사

❶ voca    ❷ text    ❸ [ / ]    ❹ ____    ❺ quiz 1    ❻ quiz 2    ❼ quiz 3    ❽ quiz 4    ❾ quiz 5    ❿ quiz 6

\*밑줄 친 부분 중, 어법, 혹은 문맥상 어색한 곳을 고르시오.

## 18 1)

My name is Anthony Thompson and I am writing on behalf of the residents' association. Our recycling program has been ① working well thanks to your participation. However, a problem has recently ② occurred that needs your attention. Because there is no given day for recycling, residents are ③ putting their recycling out at any time. This makes the recycling area messy, ④ which requires extra labor and cost. To deal with this problem, the residents' association has decided on a day to recycle. I would like to let you ⑤ to know that you can put out your recycling on Wednesdays only. I am sure it will make our apartment complex look much more pleasant. Thank you in advance for your cooperation.

## 19 2)

It was a day I was due to ① give a presentation at work, not something I'd do often. As I stood up to begin, I froze. A chilly 'pins-and-needles' feeling crept over me, ② started in my hands. Time seemed to stand still as I struggled to ③ start speaking, and I felt a pressure around my throat, ④ as though my voice was trapped and couldn't come out. Gazing around at the blur of faces, I ⑤ realized they were all waiting for me to begin, but by now I knew I couldn't continue.

## 20 3)

No matter ① what your situation, ② whether you are an insider or an outsider, you need to become the voice that challenges yesterday's answers. Think about the characteristics ③ that make outsiders valuable to an organization. They are the people who have the perspective to see problems that the insiders are too close to really notice. They are the ones who have the freedom to point out these problems and criticize them without risking their job or their career. Part of adopting an outsider mentality is forcing yourself to look around your organization with this ④ disassociated, less emotional perspective. If you didn't know your coworkers and feel bonded to them by your shared experiences, what would you think of them? You may not have the job security or confidence to speak your mind to management, but you can make these "outsider" assessments of your organization on your own and ⑤ uses what you determine to advance your career.

## 21 4)

The known fact of contingencies, without knowing ① precisely what those contingencies will be, shows ② what disaster preparation is not the same thing as disaster rehearsal. No matter how many mock disasters are staged according to prior plans, the real disaster will never mirror any one of them. Disaster-preparation planning is more like training for a marathon than training for a high-jump competition or a sprinting event. Marathon runners do not practice by running the full course of twenty-six miles; rather, they get into shape by running ③ shorter distances and building up their endurance with cross-training. If they ④ have prepared successfully, then they are in optimal condition to run the marathon over its predetermined course and length, ⑤ assuming a range of weather conditions, predicted or not. This is normal marathon preparation.

## 22 5)

Fears of damaging ecosystems are based on the sound conservationist ① principle that we should aim to ② minimize the disruption we cause, but there is a risk that this principle may be ③ confused with the old idea of a 'balance of nature'. This supposes a perfect order of nature that will seek to maintain ④ it and that we should not change. It is a romantic, not to say idyllic, notion, but deeply misleading because it supposes a static condition. Ecosystems are dynamic, and although some may endure, apparently unchanged, for periods that are long in comparison with the human lifespan, they must and do change eventually. Species come and go, climates change, plant and animal communities adapt to altered circumstances, and when examined in fine detail such adaptation and consequent change can be seen to be taking place constantly. The 'balance of nature' is a myth. Our planet is dynamic, and so ⑤ are the arrangements by which its inhabitants live together.

## 23 6)

Before the modern scientific era, creativity was attributed to a superhuman force; all novel ideas ① originated with the gods. After all, how could a person create something that did not exist before the divine act of creation? In fact, the Latin meaning of the verb "inspire" is "to breathe into", ② reflected the belief that creative inspiration was similar to the moment in creation when God first breathed life into man. Plato argued that the poet was possessed by divine inspiration, and Plotin wrote that art could only be beautiful if it ③ descended from God. The artist's job was not to imitate nature but rather to reveal the sacred and transcendent qualities of nature. Art could only be a pale imitation of the perfection of the world of ideas. Greek artists did not blindly imitate ④ what they saw in reality; instead they tried to represent the pure, true forms underlying reality, resulting ⑤ in a sort of compromise between abstraction and accuracy.

## 24 7)

Some beginning researchers mistakenly believe that a good hypothesis is one that ① guaranteed to be right (e.g., alcohol will slow down reaction time). However, if we already know your hypothesis is true before you test it, testing your hypothesis won't tell us anything new. Remember, research is supposed to produce new knowledge. To get new knowledge, you, as a researcher-explorer, need to leave the safety of the shore (established facts) and venture into uncharted waters (as Einstein said, "If we knew ② what we were doing, it would not be called research, would it"?). If your predictions about what will ③ happen in these uncharted waters are wrong, that's okay: Scientists ④ are allowed to make mistakes (as Bates said, "Research is the process of going up alleys to see if they are blind"). Indeed, scientists often learn more from predictions that do not turn out than from those that ⑤ do.

## 29 8)

While reflecting on the needs of organizations, leaders, and families today, we realize that one of the unique characteristics ① is inclusivity. Why? Because inclusivity supports what everyone ultimately ② wants from their relationships: collaboration. Yet the majority of leaders, organizations, and families are still using the language of the old paradigm in which one person—typically the oldest, most educated, and/or wealthiest—makes all the decisions, and their decisions rule with little discussion or inclusion of others, resulting ③ from exclusivity. Today, this person could be a director, CEO, or other senior leader of an organization. There is no need for others to present their ideas because they are considered ④ inadequate. Yet research shows that exclusivity in problem solving, even with a genius, is not as effective as inclusivity, ⑤ where everyone's ideas are heard and a solution is developed through collaboration.

## 30 9)

The objective point of view is illustrated by John Ford's "philosophy of camera". Ford considered the camera to be a window and the audience to be outside the window viewing the people and events within. We ① are asked to watch the actions ② as if they were taking place at a distance, and we are not asked to participate. The objective point of view employs a static camera as ③ many as possible in order to produce this window effect, and it concentrates on the actors and the action without drawing attention to the camera. The objective camera suggests an emotional distance between camera and subject; the camera ④ seems simply to be recording, as straightforwardly as possible, the characters and actions of the story. For the most part, the director uses natural, normal types of camera positioning and camera angles. The objective camera does not comment on or interpret the action but merely records it, letting it unfold. We see the action from the viewpoint of an impersonal observer. If the camera moves, it does so unnoticeably, ⑤ calling as little attention to itself as possible.

## 31 10)

Even the most respectable of all musical institutions, the symphony orchestra, ① carries inside its DNA the legacy of the hunt. The various instruments in the orchestra can be traced back to these primitive origins—their earliest forms ② were made either from the animal (horn, hide, gut, bone) or the weapons employed in bringing the animal under control (stick, bow). Are we wrong to hear this history in the music itself, in the formidable aggression and awe-inspiring assertiveness of those monumental symphonies that remain the core repertoire of the world's leading orchestras? ③ Listening to Beethoven, Brahms, Mahler, Bruckner, Berlioz, Tchaikovsky, Shostakovich, and other great composers, I can easily summon up images of bands of men starting to chase animals, ④ using sound as a source and symbol of ⑤ inferiority, an expression of the will to predatory power.

## 32 11)

Our brains have ① evolved to remember unexpected events because basic survival depends on the ability to perceive causes and predict effects. If the brain predicts one event and experiences another, the unusualness will be especially ② interesting and will be encoded accordingly. Neurologist and classroom teacher Judith Willis has claimed that surprise in the classroom is one of the most effective ways of teaching with brain stimulation in mind. If students are exposed to new experiences via demonstrations or through the unexpected enthusiasm of their teachers or peers, they will be much more likely to connect with the information that follows. Willis has written ③ that encouraging active discovery in the classroom allows students to interact with new information, ④ moving it beyond working memory to be processed in the frontal lobe, which is devoted to advanced cognitive functioning. Preference for novelty sets us up for learning by directing attention, providing stimulation to ⑤ develop perceptual systems, and feeding curious and exploratory behavior.

## 33 12)

Psychological research has shown ① that people naturally divide up cognitive labor, often without thinking about it. Imagine you're cooking up a special dinner with a friend. You're a great cook, but your friend is the wine expert, an amateur sommelier. A neighbor drops by and starts telling you both about the terrific new wines ② are sold at the liquor store just down the street. There are many new wines, so there's a lot to remember. How ③ hard are you going to try to remember what the neighbor has to say about which wines to buy? Why bother when the information would be better ④ retained by the wine expert sitting next to you? If your friend wasn't around, you might try harder. After all, it would be good to know ⑤ what a good wine would be for the evening's festivities. But your friend, the wine expert, is likely to remember the information without even trying.

## 34 13)

Even companies that sell physical products to make profit ① are forced by their boards and investors to reconsider their underlying motives and to collect as ② many data as possible from consumers. Supermarkets no longer make all their money selling their produce and manufactured goods. They give you loyalty cards with ③ which they track your purchasing behaviors precisely. Then supermarkets sell this purchasing behavior to ④ marketing analytics companies. The marketing analytics companies perform machine learning procedures, slicing the data in new ways, and resell behavioral data back to product manufacturers as marketing insights. When data and machine learning become currencies of value in a capitalist system, then every company's natural tendency is to maximize its ability to conduct surveillance on its own customers because the customers are ⑤ themselves the new value-creation devices.

## 35 14)

Academics, politicians, marketers and others have in the past debated whether or not it is ethically correct to market products and services directly to young consumers. This is also a dilemma for psychologists who have questioned whether they ought to help advertisers manipulate children into purchasing more products they have ① seen advertised. Advertisers have admitted to ② taking advantage of the fact that it is easy to make children feel that they are losers if they do not own the 'right' products. Clever advertising informs children that they will be viewed by their peers in an unfavorable way if they do not have the products that are advertised, thereby ③ played on their emotional vulnerabilities. The constant feelings of inadequateness created by advertising ④ have been suggested to contribute to children ⑤ becoming fixated with instant gratification and beliefs that material possessions are important.

## 36 15)

Once we recognize the false-cause issue, we see it everywhere. ① However, a recent long-term study of University of Toronto medical students ② concluded that medical school class presidents lived an average of 2.4 years less than other medical school graduates. At first glance, this seemed to imply that being a medical school class president is bad for you. Does this mean that you should avoid being medical school class president at all costs? Probably not. Just because being class president is correlated with shorter life expectancy does not mean ③ that it causes shorter life expectancy. In fact, it seems likely that the sort of person who becomes medical school class president is, on average, extremely hard-working, serious, and ambitious. Perhaps this extra stress, and the corresponding lack of social and relaxation time—rather than being class president per se—④ contributes to lower life expectancy. If so, the real lesson of the study is that we should all relax a little and not let our work ⑤ to take over our lives.

## 37 16)

We commonly argue about the fairness of taxation—whether this or that tax will fall more heavily on the rich or the poor. But the expressive dimension of taxation goes beyond debates about fairness, to the moral judgements societies make about which activities are worthy of honor and recognition, and which ones should be discouraged. Sometimes, these judgements are ① explicit. Taxes on tobacco, alcohol, and casinos ② are called "sin taxes" because they seek to discourage activities considered harmful or undesirable. Such taxes express society's disapproval of these activities by ③ raising the cost of engaging in them. Proposals to tax sugary sodas (to combat obesity) or carbon emissions (to address climate change) likewise seek to change norms and shape behavior. Not all taxes have this aim. We do not tax income to express disapproval of paid employment or to discourage people from engaging in it. Nor is a general sales tax intended as a deterrent to ④ buy things. These are simply ways of ⑤ raising revenue.

## 38 17)

Most beliefs—but not all—are open to tests of verification. This means ① what beliefs can be tested to see if they are correct or false. Beliefs can be verified or falsified with objective criteria external to the person. There are people who believe the Earth is flat and not a sphere. Because we have objective evidence ② that the Earth is in fact a sphere, the flat Earth belief can be shown to be false. Also, the belief that it will rain tomorrow can be tested for truth by ③ waiting until tomorrow and seeing whether it rains or not. ④ However, some types of beliefs cannot be tested for truth because we cannot get external evidence in our lifetimes (such as a belief that the Earth will stop spinning on its axis by the year 9999 or that there is life on a planet 100-million light-years away). Also, meta-physical beliefs (such as the existence and nature of a god) present ⑤ considerable challenges in generating evidence that everyone is willing to use as a truth criterion.

## 39 18)

Everyone automatically categorizes and generalizes all the time. Unconsciously. It is not a question of ① prejudicing or enlightened. Categories are absolutely necessary for us to ② function. They give structure to our thoughts. Imagine if we saw every item and every scenario as truly unique—we would not even have a language to describe the world around us. But the necessary and useful instinct to generalize can distort our world view. It can make us mistakenly ③ group together things, or people, or countries that are actually very different. It can make us ④ assume everything or everyone in one category is similar. And, maybe, most unfortunate of all, it can make us ⑤ jump to conclusions about a whole category based on a few, or even just one, unusual example.

## 40 19)

At the University of Iowa, students were briefly shown numbers that they had to memorize. Then they were offered the choice of either a fruit salad or a chocolate cake. When the number the students memorized was seven digits long, 63% of them chose the cake. When the number they ① were asked to remember had just two digits, however, 59% ② were opted for the fruit salad. Our reflective brains know that the fruit salad is better for our health, but our reflexive brains desire that soft, fattening chocolate cake. If the reflective brain is busy ③ figuring something else out—like trying to remember a seven-digit number—then impulse can easily win. On the other hand, if we're not thinking ④ too hard about something else (with only a minor distraction like memorizing two digits), then the reflective system can ⑤ deny the emotional impulse of the reflexive side.

## 41~42<sup>20)</sup>

Test scores are not a measure of self-worth; however, we often associate our sense of worthiness with our performance on an exam. Thoughts such as "If I don't pass this test, I'm a failure" ① are mental traps not rooted in truth. Failing a test is failing a test, nothing more. It is in no way descriptive of your value as a person. Believing that test performance is a reflection of your virtue places unreasonable pressure on your performance. Not passing the certification test only means ② that your certification status has been delayed. Maintaining a positive attitude is therefore important. If you have studied hard, reaffirm this mentally and believe that you will do well. If, on the other hand, you did not study as ③ hard as you should have or wanted to, accept that as beyond your control for now and attend to the task of doing the best you can. If things do not go well this time, you know ④ what needs to be done in preparation for the next exam. Talk to yourself in positive terms. Avoid ⑤ to rationalize past or future test performance by placing the blame on secondary variables. Thoughts such as, "I didn't have enough time", or "I should have ...", compound the stress of test-taking. Take control by affirming your value, self-worth, and dedication to meeting the test challenge head on. Repeat to yourself "I can and I will pass this exam".

## 43~45<sup>21)</sup>

Once upon a time there lived a poor but cheerful shoemaker. He was so happy, he sang all day long. The children loved to stand around his window to listen to him. Next door to the shoemaker lived a rich man. He ① used to sit up all night to count his gold. In the morning, he went to bed, but he could not sleep because of the sound of the shoemaker's singing. One day, he thought of a way of stopping the singing. He wrote a letter to the shoemaker asking him to visit. The shoemaker came at once, and to his surprise the rich man gave him a bag of gold. When he got home again, the shoemaker opened the bag. He had never seen so much gold before! When he sat down at his bench and began, carefully, to count it, the children watched through the window. There ② was so much there that the shoemaker was afraid to let it out of his sight. So he took it to bed with him. But he could not sleep for worrying about it. Very early in the morning, he got up and brought his gold down from the bedroom. He had decided to hide it up the chimney instead. But he was still uneasy, and in a little while he dug a hole in the garden and buried his bag of gold in it. It was no use ③ trying to work. He was too worried about the safety of his gold. And as for singing, he was too miserable to utter a note. He could not sleep, or work, or sing—and, worst of all, the children no longer came to see him. At last, the shoemaker felt so ④ unhappily that he seized his bag of gold and ran next door to the rich man. "Please take back your gold", he said. "The worry of it is making me ill, and I have lost all of my friends. I would rather be a poor shoemaker, as I ⑤ was before". And so the shoemaker was happy again and sang all day at his work.

# 2021 고2 3월 모의고사

❶ voca  ❷ text  ❸ [ / ]  ❹ ____  ❺ quiz 1  ❻ quiz 2  ❼ quiz 3  ❽ quiz 4  ❾ quiz 5  ❿ quiz 6

## 18 다음 글의 내용과 일치하지 않는 것을 모두 고르시오.1)

My name is Anthony Thompson and I am writing on behalf of the residents' association. Our recycling program has been working well thanks to your participation. However, a problem has recently occurred that needs your attention. Because there is no given day for recycling, residents are putting their recycling out at any time. This makes the recycling area messy, which requires extra labor and cost. To deal with this problem, the residents' association has decided on a day to recycle. I would like to let you know that you can put out your recycling on Wednesdays only. I am sure it will make our apartment complex look much more pleasant. Thank you in advance for your cooperation.

① 필자의 이름은 Anthony Thompson이며, 입주민 조합을 대표하여 편지를 쓰고 있다.
② 재활용 프로그램은 입주민들의 참여가 저조해 잘 운영되지 않았고, 최근에 입주민들의 관심이 필요한 문제가 생겼다.
③ 재활용을 위해 정해진 날이 있는데도 입주민들은 아무 때나 자신들의 재활용품을 내놓는다.
④ 재활용 구역이 어질러지면 추가 노동과 비용이 필요하기 때문에, 입주민 조합은 재활용하는 날을 결정했다.
⑤ 수요일에만 재활용품을 내놓을 수 있다.

## 19 다음 글의 내용과 일치하는 것을 모두 고르시오.2)

It was a day I was due to give a presentation at work, not something I'd do often. As I stood up to begin, I froze. A chilly 'pins-and-needles' feeling crept over me, starting in my hands. Time seemed to stand still as I struggled to start speaking, and I felt a pressure around my throat, as though my voice was trapped and couldn't come out. Gazing around at the blur of faces, I realized they were all waiting for me to begin, but by now I knew I couldn't continue.

① 나는 직장에서 발표를 자주 했지만, 그날은 시작하려고 일어섰을 때 얼어붙었다.
② '핀과 바늘로 찌르는 듯한' 차가운 느낌이 손에서 시작해서 나를 엄습했다.
③ 내가 말하기 시작하려고 애쓸 때 시간이 정지해 있는 것 같았고 나는 목과 가슴 부근에서 압박감을 느꼈다.

④ 그것은 마치 목소리가 갇혀서 빠져나올 수 없는 것 같았다.
⑤ 흐릿한 형체의 얼굴들이 나를 둘러싸고 발표를 시작하기를 재촉하고 있었지만 그때쯤 나는 내가 계속할 수 없다는 것을 알았다.

## 20 다음 글의 내용과 일치하지 않는 것을 모두 고르시오.3)

No matter what your situation, whether you are an insider or an outsider, you need to become the voice that challenges yesterday's answers. Think about the characteristics that make outsiders valuable to an organization. They are the people who have the perspective to see problems that the insiders are too close to really notice. They are the ones who have the freedom to point out these problems and criticize them without risking their job or their career. Part of adopting an outsider mentality is forcing yourself to look around your organization with this disassociated, less emotional perspective. If you didn't know your coworkers and feel bonded to them by your shared experiences, what would you think of them? You may not have the job security or confidence to speak your mind to management, but you can make these "outsider" assessments of your organization on your own and use what you determine to advance your career.

① 여러분의 상황이 어떠하든, 여러분이 내부자이건 외부자이건, 여러분은 어제의 정답에 이의를 제기하는 목소리가 될 필요가 있다.
② 외부자는 내부자가 너무 가까이 있어서 정말 알아차릴 수 없는 문제들을 볼 수 있는 관점을 가진 사람들이기 때문에 조직에 위협이 된다.
③ 그들은 종종 문제를 지적하고 비판하다가 자신의 일자리나 자신의 경력을 위태롭게 한다.
④ 외부자의 사고방식을 채택하는 것의 일부는 이렇게 분리된, 덜 감정적인 관점으로 여러분의 조직을 스스로 둘러보게 하는 것이다.
⑤ 자신의 조직에 관해 이런 '외부자의' 평가를 독자적으로 하거나, 판단한 사실을 자신의 경력을 발전시키기 위해 이용하기 위해서는 먼저 직업 안정성과 경력을 가지고 있어야 한다.

## 21 다음 글의 내용과 일치하지 않는 것을 모두 고르시오.4)

The known fact of contingencies, without knowing precisely what those contingencies will be, shows that disaster preparation is not the same thing as disaster rehearsal. No matter how many mock disasters are staged according to prior plans, the real disaster will never mirror any one of them. Disaster-preparation planning is more like training for a marathon than training for a high-jump competition or a sprinting event. Marathon runners do not practice by running the full course of twenty-six miles; rather, they get into shape by running shorter distances and building up their endurance with cross-training. If they have prepared successfully, then they are in optimal condition to run the marathon over its predetermined course and length, assuming a range of weather conditions, predicted or not. This is normal marathon preparation.

① 재난 대비는 재난 예행연습과 똑같은 것이다.
② 더 많은 모의 재난이 사전 계획에 따라 조직될수록, 실제 재난은 그런 것들 중 어느 하나라도 비슷하게 반영하게 될 것이다..
③ 재난 대비 계획 세우기는 높이뛰기 시합이나 단거리 달리기 경주를 위해 훈련하는 것이라기보다는 마라톤을 위해 훈련하는 것과 더 비슷하다.
④ 마라톤 선수들은 26마일 전체 코스를 달리는 것으로 연습하는 것이 아니라 오히려 더 짧은 거리를 달리고 여러 가지 운동을 조합하여 행하는 훈련법으로 자신의 지구력을 강화함으로써 몸 상태를 좋게 만든다.
⑤ 만약 그들이 성공적으로 준비했다면 그들은 마라톤의 미리 정해진 코스와 길이에 걸쳐 예상되었든 아니든 다양한 기상 조건을 가정하면서 마라톤을 달릴 수 있는 최적의 상태에 있다. 이것이 보통의 마라톤 준비이다.

## 22 다음 글의 내용과 일치하지 않는 것을 모두 고르시오.[5]

Fears of damaging ecosystems are based on the sound conservationist principle that we should aim to minimize the disruption we cause, but there is a risk that this principle may be confused with the old idea of a 'balance of nature.' This supposes a perfect order of nature that will seek to maintain itself and that we should not change. It is a romantic, not to say idyllic, notion, but deeply misleading because it supposes a static condition. Ecosystems are dynamic, and although some may endure, apparently unchanged, for periods that are long in comparison with the human lifespan, they must and do change eventually. Species come and go, climates change, plant and animal communities adapt to altered circumstances, and when examined in fine detail such adaptation and consequent change can be seen to be taking place constantly. The 'balance of nature' is a myth. Our planet is dynamic, and so are the arrangements by which its inhabitants live together.

① 생태계를 손상하는 것에 대한 두려움은 우리가 초래하는 (환경) 파괴를 최소화하는 것을 목표로 해야 한다는 건전한 환경 보호주의자 원칙을 바탕으로 하지만,
② 이 원칙이 '자연의 균형'이라는 오래된 생각과 혼동될지도 모른다는 위험이 있다. 이것은 그 자체를 유지하려고 노력하고 우리가 바꾸어서는 안 되는 완벽한 자연의 질서를 전제로 한다.
③ 그것은 낭만적인 개념이지만 동적인 상태를 전제로 하기 때문에 매우 잘못된 인식을 준다.
④ 생태계는 역동적이고, 일부는 겉보기에는 변하지 않는 채로 인간의 수명과 비교해 보면 오랜 기간 동안 지속될지 모르지만, 그것은 결국 변할 것임에 틀림없고 정말 변한다.
⑤ 생물 종과 기후, 동식물 군집의 환경 적응과 결과적인 변화는 항상 일어나는 것처럼 보이며 이는 '자연의 균형'을 맞추기 위한 일이다. 지구는 역동적 대응하며 균형을 찾아 나가며 그것은 우리의 삶의 방식도 마찬가지이다.

## 23 다음 글의 내용과 일치하지 않는 것을 모두 고르시오.[6]

Before the modern scientific era, creativity was attributed to a superhuman force; all novel ideas originated with the gods. After all, how could a person create something that did not exist before the divine act of creation? In fact, the Latin meaning of the verb "inspire" is "to breathe into," reflecting the belief that creative inspiration was similar to the moment in creation when God first breathed life into man. Plato argued that the poet was possessed by divine inspiration, and Plotin wrote that art could only be beautiful if it descended from God. The artist's job was not to imitate nature but rather to reveal the sacred and transcendent qualities of nature. Art could only be a pale imitation of the perfection of the world of ideas. Greek artists did not blindly imitate what they saw in reality; instead they tried to represent the pure, true forms underlying reality, resulting in a sort of compromise between abstraction and accuracy.

① 근대의 과학적인 시대 이전에 창의성은 초인적인 힘, 즉 신의 생각에서 기인하는 것으로 여겨졌다.
② '영감을 주다'라는 동사의 라틴어 의미는 '숨결을 불어넣다'이고 창의적 영감은 신이 처음에 인간에게 생명을 불어 넣었을 때 창조의 순간과 비슷했다는 믿음을 반영한다.
③ Plato는 시인은 신이 내린 영감에 사로잡혔다고 주장했고 Plotin은 예술은 그것이 신으로부터 내려온 경우에만 아름다울 수 있다고 썼다.
④ 예술가의 일은 자연을 모방함으로써 자연의 신성하고 초월적인 특성을 드러내는 것으로, 근본적으로 완벽한 관념[이데아]의 세계의 어설프게 흉내 낸 것에 불과했다.
⑤ 그리스의 예술가들은 그들이 현실에서 본 것을 맹목적으로 모방하기보다는 현실의 근저에 있는 순수하고 진정한 형태를 나타내려고 애썼는데 그 결과 추상과 정확성 간의 일종의 타협을 발생시켰다.

## 24 다음 글의 내용과 일치하지 않는 것을 모두 고르시오.⁷⁾

Some beginning researchers mistakenly believe that a good hypothesis is one that is guaranteed to be right (e.g., alcohol will slow down reaction time). However, if we already know your hypothesis is true before you test it, testing your hypothesis won't tell us anything new. Remember, research is supposed to produce new knowledge. To get new knowledge, you, as a researcher-explorer, need to leave the safety of the shore (established facts) and venture into uncharted waters (as Einstein said, "If we knew what we were doing, it would not be called research, would it?"). If your predictions about what will happen in these uncharted waters are wrong, that's okay: Scientists are allowed to make mistakes (as Bates said, "Research is the process of going up alleys to see if they are blind"). Indeed, scientists often learn more from predictions that do not turn out than from those that do.

① 일부 처음 시작하는 연구자들은 '좋은 가설은 옳음이 보장된 것'이라고 생각한다.
② 가설을 검사해 보기도 전에 그것이 사실임을 알고 있다면, 그 가설은 우리에게 새로운 지식을 알려주지 않으므로 연구가 될 수 없다.
③ 새로운 지식을 얻기 위해서 연구자이자 탐험가로서 여러분은 해변의 안전함(가정 사실)을 떠나 미개척 영역으로 과감히 들어가 볼 필요가 있다
④ 이런 미개척 영역에서 무엇이 일어날 것인지에 관한 여러분의 예측이 틀리면 안 된다. 과학자는 실수를 저지르면 안 되기 때문이다.
⑤ 과학자는 흔히 결과를 내지 않는 예측들보다는 결과를 내는 예측들로부터 더 많이 배운다.

## 28 다음 글의 내용과 일치하는 것을 모두 고르시오.⁸⁾

Ingrid Bergman was born in Stockholm, Sweden on August 29, 1915. Her mother was German and her father Swedish. Her mother died when she was three, and her father passed away when she was 12. Eventually she was brought up by her Uncle Otto and Aunt Hulda. She was interested in acting from an early age. When she was 17, she attended the Royal Dramatic Theater School in Stockholm. She made her debut on the stage but was more interested in working in films. In the early 1940s, she gained star status in Hollywood, playing many roles as the heroine of the film. Bergman was considered to have tremendous acting talent, an angelic natural beauty and the willingness to work hard to get the best out of films. She was fluent in five languages and appeared in a range of films, plays and TV productions.

① Ingrid Bergman은 1915년 8월 29일에 스웨덴의 스톡홀름에 사는 독일인 부모님 밑에서 태어났다.
② 그녀는 어릴 때 부모를 잃었고, 조부모에 의해 키워졌다.
③ 그녀는 어릴 때부터 연기에 관심이 있었다. 그녀가 열아홉 살 때 스톡홀름에 있는 Royal Dramatic Theater School에 다녔다. 그녀는 연극으로 데뷔했지만 영화계에서 일하는 데 더 관심이 있었다.
④ 1940년대 초에 그녀는 할리우드에서 스타의 지위를 얻었고 영화의 여주인공으로 많은 역할을 맡았다. Bergman은 연기 재능은 평범했지만 천사 같은 자연적인 미모와, 최고의 결과를 얻기 위해 열심히 일하는 태도를 가지고 있다는 칭찬을 받았다.
⑤ 그녀는 다섯 개의 언어에 유창했고 다양한 영화, 연극, 그리고 TV 작품에 출연했다.

## 29 다음 글의 내용과 일치하지 않는 것을 모두 고르시오.⁹⁾

While reflecting on the needs of organizations, leaders, and families today, we realize that one of the unique characteristics is inclusivity. Why? Because inclusivity supports what everyone ultimately wants from their relationships: collaboration. Yet the majority of leaders, organizations, and families are still using the language of the old paradigm in which one person — typically the oldest, most educated, and/or wealthiest — makes all the decisions, and their decisions rule with little discussion or inclusion of others, resulting in exclusivity. Today, this person could be a director, CEO, or other senior leader of an organization. There is no need for others to present their ideas because they are considered inadequate. Yet research shows that exclusivity in problem solving, even with a genius, is not as effective as inclusivity, where everyone's ideas are heard and a solution is developed through collaboration.

① 오늘날 조직, 지도자, 그리고 가족의 요구에 관해 곰곰이 생각할 때 우리는 독특한 특성 중 하나가 배타성이라는 것을 깨닫는다.
② 포용성은 모든 사람이 자신의 관계에서 궁극적으로 원하는 것인 협력을 뒷받침한다.
③ 그러나 대다수의 지도자, 조직, 그리고 가족은 여전히 낡은 패러다임의 언어를 사용하고 있다. 한 사람이 토론이나 다른 사람을 포함시키는 과정을 통해 모든 결정을 내리면 그들의 결정이 집단을 지배하고 결과적으로 배타성을 초래한다.
④ 오늘날 이 사람은 어떤 조직의 관리자, 최고 경영자, 또는 다른 상급 지도자일 수 있다. 다른 사람들이 자신의 생각을 제시할 필요가 없는데 왜냐하면 그것은 부적절한 것으로 여겨지기 때문이다.
⑤ 그러나 연구에 따르면 문제 해결에 있어서 배타성은, 심지어 천재와 함께하는 것이더라도, 포용성만큼 효과적이지 않은데, 포용성이 있는 경우

에는 모든 사람의 생각을 듣게 되고 해결책은 협력을 통해 발전된다.

# 30 다음 글의 내용과 일치하는 것을 모두 고르시오.10)

The objective point of view is illustrated by John Ford's "philosophy of camera." Ford considered the camera to be a window and the audience to be outside the window viewing the people and events within. We are asked to watch the actions as if they were taking place at a distance, and we are not asked to participate. The objective point of view employs a static camera as much as possible in order to produce this window effect, and it concentrates on the actors and the action without drawing attention to the camera. The objective camera suggests an emotional distance between camera and subject; the camera seems simply to be recording, as straightforwardly as possible, the characters and actions of the story. For the most part, the director uses natural, normal types of camera positioning and camera angles. The objective camera does not comment on or interpret the action but merely records it, letting it unfold. We see the action from the viewpoint of an impersonal observer. If the camera moves, it does so unnoticeably, calling as little attention to itself as possible.

① John Ford는 카메라를 창문이라고 생각했고 관객은 창문 안에 있는 사람과 사건을 바라보면서 창문 밖에 있다고 생각했다.

② 우리는 사건들이 멀리서 일어나고 있는 것처럼 그것들을 바라보고, 참여하지 않는다. 객관적인 관점은 이런 창문 효과를 만들기 위해 역동적인 카메라를 가능한 한 많이 이용하고, 그것은 카메라에 관심을 끄는 것 없이 배우와 사건에 집중한다.

③ 객관적인 카메라는 카메라와 대상 간의 물리적인 거리를 보여 주는데, 카메라는 이야기의 등장인물과 사건을 가능한 한 있는 그대로 그저 기록하고 있는 것으로 보인다.

④ 대부분의 경우, 감독은 자연스럽고 일반적인 종류의 카메라 위치 선정과 카메라 각도를 사용한다. 객관적인 카메라는 사건에 관해 논평하거나 해석하지 않고 그것이 전개되게 하면서 그저 그것을 기록한다.

⑤ 우리는 온정적인 관찰자의 관점에서 사건을 본다. 만약 카메라가 움직인다면 그것은 눈에 띄지만 가능한 한 관심을 끌지 않는 방향으로 움직인다.

# 31 다음 글의 내용과 일치하지 않는 것을 모두 고르시오.11)

Even the most respectable of all musical institutions, the symphony orchestra, carries inside its DNA the legacy of the hunt. The various instruments in the orchestra can be traced back to these primitive origins — their earliest forms were made either from the animal (horn, hide, gut, bone) or the weapons employed in bringing the animal under control (stick, bow). Are we wrong to hear this history in the music itself, in the formidable aggression and awe-inspiring assertiveness of those monumental symphonies that remain the core repertoire of the world's leading orchestras? Listening to Beethoven, Brahms, Mahler, Bruckner, Berlioz, Tchaikovsky, Shostakovich, and other great composers, I can easily summon up images of bands of men starting to chase animals, using sound as a source and symbol of dominance, an expression of the will to predatory power.

① 모든 음악 단체 중 가장 훌륭한 단체인 교향악단도 자신의 DNA 안에 수렵과 채집의 유산을 지니고 있다.

② 교향악단에 있는 다양한 악기들은 모두 원시적인 기원을 가지고 있다.

③ 그것들의 초기 형태는 동물(뿔, 가죽, 내장, 뼈) 또는 동물을 진압하기 위해 사용된 무기(막대, 활)로 만들어졌다.

④ 하지만 음악 그 자체에서, 세계의 주요한 교향악단의 핵심 레퍼토리로 남아 있는 기념비적인 교향곡들의 강력한 공격성과 경외감을 자아내는 당당함에서 이러한 역사를 들을 수는 없다. 만약 들린다면 틀린 것이다.

⑤ 위대한 작곡가들의 음악을 들으며, 나는 소리를 지배의 원천이자 상징으로, 공격적인 힘에 대한 의지의 표현으로 사용하면서 동물을 쫓기 시작하는 사람들 무리의 이미지를 쉽게 떠올릴 수 있다.

## 32 다음 글의 내용과 일치하지 않는 것을 모두 고르시오.12)

Our brains have evolved to remember unexpected events because basic survival depends on the ability to perceive causes and predict effects. If the brain predicts one event and experiences another, the unusualness will be especially interesting and will be encoded accordingly. Neurologist and classroom teacher Judith Willis has claimed that surprise in the classroom is one of the most effective ways of teaching with brain stimulation in mind. If students are exposed to new experiences via demonstrations or through the unexpected enthusiasm of their teachers or peers, they will be much more likely to connect with the information that follows. Willis has written that encouraging active discovery in the classroom allows students to interact with new information, moving it beyond working memory to be processed in the frontal lobe, which is devoted to advanced cognitive functioning. Preference for novelty sets us up for learning by directing attention, providing stimulation to developing perceptual systems, and feeding curious and exploratory behavior.

① 우리의 뇌는 예상치 못한 사건들을 기억하도록 진화해 왔는데, 왜냐하면 기본적인 생존이 원인을 인식하고 결과를 예측하는 능력에 달려 있기 때문이다.

② 만약 뇌가 예측과 다른 사건을 경험한다면, 그 특이함은 특히 흥미로울 것이고 그에 따라 정보가 입력될 것이다. 따라서 교실에서 놀라움을 느끼게 하는 것은 자극을 염두에 두고 가르치는 유일한 효과적인 방법이다.

③ 학생들이 실연, 혹은 교사나 또래 친구의 예상치 못한 열의를 통해 새로운 경험에 노출되면, 그들은 뒤따르는 정보와 연결될 가능성이 훨씬 더 클 것이다.

④ Willis는 교실에서의 능동적인 발견을 장려하는 것이 학생들로 하여금 새로운 정보와 상호 작용하게 해 주어서, 그것이 고도의 인지 기능을 넘어 작동 기억을 전담하는 전두엽에서 처리되도록 한다고 기술했다.

⑤ 새로움에 대한 선호는, 주의를 이끌고, 지각 체계를 발전시키는 데 자극을 제공하며, 호기심 많고 탐구적인 행동을 충족함으로써 우리를 학습하도록 준비시킨다.

## 33 다음 글의 내용과 일치하지 않는 것을 모두 고르시오.13)

Psychological research has shown that people naturally divide up cognitive labor, often without thinking about it. Imagine you're cooking up a special dinner with a friend. You're a great cook, but your friend is the wine expert, an amateur sommelier. A neighbor drops by and starts telling you both about the terrific new wines being sold at the liquor store just down the street. There are many new wines, so there's a lot to remember. How hard are you going to try to remember what the neighbor has to say about which wines to buy? Why bother when the information would be better retained by the wine expert sitting next to you? If your friend wasn't around, you might try harder. After all, it would be good to know what a good wine would be for the evening's festivities. But your friend, the wine expert, is likely to remember the information without even trying.

① 심리학 연구에 따르면, 사람들은 의식적으로 자연스럽게 인지 노동을 나눈다.

② 아마추어 소믈리에라고 할 수 있는 와인 전문가 친구와 함께 있을 때, 이웃이 와인에 대해 말한다고 생각해 보자. 여러분만 그 자리에 있었다면 그 말을 기억하기 위해 아주 열심히 노력해야 할 것이다.

③ 와인 전문가인 그 친구는 그럴 필요가 없다. 그 정보를 더 잘 기억할 수 있기 때문이다.

④ 저녁 만찬을 위해 뭐가 좋은 와인이 될지 아는 것은 좋은 일이다.

⑤ 하지만, 와인 전문가인 여러분의 친구는 애쓰지 않아도 이미 그 정보를 알고 있다.

## 34 다음 글의 내용과 일치하지 않는 것을 모두 고르시오.14)

Even companies that sell physical products to make profit are forced by their boards and investors to reconsider their underlying motives and to collect as much data as possible from consumers. Supermarkets no longer make all their money selling their produce and manufactured goods. They give you loyalty cards with which they track your purchasing behaviors precisely. Then supermarkets sell this purchasing behavior to marketing analytics companies. The marketing analytics companies perform machine learning procedures, slicing the data in new ways, and resell behavioral data back to product manufacturers as marketing insights. When data and machine learning become currencies of value in a capitalist system, then every company's natural tendency is to maximize its ability to conduct surveillance on its own customers because the customers are themselves the new value-creation devices.

① 수익을 내기 위해 물적 제품을 판매하는 기업들은 이사회와 투자자가 있어야만 고객에게서 가능한 한 많은 정보를 수집하려는 자신들의 근원적인 동기를 파악할 수 있다.
② 슈퍼마켓의 수익에는 농산물과 제조된 물품을 판매한 것만이 아니라 다른 것들도 포함된다..
③ 슈퍼마켓은 고객 우대 카드를 통해 대략적으로 추적한 고객들의 구매 행위에 대한 정보를 마케팅 분석 기업에 판매한다.
④ 마케팅 분석 기업은 기계 학습 절차를 수행하고 그 정보를 새로운 방식으로 쪼개서 행동 정보를 제품 제조 기업에 통찰력 있는 마케팅 정보로 다시 되판다.
⑤ 정보와 기계 학습이 자본주의 체제에서 가치 있는 통화가 될 때, 고객 자체가 새로운 가치 창출 장치이기 때문에 모든 기업의 자연스러운 경향은 자신의 고객을 관찰하는 능력을 최대화하는 것이다.

## 35 다음 글의 내용과 일치하지 않는 것을 모두 고르시오.15)

Academics, politicians, marketers and others have in the past debated whether or not it is ethically correct to market products and services directly to young consumers. This is also a dilemma for psychologists who have questioned whether they ought to help advertisers manipulate children into purchasing more products they have seen advertised. Advertisers have admitted to taking advantage of the fact that it is easy to make children feel that they are losers if they do not own the 'right' products. Clever advertising informs children that they will be viewed by their peers in an unfavorable way if they do not have the products that are advertised, thereby playing on their emotional vulnerabilities. The constant feelings of inadequateness created by advertising have been suggested to contribute to children becoming fixated with instant gratification and beliefs that material possessions are important.

① 많은 사람들이 제품과 서비스를 어린 소비자들에게 직접 판촉하는 것이 윤리적으로 옳은지 그렇지 않은지를 논쟁해 왔다.
② 이것은 또한, 아이들을 조종해서 광고되는 제품을 보고 더 많이 구매하게 하는 광고 업자들을 돕는 심리학자들에게도 딜레마이다.
③ 광고주들은 아이들이 그 '적절한' 제품을 소유하고 있지 않으면 자신이 패배자라고 느낀다는 사실을 이용한 것을 인정하려고 하지 않는다.
④ 영리한 광고는 아이들에게 만약 그들이 광고되는 제품을 가지고 있지 않으면 자신의 또래 친구들에게 부정적으로 보일 것이라고 알려 주고, 그로 인해 아이들의 정서적인 취약성을 이용한다.
⑤ 광고가 만들어 내는, 끊임없이 부적절하다고 느끼는 감정은, 아이들이 즉각적인 만족감과 물질적 소유물이 중요하다는 믿음에 집착하게 되는 데 기여한다고 언급되어 왔다.

## 36 다음 글의 내용과 일치하지 않는 것을 모두 고르시오.[16]

Once we recognize the false-cause issue, we see it everywhere. For example, a recent long-term study of University of Toronto medical students concluded that medical school class presidents lived an average of 2.4 years less than other medical school graduates. At first glance, this seemed to imply that being a medical school class president is bad for you. Does this mean that you should avoid being medical school class president at all costs? Probably not. Just because being class president is correlated with shorter life expectancy does not mean that it causes shorter life expectancy. In fact, it seems likely that the sort of person who becomes medical school class president is, on average, extremely hard-working, serious, and ambitious. Perhaps this extra stress, and the corresponding lack of social and relaxation time — rather than being class president per se — contributes to lower life expectancy. If so, the real lesson of the study is that we should all relax a little and not let our work take over our lives.

① 토론토 대학의 의대생들에 대한 최근의 장기간의 연구는 의대 학년 대표들이 다른 의대 졸업생들보다 평균 2.4년 더 적게 살았다는 결론을 내렸다.
② 의대 학년 대표인 것이 여러분에게 해로우므로, 무슨 수를 써서라도 의대 학년 대표가 되는 것을 피해야 한다.
③ 학년 대표인 것이 더 짧은 평균 수명과 서로 관련된다는 사실은 그것이 더 짧은 평균 수명을 '유발한다'는 의미로 해석될 수 있다.
④ 의대 학년 대표가 되는 그런 부류의 사람은 평균적으로 몹시 열심히 공부하고, 진지하며, 야망이 있으며 이런 점으로 인해 가중된 스트레스와 그에 상응하는 사교와 휴식 시간의 부족이 더 짧은 평균 수명의 원인이 된다.
⑤ 우리 모두는 약간의 휴식을 취해야 하고 우리의 일이 우리의 삶을 장악하게 두어서는 안 된다.

## 37 다음 글의 내용과 일치하지 않는 것을 모두 고르시오.[17]

We commonly argue about the fairness of taxation — whether this or that tax will fall more heavily on the rich or the poor. But the expressive dimension of taxation goes beyond debates about fairness, to the moral judgements societies make about which activities are worthy of honor and recognition, and which ones should be discouraged. Sometimes, these judgements are explicit. Taxes on tobacco, alcohol, and casinos are called "sin taxes" because they seek to discourage activities considered harmful or undesirable. Such taxes express society's disapproval of these activities by raising the cost of engaging in them. Proposals to tax sugary sodas (to combat obesity) or carbon emissions (to address climate change) likewise seek to change norms and shape behavior. Not all taxes have this aim. We do not tax income to express disapproval of paid employment or to discourage people from engaging in it. Nor is a general sales tax intended as a deterrent to buying things. These are simply ways of raising revenue.

① 과세의 표현적 차원은 공정성에 대한 논쟁을 넘어, 어떤 활동이 명예와 인정을 받을 가치가 있고 어떤 활동이 억제되어야 하는지에 대해 사회가 내리는 도덕적 판단에까지 이를 수 있다. 모든 세금이 이런 목적을 가지고 있다.
② 담배, 술, 그리고 카지노에 대한 세금은 해롭거나 바람직하지 않은 것으로 간주되는 활동들을 억제하려고 하기 때문에 '죄악세'라고 불린다. 그런 세금은 이러한 활동을 하는 데 드는 비용을 증가시킴으로써 그것에 대한 사회의 반대를 표현한다.
③ 마찬가지로 설탕이 든 탄산음료에 세금을 부과하는 제안이나 탄소 배출에 세금을 부과하는 제안은 규범을 바꾸고 행동을 형성하려 한다.
④ 우리는 유급 고용에 대한 반대를 표명하거나 사람들이 그것을 하는 것을 막기 위해 소득에 세금을 부과한다.
⑤ 하지만 일반 판매세는 물건을 사는 것의 억제책으로서 의도된 것이 아니다. 이것들은 단순히 세입을 올리는 방법이다.

## 38 다음 글의 내용과 일치하지 않는 것을 모두 고르시오.[18]

Most beliefs — but not all — are open to tests of verification. This means that beliefs can be tested to see if they are correct or false. Beliefs can be verified or falsified with objective criteria external to the person. There are people who believe the Earth is flat and not a sphere. Because we have objective evidence that the Earth is in fact a sphere, the flat Earth belief can be shown to be false. Also, the belief that it will rain tomorrow can be tested for truth by waiting until tomorrow and seeing whether it rains or not. However, some types of beliefs cannot be tested for truth because we cannot get external evidence in our lifetimes (such as a belief that the Earth will stop spinning on its axis by the year 9999 or that there is life on a planet 100-million light-years away). Also, meta-physical beliefs (such as the existence and nature of a god) present considerable challenges in generating evidence that everyone is willing to use as a truth criterion.

① 모든 믿음은 그것이 옳거나 그른지를 확인하기 위해 시험될 수 있다.
② 믿음은 그 사람의 외부에 있는 객관적인 기준을 통해 진실임이 입증되거나 거짓임이 입증될 수 있다.
③ 우리는 지구가 구라는 객관적인 증거를 가지고 있기 때문에, 지구가 평평하다는 믿음은 거짓임이 증명된다. 또한, 내일 비가 올 것이라는 믿음도 내일까지 기다려 비가 오는지 안 오는지 봄으로써 진실인지 확인될 수 있다.
④ 비슷하게, 9999년이 되면 지구가 자전하는 것을 멈출 것이라는 믿음이나 1억 광년 떨어진 행성에 생명체가 있다는 것 같은 믿음도 그때까지 기다려서 확인함으로써 입증할 수 있다.
⑤ 또한, 형이상학적 믿음은 모든 사람이 진리 기준으로 기꺼이 사용할 증거를 만드는 데 있어서 상당한 난제가 된다.

## 39 다음 글의 내용과 일치하지 않는 것을 모두 고르시오.[19]

Everyone automatically categorizes and generalizes all the time. Unconsciously. It is not a question of being prejudiced or enlightened. Categories are absolutely necessary for us to function. They give structure to our thoughts. Imagine if we saw every item and every scenario as truly unique — we would not even have a language to describe the world around us. But the necessary and useful instinct to generalize can distort our world view. It can make us mistakenly group together things, or people, or countries that are actually very different. It can make us assume everything or everyone in one category is similar.

And, maybe, most unfortunate of all, it can make us jump to conclusions about a whole category based on a few, or even just one, unusual example.

① 모든 사람들은 항상 무의식적으로 자동적으로 분류하고 일반화한다. 이것은 편견이나 계몽의 문제가 아니다.
② 범주는 우리의 사고에 체계를 주기 때문에, 정상적으로 활동하는 데 반드시 필요하다.
③ 만일 우리가 모든 품목과 모든 있을 법한 상황을 유일무이하다고 생각한다면, 우리 주변의 세계를 설명하는 언어가 너무 많아질 것이다.
④ 그러나 필요하고 유용한 일반화하려는 본능은 우리의 세계관을 왜곡할 수 있다. 그것은 우리가 하나의 범주 안에 있는 모든 것이나 모든 사람이 비슷하다고 가정하게 만들기 때문에 대동소이한 것들 사이의 차이점을 볼 수 없게 만든다.
⑤ 그리고 가장 유감스러운 문제는, 그것이 우리로 하여금 몇 가지, 또는 심지어 고작 하나의 특이한 사례를 바탕으로 전체 범주에 대해 성급하게 결론을 내리게 만들 수 있다는 것이다.

## 40 다음 글의 내용과 일치하지 않는 것을 모두 고르시오.[20]

At the University of Iowa, students were briefly shown numbers that they had to memorize. Then they were offered the choice of either a fruit salad or a chocolate cake. When the number the students memorized was seven digits long, 63% of them chose the cake. When the number they were asked to remember had just two digits, however, 59% opted for the fruit salad. Our reflective brains know that the fruit salad is better for our health, but our reflexive brains desire that soft, fattening chocolate cake. If the reflective brain is busy figuring something else out — like trying to remember a seven-digit number — then impulse can easily win. On the other hand, if we're not thinking too hard about something else (with only a minor distraction like memorizing two digits), then the reflective system can deny the emotional impulse of the reflexive side.

① Iowa 대학교에서는 학생들에게 그들이 암기해야 하는 숫자를 잠시 보여준 뒤 과일 샐러드나 초콜릿 케이크 중 하나를 선택하게 했다.
② 학생들이 외운 숫자가 두 자리일 때는 그들 중 59%가 케이크를 골랐다. 외운 숫자가 일곱 자리였을 때는, 63%가 과일 샐러드를 골랐다.
③ 우리의 반사적인 뇌는 과일 샐러드가 건강에 더 좋다는 것을 알지만, 우리의 숙고하는 뇌는 부드럽고 살이 찌는 초콜릿 케이크를 원한다.
④ 만약 숙고하는 뇌가 일곱 자리 숫자를 기억하려고 애쓰는 일과 같은 다른 어떤 것을 해결하느라 바쁘다면, 충동이 쉽게 이길 수 있다.
⑤ 다른 한편, 우리가 다른 것에 관해 너무 열심히 생각하고 있지 않다면, 숙고하는 계통이 반사적인 쪽의 감정적인 충동을 억제할 수 있다.

# 41~42

Test scores are not a measure of self-worth; however, we often associate our sense of worthiness with our performance on an exam. Thoughts such as "If I don't pass this test, I'm a failure" are mental traps not rooted in truth. Failing a test is failing a test, nothing more. It is in no way descriptive of your value as a person. Believing that test performance is a reflection of your virtue places unreasonable pressure on your performance. Not passing the certification test only means that your certification status has been delayed. Maintaining a positive attitude is therefore important. If you have studied hard, reaffirm this mentally and believe that you will do well. If, on the other hand, you did not study as hard as you should have or wanted to, accept that as beyond your control for now and attend to the task of doing the best you can. If things do not go well this time, you know what needs to be done in preparation for the next exam. Talk to yourself in positive terms. Avoid rationalizing past or future test performance by placing the blame on secondary variables. Thoughts such as, "I didn't have enough time," or "I should have ...," compound the stress of test-taking. Take control by affirming your value, self-worth, and dedication to meeting the test challenge head on. Repeat to yourself "I can and I will pass this exam."

**A. 다음 글의 내용과 일치하는 것을 모두 고르시오.** 21)
① 시험 점수는 흔히 우리의 자부심과 연관된다.
② "이 시험에 합격하지 못하면 나는 실패자야."와 같은 생각은 사실에 뿌리를 두는 정신적 함정이다.
③ 시험에 실패하는 것은 사람으로서의 여러분의 가치를 설명하는 것으로 받아들여진다.
④ 시험 성적은 보통 여러분의 미덕을 반영하는 것이라고 여겨지기 때문에, 여러분의 수행에는 부당한 압력이 가해진다.
⑤ 자격 시험을 통과하지 못한 것은 단지 여러분의 자격 지위가 지연되었다는 것을 의미할 따름이다. 그러므로 긍정적인 태도를 유지하는 것이 중요하다.

**B. 다음 글의 내용과 일치하지 않는 것을 모두 고르시오.** 22)
① 만약 여러분이 열심히 공부했다면, 마음속으로 이것을 재확인하고 좋은 성적이 나올 것이라고 믿으라.
② 다른 한편, 만약 여러분이 했어야 하거나 원하는 만큼 열심히 공부하지 않았다면, 당신은 게으름뱅이지만 이제 와서 어찌할 수 없으므로 그저 할 수 있는 최선의 것을 해야 한다.
③ 만약 이번에 잘 되지 않는다면, 다음 시험 준비에서는 무엇을 해야 될지 알게 된다. 긍정적인 말로 자신에게 이야기하라. 부차적인 변수에 책임을 지움으로써 과거 또는 미래의 시험 성적을 합리화하는 것은 멘

탈 유지에 도움이 될 수 있다.
④ "나는 시간이 충분하지 않았어."라거나 "내가 그랬어야 했는데…"와 같은 생각은 시험을 보는 것의 스트레스를 악화시킨다.
⑤ 자신의 가치, 자부심, 그리고 시험 과제에 정면으로 맞서는 것에 대한 헌신을 확인함으로써 통제권을 잡으라. "난 할 수 있고 이 시험에 합격할 거야."라고 자신에게 되풀이해 말하라.

# 43~45

Once upon a time there lived a poor but cheerful shoemaker. He was so happy, he sang all day long. The children loved to stand around his window to listen to him. Next door to the shoemaker lived a rich man. He used to sit up all night to count his gold. In the morning, he went to bed, but he could not sleep because of the sound of the shoemaker's singing. One day, he thought of a way of stopping the singing. He wrote a letter to the shoemaker asking him to visit. The shoemaker came at once, and to his surprise the rich man gave him a bag of gold. When he got home again, the shoemaker opened the bag. He had never seen so much gold before! When he sat down at his bench and began, carefully, to count it, the children watched through the window. There was so much there that the shoemaker was afraid to let it out of his sight. So he took it to bed with him. But he could not sleep for worrying about it. Very early in the morning, he got up and brought his gold down from the bedroom. He had decided to hide it up the chimney instead. But he was still uneasy, and in a little while he dug a hole in the garden and buried his bag of gold in it. It was no use trying to work. He was too worried about the safety of his gold. And as for singing, he was too miserable to utter a note. He could not sleep, or work, or sing — and, worst of all, the children no longer came to see (b) him. At last, the shoemaker felt so unhappy that he seized his bag of gold and ran next door to the rich man. "Please take back your gold," he said. "The worry of it is making me ill, and I have lost all of my friends. I would rather be a poor shoemaker, as I was before." And so the shoemaker was happy again and sang all day at his work.

### A. 다음 글의 내용과 일치하지 않는 것을 모두 고르시오.²³⁾

① 옛날 옛적에 가난하지만 쾌활한 구두 만드는 사람이 살았다. 그는 불행을 잊기 위해 하루 종일 노래를 불렀다.

② 구두 만드는 사람 옆집에는 부자가 살았다. 그는 구두 만드는 사람의 노랫소리 때문에 잠을 잘 수 없었다.

③ 어느 날, 부자는 구두 만드는 사람의 노래를 멈추기 위해 그에게 금화가 든 가방을 주었다.

④ 구두장이가 의자에 앉아 조심스럽게 금화를 세기 시작했을 때, 아이들이 창문을 통해서 지켜보고는 금화라고 소리쳤다.

⑤ 구두 만드는 사람은 금화 주머니를 자신에게 보이지 않는 곳에 두기가 겁이 났고, 그래서 잠자리에 가져갔다.

### B. 다음 글의 내용과 일치하는 것을 모두 고르시오.²⁴⁾

① 구두장이는 계속 불안했고, 잠시 후에 정원에 구멍을 파고 그 안에 금화가 든 가방을 묻었다. 그 다음에는 굴뚝에 숨겨도 봤지만 구두장이는 여전히 불안했고, 금화가 너무 걱정이 되었다.

② 그는 잠을 잘 수도, 일을 할 수도, 노래를 부를 수도 없었고, 최악은, 아이들이 금화를 훔치려 했다.

③ 구두 만드는 사람은 너무 불행해져서 그의 금화가 든 가방을 움켜쥐고 옆집 부자에게 달려갔다.

④ "제발 당신의 금화를 다시 가져가세요."라고 그가 말했다. "그것에 대한 걱정이 저를 아프게 하고 있고, 저는 제 친구들을 모두 잃었어요. 저는 예전처럼 차라리 가난한 구두 만드는 사람이 되겠어요."

⑤ 그래서 구두 만드는 사람은 다시 행복해졌고 일을 하면서 하루 종일 노래를 불렀다.

## 2021 고2 3월 모의고사

❶ voca   ❷ text   ❸ [ / ]   ❹ ____   ❺ quiz 1   ❻ quiz 2   ❼ quiz 3   ❽ quiz 4   ❾ quiz 5   ❿ quiz 6

### 19 다음 중 상사가 화자에게 해줬을 위로의 격언으로 가장 적절한 것은? 1)

It was a day I was due to give a presentation at work, not something I'd do often. As I stood up to begin, I froze. A chilly 'pins-and-needles' feeling crept over me, starting in my hands. Time seemed to stand still as I struggled to start speaking, and I felt a pressure around my throat, as though my voice was trapped and couldn't come out. Gazing around at the blur of faces, I realized they were all waiting for me to begin, but by now I knew I couldn't continue. When I was about to give up on this, I remembered what my reliable boss had said before. To get started is the hardest thing but once you get started, thing will go as well as you expect. I regained my courage again.

① Good past is memory, bad past is experience.
② One cannot put back the clock.
③ One mischief comes on the neck of another.
④ Well begun is half done.
⑤ All the glitters in not gold.

### 20 다음 빈칸에 들어갈 말로 가장 적절한 것은? 2)

No matter what your situation, whether you are an insider or an outsider, you need to _____. Think about the characteristics that make outsiders valuable to an organization. They are the people who have the perspective to see problems that the insiders are too close to really notice. They are the ones who have the freedom to point out these problems and criticize them without risking their job or their career. Part of adopting an outsider mentality is forcing yourself to look around your organization with this disassociated, less emotional perspective. If you didn't know your coworkers and feel bonded to them by your shared experiences, what would you think of them? You may not have the job security or confidence to speak your mind to management, but you can make these "outsider" assessments of your organization on your own and use what you determine to advance your career.

① truly assimilate into the organization
② view your organization critically from an outsider's point of view
③ be flexible to accept the situation even if it is problematic
④ prioritize the stability before evaluation or judgment is pursued
⑤ contribute to active communication within the organization

### 21 다음 글의 내용을 한 문장으로 요약하고자 한다. 빈칸 (A), (B)에 들어갈 말로 가장 적절한 것은? 3)

The known fact of contingencies, without knowing precisely what those contingencies will be, shows that disaster preparation is not the same thing as disaster rehearsal. No matter how many mock disasters are staged according to prior plans, the real disaster will never mirror any one of them. Disaster-preparation planning is more like training for a marathon than training for a high-jump competition or a sprinting event. Marathon runners do not practice by running the full course of twenty-six miles; rather, they get into shape by running shorter distances and building up their endurance with cross-training. If they have prepared successfully, then they are in optimal condition to run the marathon over its predetermined course and length, assuming a range of weather conditions, predicted or not. This is normal marathon preparation.

↓

Although disaster rehearsal is not a true _____(A)_____ of real disasters but it is like training for real situation in order for you to be ___(B)___ successfully.

|     | {A} | {B} |
| --- | --- | --- |
| ① | representation | ... ruined |
| ② | representation | ... prepared |
| ③ | differentiation | ... champion |
| ④ | differentiation | ... ruined |
| ⑤ | differentiation | ... prepared |

**22** 다음 글의 밑줄 친 부분 중, 문맥상 낱말의 쓰임이 적절하지 않은 것을 모두 고르시오. 4)

Fears of damaging ecosystems are based on the sound conservationist principle that we should aim to ① minimize the disruption we cause, but there is a risk that this principle may be ② confused with the old idea of a 'balance of nature'. This supposes a perfect order of nature that will seek to maintain itself and that we should not ③ change. It is a romantic, not to say idyllic, notion, but deeply ④ straightforward because it supposes a static condition. Ecosystems are dynamic, and although some may endure, apparently ⑤ constant, for periods that are long in comparison with the human lifespan, they must and do ⑥ change eventually. Species come and go, climates change, plant and animal communities adapt to ⑦ altered circumstances, and when examined in fine detail such adaptation and consequent ⑧ change can be seen to be taking place constantly. The 'balance of nature' is a myth. Our planet is dynamic, and so are the arrangements by which its inhabitants live together.

**23** 다음 글의 밑줄 친 부분 중, 문맥상 낱말의 쓰임이 적절하지 않은 것을 고르시오. 5)

Before the modern scientific era, creativity was attributed to a superhuman force; all novel ideas ① originated with the gods. After all, how could a person create something that did not exist before the divine act of creation? In fact, the Latin meaning of the verb "inspire" is "to breathe into", reflecting the belief that creative inspiration was similar to the moment in creation when God first breathed life into man. Plato argued that the poet was ② possessed by divine inspiration, and Plotin wrote that art could only be beautiful if it ③ descended from God. The artist's job was not to imitate nature but rather to reveal the sacred and transcendent qualities of nature. Art could only be a pale imitation of the perfection of the world of ideas. Greek artists did not blindly imitate what they saw in reality; instead they tried to ④ avoid the pure, true forms underlying reality, resulting in a sort of compromise between ⑤ abstraction and accuracy.

**24** 다음 글의 빈칸 (A), (B)에 들어갈 말로 가장 적절한 것을 고르시오. 6)

Some beginning researchers mistakenly believe that a good hypothesis is one that is guaranteed to be right (e.g., alcohol will slow down reaction time).     (A)    , if we already know your hypothesis is true before you test it, testing your hypothesis won't tell us anything new. Remember, research is supposed to produce new knowledge. To get new knowledge, you, as a researcher-explorer, need to leave the safety of the shore (established facts) and venture into uncharted waters (as Einstein said "If we knew what we were doing, it would not be called research, would it"?). If your predictions about what will happen in these uncharted waters are wrong, that's okay: Scientists are allowed to make mistakes (as Bates said, "Research is the process of going up alleys to see if they are blind").      (B)      , scientists often learn more from predictions that do not turn out than from those that do.

|  | {A} | {B} |
|---|---|---|
| ① | For example | ... Indeed |
| ② | For example | ... Therefore |
| ③ | However | ... Therefore |
| ④ | However | ... Moreover |
| ⑤ | However | ... Indeed |

## 29 다음 빈칸에 공통으로 들어갈 단어로 적절한 것을 고르시오. 7)

While reflecting on the needs of organizations, leaders, and families today, we realize that one of the unique characteristics is _____. Why? Because _____ supports what everyone ultimately wants from their relationships: collaboration. Yet the majority of leaders, organizations, and families are still using the language of the old paradigm in which one person—typically the oldest, most educated, and/or wealthiest—makes all the decisions, and their decisions rule with little discussion or inclusion of others, resulting in exclusivity. Today, this person could be a director, CEO, or other senior leader of an organization. There is no need for others to present their ideas because they are considered inadequate. Yet research shows that exclusivity in problem solving, even with a genius, is not as effective as _____, where everyone's ideas are heard and a solution is developed through collaboration.

① reflexivity
② passivity
③ conductivity
④ inclusivity
⑤ transitivity

## 30 다음 중 윗글에 나온 카메라 기법을 사용하지 못한 감독을 고르시오. 8)

The objective point of view is illustrated by John Ford's "philosophy of camera". Ford considered the camera to be a window and the audience to be outside the window viewing the people and events within. We are asked to watch the actions as if they were taking place at a distance, and we are not asked to participate. The objective point of view employs a static camera as much as possible in order to produce this window effect, and it concentrates on the actors and the action without drawing attention to the camera. The objective camera suggests an emotional distance between camera and subject; the camera seems simply to be recording, as straightforwardly as possible, the characters and actions of the story. For the most part, the director uses natural, normal types of camera positioning and camera angles. The objective camera does not comment on or interpret the action but merely records it, letting it unfold. We see the action from the viewpoint of an impersonal observer. If the camera moves, it does so unnoticeably, calling as little attention to itself as possible.

① 잔잔한 카메라 움직임으로 등장인물의 삶을 그대로 보여준 박 감독
② 정적인 화면 연출로 가감 없는 화면 묘사를 한 장 감독
③ 현란한 카메라 기법으로 시청자가 장면에 빠져들게 한 크 감독
④ 제 3자의 입장에서 인물들의 삶을 그려낸 봉 감독
⑤ 적당한 거리감을 유지하며 사건의 발생을 바라보게 하는 쿠 감독

## 31 다음 글의 내용을 한 문장으로 요약하고자 한다. 빈칸 (A), (B), (C)에 들어갈 말로 가장 적절한 것은? 9)

Even the most respectable of all musical institutions, the symphony orchestra, carries inside its DNA the legacy of the hunt. The various instruments in the orchestra can be traced back to these primitive origins—their earliest forms were made either from the animal (horn, hide, gut, bone) or the weapons employed in bringing the animal under control (stick, bow). Are we wrong to hear this history in the music itself, in the formidable aggression and awe-inspiring assertiveness of those monumental symphonies that remain the core repertoire of the world's leading orchestras? Listening to Beethoven, Brahms, Mahler, Bruckner, Berlioz, Tchaikovsky, Shostakovich, and other great composers, I can easily summon up images of bands of men starting to chase animals, using sound as a source and symbol of dominance, an expression of the will to predatory power.

↓

We can easily ___(A)___ images of group of men ___(B)___ animals, using sound as a source and symbol of ___(C)___.

|  | {A} | {B} | (C) |
|---|---|---|---|
| ① | evoke | pursuing | ascendancy |
| ② | evoke | pursuing | collaboration |
| ③ | evoke | slaughtering | expression |
| ④ | erase | pursuing | collaboration |
| ⑤ | erase | slaughtering | expression |

## 32 다음 글의 제목으로 가장 적절한 것은? 10)

Our brains have evolved to remember unexpected events because basic survival depends on the ability to perceive causes and predict effects. If the brain predicts one event and experiences another, the unusualness will be especially interesting and will be encoded accordingly. Neurologist and classroom teacher Judith Willis has claimed that surprise in the classroom is one of the most effective ways of teaching with brain stimulation in mind. If students are exposed to new experiences via demonstrations or through the unexpected enthusiasm of their teachers or peers, they will be much more likely to connect with the information that follows. Willis has written that encouraging active discovery in the classroom allows students to interact with new information, moving it beyond working memory to be processed in the frontal lobe, which is devoted to advanced cognitive functioning. Preference for novelty sets us up for learning by directing attention, providing stimulation to developing perceptual systems, and feeding curious and exploratory behavior.

① Human Evolution Unrelated to Predictive Ability
② Competition: Tool for Memorizing
③ Effective Learning: Find Unexpected Novelty
④ Stimulation: Efficient Way to Explore Facts
⑤ Perceptual Process Influenced by Conventional Information

## 33 다음 각 괄호 (A), (B), (C)에 올바른 것으로 짝지은 것을 고르시오. 11)

Psychological research has shown that people naturally (A) [ discard / split ] cognitive labor, often without thinking about it. Imagine you're cooking up a special dinner with a friend. You're a great cook, but your friend is the wine expert, an amateur sommelier. A neighbor drops by and starts telling you both about the terrific new wines being sold at the liquor store just down the street. There are many new wines, so there's a lot to remember. How hard are you going to try to remember what the neighbor has to say about which wines to buy? Why bother when the information would be better (B) [ retained / ascertained ] by the wine expert sitting next to you? If your friend wasn't around, you might try harder.

After all, it would be good to know what a good wine would be for the evening's festivities. But your friend, the wine expert, is likely to remember the information without even (C) [ neglecting / trying ].

| | {A} | {B} | (C) |
|---|---|---|---|
| ① | discard | ... retained | ... trying |
| ② | discard | ... ascertained | ... neglecting |
| ③ | split | ... retained | ... neglecting |
| ④ | split | ... retained | ... trying |
| ⑤ | split | ... ascertained | ... neglecting |

## 34 다음 글의 밑줄 친 부분에 들어갈 단어로 적절하지 않은 것을 모두 고르시오. 12)

Even companies that sell ① physical products to make profit are forced by their boards and investors to reconsider their underlying motives and to collect as much data as possible from ② consumers. Supermarkets no longer make all their money selling their produce and manufactured goods. They give you loyalty cards with which they ③ trace your purchasing behaviors ④ concisely. Then supermarkets sell this purchasing behavior to marketing ⑤ analogical companies. The marketing analytics companies perform machine learning procedures, slicing the data in new ways, and resell behavioral data back to product manufacturers as marketing insights. When data and machine learning become ⑥ currencies of value in a capitalist system, then every company's natural tendency is to ⑦ maximize its ability to conduct ⑧ observation on its own customers because the customers are themselves the new value-creation devices.

## 35 다음 글의 밑줄 친 부분 중, 문맥상 낱말의 쓰임이 적절하지 않은 것을 고르시오. 13)

Academics, politicians, marketers and others have in the past debated whether or not it is ethically ① correct to market products and services directly to young consumers. This is also a dilemma for psychologists who have questioned whether they ought to help advertisers manipulate children into purchasing more products they have seen advertised. Advertisers have admitted to taking advantage of the fact that it is ② uncomplicated to make children feel that they are losers if they do not own the 'right' products. Clever advertising informs children that they will be viewed by their peers in an ③ favorable way if they do not have the products that are advertised, thereby playing on their emotional ④ vulnerabilities. The constant feelings of ⑤ inadequateness created by advertising have been suggested to contribute to children becoming fixated with instant gratification and beliefs that material possessions are important.

## 36 다음 빈칸에 들어갈 말로 가장 적절한 것은?14)

Once we recognize the false-cause issue, we see it everywhere. However, a recent long-term study of University of Toronto medical students concluded that medical school class presidents lived an average of 2.4 years less than other medical school graduates. At first glance, this seems to imply that being a medical school class president is bad for you. Does this mean that you should avoid being medical school class president at all costs? Probably not. Just because being class president is correlated with shorter life expectancy does not mean that it causes shorter life expectancy. In fact, it seemed likely that the sort of person who becomes medical school class president is, on average, extremely hard-working, serious, and ambitious. Perhaps this extra stress, and _____—rather than being class president per se—contributes to lower life expectancy. If so, the real lesson of the study is that we should all relax a little and not let our work take over our lives.

① the lack of responsibility and seriousness
② the overwhelming feeling of loneliness
③ the corresponding lack of social and relaxation time
④ the manipulation caused by colleagues
⑤ the sufficient amount of relaxation

## 37 다음 글의 밑줄 친 부분 중, 문맥상 낱말의 쓰임이 적절하지 않은 것은 ?15)

We commonly argue about the fairness of taxation—whether this or that tax will fall more heavily on the rich or the poor. But the expressive dimension of taxation goes beyond debates about ① fairness, to the moral judgements societies make about which activities are worthy of honor and recognition, and which ones should be discouraged. Sometimes, these judgements are ② explicit. Taxes on tobacco, alcohol, and casinos are called "sin taxes" because they seek to ③ courage activities considered harmful or undesirable. Such taxes express society's ④ disapproval of these activities by raising the cost of engaging in them. Proposals to tax sugary sodas (to combat obesity) or carbon emissions (to address climate change) likewise seek to change norms and shape behavior. Not all taxes have this aim. We do not tax income to express disapproval of paid employment or to discourage people from engaging in it. Nor is a general sales tax intended as a ⑤ deterrent to buying things. These are simply ways of raising revenue.

## 38 다음 글의 밑줄 친 부분 중, 문맥상 낱말의 쓰임이 적절하지 않은 것은 ? 16)

Most beliefs—but not all—are open to tests of ① verification. This means that beliefs can be tested to see if they are correct or false. Beliefs can be verified or falsified with objective criteria ② external to the person. There are people who believe the Earth is flat and not a sphere. Because we have ③ objective evidence that the Earth is in fact a sphere, the flat Earth belief can be shown to be false. Also, the belief that it will rain tomorrow can be tested for truth by waiting until tomorrow and seeing whether it rains or not. However, some types of beliefs ④ cannot be tested for truth because we cannot get external evidence in our lifetimes (such as a belief that the Earth will stop spinning on its axis by the year 9999 or that there is life on a planet 100-million light-years away). Also, meta-physical beliefs (such as the existence and nature of a god) present ⑤ considerate challenges in generating evidence that everyone is willing to use as a truth criterion.

## 39  다음 빈칸에 들어갈 말로 가장 적절한 것은?[17)]

Everyone automatically categorizes and generalizes all the time. Unconsciously. It is not a question of being prejudiced or enlightened. Categories are absolutely necessary for us to function. They give structure to our thoughts. Imagine if we saw every item and every scenario as truly unique—we would not even have a language to describe the world around us. But the necessary and useful instinct to generalize can _____. It can make us mistakenly group together things, or people, or countries that are actually very different. It can make us assume everything or everyone in one category is similar. And, maybe, most unfortunate of all, it can make us jump to conclusions about a whole category based on a few, or even just one, unusual example.

① be used to widen our point of view
② strengthen our existing feeling
③ compel us to yield to other people's opinion
④ manipulate our world view
⑤ help us to spread our imagination about ourselves

## 40  다음 글의 주제로 가장 적절한 것은? [18)]

At the University of Iowa, students were briefly shown numbers that they had to memorize. Then they were offered the choice of either a fruit salad or a chocolate cake. When the number the students memorized was seven digits long, 63% of them chose the cake. When the number they were asked to remember had just two digits, however, 59% opted for the fruit salad. Our reflective brains know that the fruit salad is better for our health, but our reflexive brains desire that soft, fattening chocolate cake. If the reflective brain is busy figuring something else out—like trying to remember a seven-digit number—then impulse can easily win. On the other hand, if we're not thinking too hard about something else (with only a minor distraction like memorizing two digits), then the reflective system can deny the emotional impulse of the reflexive side.

① the close relationship between left and right brains
② the food that makes our reflective brains confused
③ the correlation between an intellectual burden on brain and impulsive chocies
④ our reflective choices regarding memorization and food selection
⑤ the faulty statistics about the relationship between our reflexive brains and food choices

## 41~42

Test scores are not a measure of self-worth;     (A)     , we often associate our sense of worthiness with our performance on an exam. Thoughts such as "If I don't pass this test, I'm a failure" are mental traps not rooted in truth. Failing a test is failing a test, nothing more. It is in no way descriptive of your value as a person. Believing that test performance is a reflection of your virtue places unreasonable pressure on your performance. Not passing the certification test only means that your certification status has been delayed. Maintaining a positive attitude is therefore important. If you have studied hard, reaffirm this mentally and believe that you will do well. If,     (B)     , you did not study as hard as you should have or wanted to, accept that as beyond your control for now and attend to the task of doing the best you can. If things do not go well this time, you know what needs to be done in preparation for the next exam. Talk to yourself in positive terms. Avoid rationalizing past or future test performance by placing the blame on secondary variables. Thoughts such as, "I didn't have enough time", or "I should have ...", compound the stress of test-taking. Take control by affirming your value, self-worth, and dedication to meeting the test challenge head on. Repeat to yourself "I can and I will pass this exam".

**A. 다음 글의 빈칸 (A), (B)에 들어갈 말로 가장 적절한 것을 고르시오.** 19)

|   | {A} | {B} |
|---|-----|-----|
| ① | For example | ... nevertheless |
| ② | For example | ... indeed |
| ③ | However | ... therefore |
| ④ | However | ... for example |
| ⑤ | However | ... on the other hand |

**B. 당신이 시험 성적 때문에 힘들어하고 있을 때, 가장 적절하게 위로한 친구는 누구일까요?** 20)

① 정국: Someone said that he was afraid of falling, but not landing. It is not bad to slowly prepare for the end.

② 호석: You can bow down because of failure or frustraion. A rock that doesn't roll has moss, so I hope you work hard constantly.

③ 태형: I believe you. You may be weak now, but the end is a great leap. It's just the beginning, so don't be too scared and try.

④ 지민: There are stars that shine more at the deepest night. Your hard times will eventually be the process of growing up to shine on you.

⑤ 윤기: The past is in the past. Forget everything that is gone and then make positive commitment to yourself.

# 2021 고2 3월 모의고사

❶ voca   ❷ text   ❸ [ / ]   ❹ _____   ❺ quiz 1   ❻ quiz 2   ❼ quiz 3   ❽ quiz 4   ❾ quiz 5   ❿ quiz 6

## 18 밑줄 부분 중 어법, 혹은 문맥상 어휘의 쓰임이 어색한 것을 올바르게 고쳐 쓰시오. (1개)1)

My name is Anthony Thompson and I am writing on behalf of the residents' association. Our recycling program has been ① working well thanks to your participation. However, a problem has recently ② occurred that needs your attention. Because there is no given day for recycling, residents are ③ putting their recycling out at any time. This makes the recycling area messy, ④ that requires extra labor and cost. To deal with this problem, the residents' association has decided on a day to recycle. I would like to let you ⑤ know that you can put out your recycling on Wednesdays only. I am sure it will make our apartment complex ⑥ look much more pleasant. Thank you in advance for your cooperation.

| 기호 | 어색한 표현 | | 올바른 표현 |
|---|---|---|---|
| (      ) | _____ | ⇨ | _____ |

## 19 밑줄 부분 중 어법, 혹은 문맥상 어휘의 쓰임이 어색한 것을 올바르게 고쳐 쓰시오. (2개)2)

It was a day I was due to ① giving a presentation at work, not something I'd do often. As I stood up to begin, I froze. A chilly 'pins-and-needles' feeling crept over me, ② started in my hands. Time seemed to stand still as I struggled to ③ start speaking, and I felt a pressure around my throat, ④ as though my voice ⑤ was trapped and couldn't come out. Gazing around at the blur of faces, I ⑥ realized they were all ⑦ waiting for me to begin, but by now I knew I couldn't continue.

| 기호 | 어색한 표현 | | 올바른 표현 |
|---|---|---|---|
| (      ) | _____ | ⇨ | _____ |
| (      ) | _____ | ⇨ | _____ |

## 20 밑줄 부분 중 어법, 혹은 문맥상 어휘의 쓰임이 어색한 것을 올바르게 고쳐 쓰시오. (6개)3)

No matter ① how your situation, ② if you are an insider or an outsider, you need to become the voice that challenges yesterday's answers. Think about the characteristics ③ what make outsiders valuable to an organization. They are the people who have the perspective to see problems that the insiders are ④ too close to really notice. They are the ones who have the freedom to point out these problems and criticize them without risking their job or their career. Part of ⑤ adapting an outsider mentality is forcing yourself ⑥ to look around your organization with this ⑦ disassociating, less emotional perspective. If you didn't know your coworkers and feel bonded to them by your shared experiences, what would you think of them? You may not have the job security or confidence to speak your mind to management, but you can make these "outsider" assessments of your organization on your own and ⑧ uses what you determine to advance your career.

| 기호 | 어색한 표현 | | 올바른 표현 |
|---|---|---|---|
| (      ) | _____ | ⇨ | _____ |
| (      ) | _____ | ⇨ | _____ |
| (      ) | _____ | ⇨ | _____ |
| (      ) | _____ | ⇨ | _____ |
| (      ) | _____ | ⇨ | _____ |
| (      ) | _____ | ⇨ | _____ |

## 21

밑줄 부분 중 어법, 혹은 문맥상 어휘의 쓰임이 어색한 것을 올바르게 고쳐 쓰시오. (1개)4)

The known fact of contingencies, without knowing ① concisely what those contingencies will be, shows ② that disaster preparation is not the same thing as disaster rehearsal. No matter ③ how many mock disasters are staged according to prior plans, the real disaster will never mirror any one of them. Disaster-preparation planning is more like training for a marathon than training for a high-jump competition or a sprinting event. Marathon runners do not practice by running the full course of twenty-six miles; rather, they get into shape by running ④ shorter distances and building up their endurance with cross-training. If they ⑤ have prepared successfully, then they are in optimal condition to run the marathon over its predetermined course and length, ⑥ assuming a range of weather conditions, predicted or not. This is normal marathon preparation.

| 기호 | 어색한 표현 | | 올바른 표현 |
|---|---|---|---|
| ( ) | _____ | ⇨ | _____ |

## 22

밑줄 부분 중 어법, 혹은 문맥상 어휘의 쓰임이 어색한 것을 올바르게 고쳐 쓰시오. (4개)5)

Fears of damaging ecosystems are based on the sound conservationist ① principal that we should aim to ② minimizing the disruption we cause, but there is a risk that this principle may be ③ confused with the old idea of a 'balance of nature'. This supposes a perfect order of nature ④ that will seek to maintain ⑤ itself and that we should not change. It is a romantic, not to say idyllic, notion, but deeply misleading because it supposes a static condition. Ecosystems are dynamic, and ⑥ although some may endure, apparently unchanged, for periods that are long in comparison with the human lifespan, they must and do change eventually. Species come and go, climates change, plant and animal communities ⑦ adapt to ⑧ altered circumstances, and when ⑨ examined in fine detail such ⑩ adoption and consequent change can be seen to be taking place constantly. The 'balance of nature' is a myth. Our planet is dynamic, and so ⑪ do the arrangements by which its inhabitants live together.

| 기호 | 어색한 표현 | | 올바른 표현 |
|---|---|---|---|
| ( ) | _____ | ⇨ | _____ |
| ( ) | _____ | ⇨ | _____ |
| ( ) | _____ | ⇨ | _____ |
| ( ) | _____ | ⇨ | _____ |

## 23

밑줄 부분 중 어법, 혹은 문맥상 어휘의 쓰임이 어색한 것을 올바르게 고쳐 쓰시오. (3개)6)

Before the modern scientific era, creativity ① attributed to a superhuman force; all novel ideas ② were originated with the gods. After all, how could a person create something that did not exist before the divine act of creation? In fact, the Latin meaning of the verb "inspire" is "to breathe into", ③ reflecting the belief that creative inspiration was similar to the moment in creation when God first breathed life into man. Plato argued that the poet was possessed by divine inspiration, and Plotin wrote that art could only be beautiful if it ④ descended from God. The artist's job was not to imitate nature but rather to reveal the sacred and transcendent qualities of nature. Art could only be a pale imitation of the perfection of the world of ideas. Greek artists did not blindly imitate ⑤ which they saw in reality; instead they tried to represent the pure, true forms underlying reality, resulting ⑥ in a sort of compromise between abstraction and accuracy.

| 기호 | 어색한 표현 | | 올바른 표현 |
|---|---|---|---|
| ( ) | _____ | ⇨ | _____ |
| ( ) | _____ | ⇨ | _____ |
| ( ) | _____ | ⇨ | _____ |

## 24 밑줄 부분 중 어법, 혹은 문맥상 어휘의 쓰임이 어색한 것을 올바르게 고쳐 쓰시오. (4개)7)

Some beginning researchers mistakenly believe that a good hypothesis is one that ① guaranteed to be right (e.g., alcohol will slow down reaction time). However, if we already know your hypothesis is true before you test it, testing your hypothesis won't tell us anything new. Remember, research is supposed to ② producing new knowledge. To get new knowledge, you, as a researcher-explorer, need to leave the safety of the shore (established facts) and venture into uncharted waters (as Einstein said, "If we knew ③ what we were doing, it would not be called research, would it"?). If your predictions about what will ④ happen in these uncharted waters are wrong, that's okay: Scientists ⑤ allowed to make mistakes (as Bates said, "Research is the process of going up alleys to see if they are blind"). Indeed, scientists often learn more from predictions that do not turn out than from those that ⑥ are.

| 기호 | 어색한 표현 | | 올바른 표현 |
|---|---|---|---|
| ( ) | _____ | ⇨ | _____ |
| ( ) | _____ | ⇨ | _____ |
| ( ) | _____ | ⇨ | _____ |
| ( ) | _____ | ⇨ | _____ |

## 29 밑줄 부분 중 어법, 혹은 문맥상 어휘의 쓰임이 어색한 것을 올바르게 고쳐 쓰시오. (9개)8)

While ① reflected on the needs of organizations, leaders, and families today, we realize that one of the unique characteristics ② are inclusivity. Why? Because inclusivity supports what everyone ultimately ③ wanted from their relationships: collaboration. Yet the majority of leaders, organizations, and families ④ is still using the language of the old paradigm ⑤ which one person—typically the oldest, most educated, and/or wealthiest—makes all the decisions, and their decisions rule with little discussion or inclusion of others, resulting ⑥ from exclusivity. Today, this person could be a director, CEO, or other senior leader of an organization. There is no need for others to present their ideas because they are considered ⑦ inadequately. Yet research shows that ⑧ diversity in problem solving, even with a genius, is not as effective as inclusivity, ⑨ which everyone's ideas are heard and a solution is developed through collaboration.

| 기호 | 어색한 표현 | | 올바른 표현 |
|---|---|---|---|
| ( ) | _____ | ⇨ | _____ |
| ( ) | _____ | ⇨ | _____ |
| ( ) | _____ | ⇨ | _____ |
| ( ) | _____ | ⇨ | _____ |
| ( ) | _____ | ⇨ | _____ |
| ( ) | _____ | ⇨ | _____ |
| ( ) | _____ | ⇨ | _____ |
| ( ) | _____ | ⇨ | _____ |
| ( ) | _____ | ⇨ | _____ |

## 30 밑줄 부분 중 어법, 혹은 문맥상 어휘의 쓰임이 어색한 것을 올바르게 고쳐 쓰시오. (6개)9)

The objective point of view is illustrated by John Ford's "philosophy of camera". Ford considered the camera to be a window and the audience to be outside the window viewing the people and events within. We ① asked to watch the actions ② even if they were ③ taken place at a distance, and we are not asked to participate. The objective point of view employs a static camera as ④ much as possible in order to produce this window effect, and it concentrates on the actors and the action without drawing attention to the camera. The objective camera suggests an emotional distance between camera and subject; the camera ⑤ is seemed simply to be recording, as straightforwardly as possible, the characters and actions of the story. For the most part, the director uses natural, normal types of camera positioning and camera angles. The objective camera does not comment on or interpret the action but merely ⑥ recording it, letting it unfold. We see the action from the viewpoint of an impersonal observer. If the camera moves, it does so unnoticeably, ⑦ called as little attention to itself as possible.

| 기호 | 어색한 표현 | | 올바른 표현 |
|---|---|---|---|
| ( ) | _____ | ⇨ | _____ |
| ( ) | _____ | ⇨ | _____ |
| ( ) | _____ | ⇨ | _____ |
| ( ) | _____ | ⇨ | _____ |
| ( ) | _____ | ⇨ | _____ |
| ( ) | _____ | ⇨ | _____ |

## 31 밑줄 부분 중 어법, 혹은 문맥상 어휘의 쓰임이 어색한 것을 올바르게 고쳐 쓰시오. (4개)[10]

Even the most respectable of all musical institutions, the symphony orchestra, ① carrying inside its DNA the legacy of the hunt. The various instruments in the orchestra can ② traced back to these primitive origins— their earliest forms ③ were made either from the animal (horn, hide, gut, bone) or the weapons employed in bringing the animal under control (stick, bow). Are we wrong to hear this history in the music itself, in the formidable aggression and awe-inspiring assertiveness of those monumental symphonies that ④ remain the core repertoire of the world's leading orchestras? ⑤ Listen to Beethoven, Brahms, Mahler, Bruckner, Berlioz, Tchaikovsky, Shostakovich, and other great composers, I can easily summon up images of bands of men starting to chase animals, ⑥ using sound as a source and symbol of ⑦ inferiority, an expression of the will to predatory power.

| 기호 | 어색한 표현 | | 올바른 표현 |
|---|---|---|---|
| ( ) | _____ | ⇨ | _____ |
| ( ) | _____ | ⇨ | _____ |
| ( ) | _____ | ⇨ | _____ |
| ( ) | _____ | ⇨ | _____ |

## 32 밑줄 부분 중 어법, 혹은 문맥상 어휘의 쓰임이 어색한 것을 올바르게 고쳐 쓰시오. (10개)[11]

Our brains have ① been evolved to remember unexpected events because basic survival depends on the ability to perceive causes and ② predicts effects. If the brain predicts one event and experiences another, the unusualness will be especially ③ intertested and will be encoded accordingly. Neurologist and classroom teacher Judith Willis has claimed that surprise in the classroom is one of the most effective ways of teaching with brain stimulation in mind. If students are exposed to new experiences via demonstrations or through the unexpected enthusiasm of their teachers or peers, they will be ④ very more likely to connect with the information that follows. Willis has written ⑤ what encouraging active discovery in the classroom allows students ⑥ interacting with new information, ⑦ moved it

beyond working memory to be processed in the frontal lobe, ⑧ that is devoted to advanced cognitive functioning. Preference for novelty sets us up for learning by directing attention, ⑨ provided stimulation to ⑩ develop perceptual systems, and feeding curious and exploratory behavior.

| 기호 | 어색한 표현 | | 올바른 표현 |
|---|---|---|---|
| ( ) | _____ | ⇨ | _____ |
| ( ) | _____ | ⇨ | _____ |
| ( ) | _____ | ⇨ | _____ |
| ( ) | _____ | ⇨ | _____ |
| ( ) | _____ | ⇨ | _____ |
| ( ) | _____ | ⇨ | _____ |
| ( ) | _____ | ⇨ | _____ |
| ( ) | _____ | ⇨ | _____ |
| ( ) | _____ | ⇨ | _____ |
| ( ) | _____ | ⇨ | _____ |

## 33 밑줄 부분 중 어법, 혹은 문맥상 어휘의 쓰임이 어색한 것을 올바르게 고쳐 쓰시오. (2개)[12]

Psychological research has shown ① that people naturally divide up cognitive labor, often without thinking about it. Imagine you're cooking up a special dinner with a friend. You're a great cook, but your friend is the wine expert, an amateur sommelier. A neighbor drops by and starts telling you both about the terrific new wines ② are sold at the liquor store just down the street. There are many new wines, so there's a lot to remember. How ③ hard are you going to try to remember ④ that the neighbor has to say about which wines to buy? Why bother when the information would be better ⑤ retained by the wine expert sitting next to you? If your friend wasn't around, you might try harder. After all, it would be good to know ⑥ what a good wine would be for the evening's festivities. But your friend, the wine expert, is likely to remember the information without even trying.

| 기호 | 어색한 표현 | | 올바른 표현 |
|---|---|---|---|
| ( ) | _____ | ⇨ | _____ |
| ( ) | _____ | ⇨ | _____ |

## 34 밑줄 부분 중 어법, 혹은 문맥상 어휘의 쓰임이 어색한 것을 올바르게 고쳐 쓰시오. (6개)13)

Even companies that sell physical products to make profit ① is forced by their boards and investors to reconsider their underlying motives and to collect as ② many data as possible from consumers. Supermarkets no longer make all their money selling their produce and manufactured goods. They give you loyalty cards with ③ what they track your purchasing behaviors precisely. Then supermarkets sell this purchasing behavior to ④ market analytics companies. The marketing analytics companies perform machine learning procedures, ⑤ sliced the data in new ways, and resell behavioral data back to product manufacturers as marketing insights. When data and machine learning ⑥ become currencies of value in a capitalist system, then every company's natural tendency is to maximize its ability to conduct surveillance on its own customers because the customers are ⑦ them the new value-creation devices.

| 기호 | 어색한 표현 | | 올바른 표현 |
|---|---|---|---|
| ( ) | _____ | ⇨ | _____ |
| ( ) | _____ | ⇨ | _____ |
| ( ) | _____ | ⇨ | _____ |
| ( ) | _____ | ⇨ | _____ |
| ( ) | _____ | ⇨ | _____ |
| ( ) | _____ | ⇨ | _____ |

## 35 밑줄 부분 중 어법, 혹은 문맥상 어휘의 쓰임이 어색한 것을 올바르게 고쳐 쓰시오. (5개)14)

Academics, politicians, marketers and others have in the past debated whether or not it is ethically correct to market products and services directly to young consumers. This is also a dilemma for psychologists who have questioned whether they ought to help advertisers manipulate children into purchasing more products they have ① been seen advertised. Advertisers have admitted to ② taking advantage of the fact that it is easy to make children feel that they are losers if they do not own the 'right' products. Clever advertising

informs children that they will be viewed by their peers in an unfavorable way if they do not have the products that are advertised, thereby ③ played on their emotional vulnerabilities. The constant feelings of inadequateness created by advertising ④ have ⑤ suggested to contribute to children ⑥ become fixated with instant ⑦ dissatisfaction and beliefs that material possessions are important.

| 기호 | 어색한 표현 | | 올바른 표현 |
|---|---|---|---|
| ( ) | _____ | ⇨ | _____ |
| ( ) | _____ | ⇨ | _____ |
| ( ) | _____ | ⇨ | _____ |
| ( ) | _____ | ⇨ | _____ |
| ( ) | _____ | ⇨ | _____ |

## 36 밑줄 부분 중 어법, 혹은 문맥상 어휘의 쓰임이 어색한 것을 올바르게 고쳐 쓰시오. (2개)15)

Once we recognize the false-cause issue, we see it everywhere. ① However, a recent long-term study of University of Toronto medical students ② included that medical school class presidents lived an average of 2.4 years less than other medical school graduates. At first glance, this seemed to imply that being a medical school class president is bad for you. Does this mean that you should avoid being medical school class president at all costs? Probably not. Just because being class president is correlated with shorter life expectancy does not mean ③ that it causes shorter life expectancy. In fact, it seems likely that the sort of person who becomes medical school class president is, on average, extremely hard-working, serious, and ambitious. Perhaps this extra stress, and the corresponding lack of social and relaxation time—rather than being class president per se—④ contributing to lower life expectancy. If so, the real lesson of the study is that we should all relax a little and not let our work ⑤ take over our lives.

| 기호 | 어색한 표현 | | 올바른 표현 |
|---|---|---|---|
| ( ) | _____ | ⇨ | _____ |
| ( ) | _____ | ⇨ | _____ |

## 37
밑줄 부분 중 어법, 혹은 문맥상 어휘의 쓰임이 어색한 것을 올바르게 고쳐 쓰시오. (1개)16)

We commonly argue about the fairness of taxation—whether this or that tax will fall more heavily on the rich or the poor. But the expressive dimension of taxation goes beyond debates about fairness, to the moral judgements societies make about ① which activities are worthy of honor and recognition, and which ones should be discouraged. Sometimes, these judgements are ② explicit. Taxes on tobacco, alcohol, and casinos ③ are called "sin taxes" because they seek to discourage activities considered harmful or undesirable. Such taxes express society's disapproval of these activities by ④ raising the cost of engaging in them. Proposals to tax sugary sodas (to combat obesity) or carbon emissions (to address climate change) likewise seek to change norms and shape behavior. Not all taxes have this aim. We do not tax income to express disapproval of ⑤ paid employment or to discourage people from engaging in it. Nor is a general sales tax intended as a deterrent to ⑥ buy things. These are simply ways of ⑦ raising revenue.

| 기호 | 어색한 표현 | 올바른 표현 |
|---|---|---|
| ( ) | _____ ⇨ | _____ |

## 38
밑줄 부분 중 어법, 혹은 문맥상 어휘의 쓰임이 어색한 것을 올바르게 고쳐 쓰시오. (3개)17)

Most beliefs—but not all—are open to tests of verification. This means ① that beliefs can be tested to see if they are correct or false. Beliefs can be verified or falsified with ② objective criteria external to the person. There are people who believe the Earth is flat and not a sphere. Because we have objective evidence ③ which the Earth is in fact a sphere, the flat Earth belief can be shown to be false. Also, the belief that it will rain tomorrow can be tested for truth by ④ awaiting until tomorrow and seeing whether it rains or not. ⑤ However, some types of beliefs cannot be tested for truth because we cannot get external evidence in our

lifetimes (such as a belief that the Earth will stop ⑥ to spin on its axis by the year 9999 or that there is life on a planet 100-million light-years away). Also, meta-physical beliefs (such as the existence and nature of a god) present ⑦ considerable challenges in generating evidence that everyone is willing to use as a truth criterion.

| 기호 | 어색한 표현 | 올바른 표현 |
|---|---|---|
| ( ) | _____ ⇨ | _____ |
| ( ) | _____ ⇨ | _____ |
| ( ) | _____ ⇨ | _____ |

## 39
밑줄 부분 중 어법, 혹은 문맥상 어휘의 쓰임이 어색한 것을 올바르게 고쳐 쓰시오. (6개)18)

Everyone automatically categorizes and generalizes all the time. Unconsciously. It is not a question of ① prejudicing or enlightened. Categories are absolutely necessary for us to ② be functioned. They give structure to our thoughts. Imagine ③ that we saw every item and every scenario as truly unique—we would not even have a language to describe the world around us. But the necessary and useful instinct to generalize can distort our world view. It can make us mistakenly ④ to group together things, or people, or countries that are actually very different. It can make us ⑤ to assume everything or everyone in one category ⑥ being similar. And, maybe, most unfortunate of all, it can make us ⑦ jump to conclusions about a whole category based on a few, or even just one, unusual example.

| 기호 | 어색한 표현 | 올바른 표현 |
|---|---|---|
| ( ) | _____ ⇨ | _____ |
| ( ) | _____ ⇨ | _____ |
| ( ) | _____ ⇨ | _____ |
| ( ) | _____ ⇨ | _____ |
| ( ) | _____ ⇨ | _____ |
| ( ) | _____ ⇨ | _____ |

## 40

밑줄 부분 중 어법, 혹은 문맥상 어휘의 쓰임이 어색한 것을 올바르게 고쳐 쓰시오. (1개)[19]

At the University of Iowa, students were briefly shown numbers that they had to memorize. Then they ① were offered the choice of either a fruit salad or a chocolate cake. When the number the students memorized was seven digits long, 63% of them chose the cake. When the number they ② asked to remember had just two digits, however, 59% ③ opted for the fruit salad. Our reflective brains know that the fruit salad is better for our health, but our reflexive brains desire that soft, fattening chocolate cake. If the reflective brain is busy ④ figuring something else out—like trying to remember a seven-digit number—then impulse can easily win. On the other hand, if we're not thinking ⑤ too hard about something else (with only a minor distraction like memorizing two digits), then the reflective system can ⑥ deny the emotional impulse of the reflexive side.

| 기호 | 어색한 표현 | | 올바른 표현 |
|---|---|---|---|
| ( ) | _____ | ⇨ | _____ |

## 41~42

밑줄 부분 중 어법, 혹은 문맥상 어휘의 쓰임이 어색한 것을 올바르게 고쳐 쓰시오. (3개)[20]

Test scores are not a measure of self-worth; however, we often ① associate our sense of worthiness with our performance on an exam. Thoughts such as "If I don't pass this test, I'm a failure" ② are mental traps not rooted in truth. Failing a test is failing a test, nothing more. It is in no way descriptive of your value as a person. ③ Believing that test performance is a reflection of your virtue places unreasonable pressure on your performance. Not passing the certification test only means ④ that your certification status has ⑤ been delayed. Maintaining a positive attitude is therefore important. If you have studied hard, reaffirm this mentally and believe that you will do well. If, ⑥ for example, you did not study as ⑦ hardly as you should have or wanted to, ⑧ accept that as beyond your control for now and attend to the task of doing the best you can. If things do not go well this time, you know ⑨ what needs to be done in preparation for the next exam. Talk to yourself in positive terms. Avoid ⑩ rationalizing past or future test performance by placing the blame on secondary variables. Thoughts such as, "I didn't have enough time", or "I should have ...", compound the stress of test-taking. Take control by affirming your value, self-worth, and dedication to ⑪ meet the test challenge head on. Repeat to yourself "I can and I will pass this exam".

| 기호 | 어색한 표현 | | 올바른 표현 |
|---|---|---|---|
| ( ) | _____ | ⇨ | _____ |
| ( ) | _____ | ⇨ | _____ |
| ( ) | _____ | ⇨ | _____ |

## 43~45 밑줄 부분 중 어법, 혹은 문맥상 어휘의 쓰임이 어색한 것을 올바르게 고쳐 쓰시오. (8개)[21]

Once upon a time there lived a poor but cheerful shoemaker. He was so happy, he sang all day long. The children loved to stand around his window to listen to him. Next door to the shoemaker lived a rich man. He ① used to sit up all night to count his gold. In the morning, he went to bed, but he could not sleep ② because the sound of the shoemaker's singing. One day, he ③ had thought of a way of stopping the singing. He wrote a letter to the shoemaker ④ asked him to visit. The shoemaker came at once, and to his surprise the rich man gave him a bag of gold. When he got home again, the shoemaker opened the bag. He ⑤ have never seen so much gold before! When he sat down at his bench and began, carefully, to count it, the children watched through the window. There ⑥ were so much there that the shoemaker was afraid to let it out of his sight. So he took it to bed with him. But he could not sleep for worrying about it. Very early in the morning, he got up and brought his gold down from the bedroom. He had decided to hide it up the chimney instead. But he was still uneasy, and in a little while he dug a hole in the garden and buried his bag of gold in it. It was no use ⑦ to try to work. He was too worried about the safety of his gold. And as for singing, he was too miserable to utter a note. He could not sleep, or work, or sing—and, worst of all, the children no longer came to see him. At last, the shoemaker felt so ⑧ unhappily that he seized his bag of gold and ran next door to the rich man. "Please take back your gold", he said. "The worry of it is making me ill, and I have lost all of my friends. I would rather be a poor shoemaker, as I ⑨ did before". And so the shoemaker was happy again and sang all day at his work.

| 기호 | 어색한 표현 | | 올바른 표현 |
|---|---|---|---|
| (   ) | _____ | ⇨ | _____ |
| (   ) | _____ | ⇨ | _____ |
| (   ) | _____ | ⇨ | _____ |
| (   ) | _____ | ⇨ | _____ |
| (   ) | _____ | ⇨ | _____ |
| (   ) | _____ | ⇨ | _____ |
| (   ) | _____ | ⇨ | _____ |
| (   ) | _____ | ⇨ | _____ |

2021 고2 3월 모의고사

❶ voca  ❷ text  ❸ [ / ]  ❹ ___  ❺ quiz 1  ❻ quiz 2  ❼ quiz 3  ❽ quiz 4  ❾ quiz 5  ❿ quiz 6

## 18

My name is Anthony Thompson and I am writing on behalf of the residents' association. ⓐ Our recycling program has been worked well thanks to your participation. However, a problem has recently been occurred that needs your attention. Because there is no given day for recycling, residents <sup>put의 올바른 형태</sup> _____ their recycling out at any time. This makes the recycling area messy, which requires extra labor and cost. To deal with this problem, the residents' association has decided on a day to recycle. (가) 수요일에만 여러분의 재활용품을 내놓을 수 있다는 것을 알려드리고 싶습니다. I am sure it will make our apartment complex look much more pleasant. Thank you in advance for your cooperation.

1. 힌트를 참고하여 각 빈칸에 알맞은 단어를 쓰시오.<sup>1)</sup>

2. 밑줄 친 ⓐ에서, 어법 혹은 문맥상 어색한 부분을 찾아 올바르게 고쳐 쓰시오.<sup>2)</sup>

ⓐ 　　잘못된 표현 　　　　　바른 표현

( 　　　　　　　) ⇨ ( 　　　　　　　)

( 　　　　　　　) ⇨ ( 　　　　　　　)

3. 위 글에 주어진 (가)의 한글과 같은 의미를 가지도록, 각각의 주어진 단어들을 알맞게 배열하시오.<sup>3)</sup>

(가) to / put / on / like / only / that / would / I / you / recycling / your / out / can / let / you / Wednesdays / know

## 19

It was a day I was due to give a presentation at work, not something I'd do often. As I stood up to begin, I froze. A chilly 'pins-and-needles' feeling <sup>엄습하다</sup> _____ me, <sup>start의 올바른 형태</sup> _____ in my hands. Time seemed to stand still as I struggled to start speaking. ⓐ And I felt a pressure around my throat, even if my voice trapped and couldn't come out. <sup>Gaze의 올바른 형태</sup> _____ around at the blur of faces, I realized they were all waiting for me to begin. But by now I knew I couldn't continue.

4. 힌트를 참고하여 각 빈칸에 알맞은 단어를 쓰시오.<sup>4)</sup>

5. 밑줄 친 ⓐ에서, 어법 혹은 문맥상 어색한 부분을 찾아 올바르게 고쳐 쓰시오.<sup>5)</sup>

ⓐ 　　잘못된 표현 　　　　　바른 표현

( 　　　　　　　) ⇨ ( 　　　　　　　)

( 　　　　　　　) ⇨ ( 　　　　　　　)

## 20

ⓐ No matter how your situation, whether you are an insider or an outsider, you need to become the voice what challenges yesterday's answers.

(A) If you didn't know your coworkers and feel [bond의 올바른 형태] _____ to them by your [share의 올바른 형태] _____ experiences, what would you think of them?

(B) They are the people who have the perspective to see problems that the insiders are too close to really notice.

(C) Part of adopting an outsider mentality is forcing yourself [look의 올바른 형태] _____ around your organization with this [dissociate의 올바른 형태] _____, less emotional perspective.

(D) Think about the characteristics that make outsiders valuable to an organization.

(E) They are the ones who have the freedom to point out these problems and criticize them without [risk의 올바른 형태] _____ their job or their career.

(F) You may not have the job security or confidence to speak your mind to management, but you can make these "outsider" [평가] _____ of your organization on your own and use what you determine to advance your career.

6. 다음 주어진 글에 이어질 순서로 바르게 짝지어진 것을 고르시오.6)

① (A)-(B)-(E)-(D)-(F)-(C)  ② (B)-(C)-(E)-(D)-(A)-(F)

③ (B)-(D)-(A)-(E)-(C)-(F)  ④ (C)-(D)-(B)-(F)-(A)-(E)

⑤ (D)-(B)-(E)-(C)-(A)-(F)

7. 힌트를 참고하여 각 빈칸에 알맞은 단어를 쓰시오.7)

8. 밑줄 친 ⓐ에서, 어법 혹은 문맥상 어색한 부분을 찾아 올바르게 고쳐 쓰시오.8)

　ⓐ　　잘못된 표현　　　　　바른 표현

　　( 　　　　　　 ) ⇨ ( 　　　　　　 )

　　( 　　　　　　 ) ⇨ ( 　　　　　　 )

## 21

The known fact of contingencies, without knowing [정확히] _____ what those [비상사태] _____ will be, shows that disaster preparation is not the same thing as disaster rehearsal. (가) 아무리 많은 모의 재난이 사전 계획에 따라 조직되더라도 실제 재난은 그런 것들 중 어느 하나라도 그대로 반영하지 않을 것이다. Disaster-preparation planning is more like training for a marathon than training for a high-jump competition or a sprinting event. Marathon runners do not practice by running the full course of twenty-six miles; [연결부사] _____, they get into shape by running shorter distances and building up their [지구력] _____ with cross-training. If they have prepared successfully, then they are in [최적의] _____ condition to run the marathon over its [predetermine의 올바른 형태] _____ course and length, [assume의 올바른 형태] _____ a range of weather conditions, [predict의 올바른 형태] _____ or not. This is normal marathon preparation.

9. 힌트를 참고하여 각 빈칸에 알맞은 단어를 쓰시오.9)

10. 위 글에 주어진 (가)의 한글과 같은 의미를 가지도록, 각각의 주어진 단어들을 알맞게 배열하시오.10)

(가) of / never / according / any / disaster / plans, / real / are / the / them / staged / mirror / to / prior / disasters / will / No / many / one / matter / how / mock

# 22

Fears of damaging ecosystems are based on the sound conservationist principle that we should aim to minimize the disruption we cause, but there is a risk that this principle may be confused with the old idea of a 'balance of nature'.

(A) Ecosystems are dynamic, and although some may endure, apparently <sup>unchange의 올바른 형태</sup> _____, for periods that are long <sup>~와</sup> <sup>비교하여</sup> _____ the human lifespan, they must and do change eventually. Species come and go, climates change, plant and animal communities <sup>적용하다</sup> _____ <sup>달라지다,변하다</sup> _____ circumstances, and when <sup>examine의 올바른 형태</sup> _____ in fine detail such <sup>adapt의 올바른 형태</sup> _____ and consequent change can be seen <sup>take의 올바른 형태</sup> _____ place constantly. The 'balance of nature' is a myth. (가) 지구는 역동적이고 지구의 서식자들이 함께 사는 모습도 그러하다.

(B) This supposes a perfect order of nature that will seek to maintain itself and that we should not change.

(C) It is a romantic, not to say idyllic, notion, but deeply <sup>mislead의 올바른 형태</sup> _____ because it supposes a <sup>정적인</sup> _____ condition.

11. 다음 주어진 글에 이어질 순서로 바르게 짝지어진 것을 고르 시오.<sup>11)</sup>

① (A)-(B)-(C)    ② (A)-(C)-(B)    ③ (B)-(C)-(A)

④ (C)-(A)-(B)    ⑤ (C)-(B)-(A)

12. 힌트를 참고하여 각 빈칸에 알맞은 단어를 쓰시오.<sup>12)</sup>

13. 위 글에 주어진 (가)의 한글과 같은 의미를 가지도록, 각각의 주어진 단어들을 알맞게 배열하시오.<sup>13)</sup>

(가) together / planet / which / Our / live / inhabitants / and / is / the / so / dynamic, / its / by / are / arrangements

# 23

Before the modern scientific era, creativity <sup>attribute의 올바른 형태</sup> _____ to a superhuman force; all novel ideas <sup>originate의 올바른 형태</sup> _____ with the gods. After all, how could a person create something that did not exist before the divine act of creation? <sup>연결부사</sup> _____, the Latin meaning of the verb "inspire" is "to breathe into", <sup>reflect의 올바른 형태</sup> _____ the belief that creative inspiration was similar to the moment in creation when God first breathed life into man. Plato argued that the poet <sup>possess의 올바른 형태</sup> _____ by divine inspiration, and Plotin wrote that art could only be beautiful if it <sup>내려가다</sup> _____ from God. (가) 예술가의 일은 자연을 모방하는 것이라기보다는 오히려 자연의 신성하고 초월적인 특성을 드러내는 것이었다. Art could only be a <sup>어설픈,힘없는</sup> _____ imitation of the perfection of the world of ideas. Greek artists did not blindly imitate what they saw in reality; instead they tried to represent the pure, true forms <sup>underly의 올바른 형태</sup> _____ reality, <sup>result의 올바른 형태</sup> _____ in a sort of <sup>타협</sup> _____ between abstraction and accuracy.

14. 힌트를 참고하여 각 빈칸에 알맞은 단어를 쓰시오.<sup>14)</sup>

15. 위 글에 주어진 (가)의 한글과 같은 의미를 가지도록, 각각의 주어진 단어들을 알맞게 배열하시오.<sup>15)</sup>

(가) to / rather / to / The artist's job / imitate / transcendent / nature / nature / was / reveal / sacred / but / qualities / and / the / of / not

## 24

Some beginning researchers mistakenly believe that a good <sup>가설</sup> _____ is one that <sup>guarantee의 올바른 형태</sup> _____ to be right (e.g., alcohol will slow down reaction time). <sup>연결부사</sup> _____, if we already know your hypothesis is true before you test it, testing your hypothesis won't tell us anything new. Remember, research <sup>suppose의 올바른 형태</sup> _____ to produce new knowledge. To get new knowledge, you, as a researcher-explorer, need to leave the safety of the shore (<sup>establish의 올바른 형태</sup> _____ facts) and venture into <sup>unchart의 올바른 형태</sup> _____ waters (as Einstein said, "(가) <u>우리가 무엇을 하고 있는지 안다면 그것은 연구라고 불리지 않을 것이다, 그렇지</u>"?). If your predictions about what will happen in these <sup>unchart의 올바른 형태</sup> _____ waters are wrong, that's okay: Scientists <sup>allow의 올바른 형태</sup> _____ to make mistakes (as Bates said, "Research is the process of going up alleys to see if they are blind"). Indeed, scientists often learn more from predictions that do not turn out than from those that do.

16. 힌트를 참고하여 각 빈칸에 알맞은 단어를 쓰시오.<sup>16)</sup>

17. 위 글에 주어진 (가)의 한글과 같은 의미를 가지도록, 각각의 주어진 단어들을 알맞게 배열하시오.<sup>17)</sup>

(가) research, / were / knew / we / not / would / it / doing, / would / we / what / called / it / be / If

## 29

While <sup>reflect의 올바른 형태</sup> _____ on the needs of organizations, leaders, and families today, we realize that one of the unique characteristics <sup>be의 올바른 형태</sup> ____ inclusivity. Why? Because inclusivity supports what everyone ultimately wants from their relationships: collaboration. <sup>연결부사</sup> ____ the majority of leaders, organizations, and families are still using the language of the old paradigm in which one person—typically the oldest, most educated, andor wealthiest—<sup>make의 올바른 형태</sup> _____ all the decisions, and their decisions rule with little discussion or inclusion of others, <sup>result의 올바른 형태</sup> _____ in exclusivity. Today, this person could be a director, CEO, or other senior leader of an organization. (가) <u>다른 사람들이 자신의 생각을 제시할 필요가 없는데 왜냐하면 그것은 부적절한 것으로 여겨지기 때문이다.</u> <sup>연결부사</sup> ____ research shows that exclusivity in problem solving, even with a genius, is not as effective as inclusivity, where everyone's ideas are heard and a solution <sup>develop의 올바른 형태</sup> _____ through collaboration.

18. 힌트를 참고하여 각 빈칸에 알맞은 단어를 쓰시오.<sup>18)</sup>

19. 위 글에 주어진 (가)의 한글과 같은 의미를 가지도록, 각각의 주어진 단어들을 알맞게 배열하시오.<sup>19)</sup>

(가) present / is / others / for / considered / ideas / to / no / because / are / There / inadequate / they / their / need

# 30

The objective point of view _____ [illustrate의 올바른 형태] by John Ford's "philosophy of camera". Ford considered the camera to be a window and the audience to be outside the window viewing the people and events within. We _____ [ask의 올바른 형태] to watch the actions as if they _____ [be의 올바른 형태] taking place at a distance, and we are not asked to participate. The objective point of view employs a _____ [정적인] camera as much as possible in order to produce this window effect, and it concentrates on the actors and the action without drawing attention to the camera. The objective camera suggests an emotional distance between camera and subject; ⓐ the camera seems simply to be recording, as straightforword as possible, the characters and actions of the story. For the most part, the director uses natural, normal types of camera _____ [position의 올바른 형태] and camera angles. The objective camera does not comment on or interpret the action but merely records it, _____ [let의 올바른 형태] it unfold. We see the action from the viewpoint of an _____ [냉담한, 비인격적인] observer. If the camera moves, it does so unnoticeably, (가) **가능한 한 자신에게 거의 관심을 불러일으키지 않으면서**.

20. 힌트를 참고하여 각 빈칸에 알맞은 단어를 쓰시오.[20]

21. 밑줄 친 ⓐ에서, 어법 혹은 문맥상 어색한 부분을 찾아 올바르게 고쳐 쓰시오.[21]

    ⓐ    잘못된 표현        바른 표현

      (          ) ⇨ (          )

      (          ) ⇨ (          )

22. 위 글에 주어진 (가)의 한글과 같은 의미를 가지도록, 각각의 주어진 단어들을 알맞게 배열하시오.[22]

(가) little / calling / as / possible / to / attention / as / itself

# 31

Even the most _____ [훌륭한,존경할만한] of all musical institutions, the symphony orchestra, _____ [carry의 올바른 형태] inside its DNA the legacy of the hunt. The various instruments in the orchestra can _____ [trace의 올바른 형태] back to these primitive origins—their earliest forms _____ [make의 올바른 형태] either from the animal (horn, hide, gut, bone) or the weapons _____ [employ의 올바른 형태] in bringing the animal under control (stick, bow). Are we wrong to hear this history in the music itself, in the _____ [강력한,만만찮은] aggression and awe-inspiring _____ [당당함] of those _____ [기념비적인] symphonies that remain the core repertoire of the world's leading orchestras? Listening to Beethoven, Brahms, Mahler, Bruckner, Berlioz, Tchaikovsky, Shostakovich, and other great composers, I can easily _____ [떠올리다,불러일으키다] images of bands of men starting to chase animals, _____ [use의 올바른 형태] sound as a source and symbol of dominance, an expression of the will to predatory power.

23. 힌트를 참고하여 각 빈칸에 알맞은 단어를 쓰시오.[23]

## 32

ⓐ <u>Our brains have been evolved to remember expected events because basic survival depending on the ability to perceive causes and predict effects.</u> If the brain predicts one event and experiences another, the unusualness will be especially <sup>interest의 올바른 형태</sup> _____ and will <sup>encode 의 올바른 형태</sup> _____ accordingly. Neurologist and classroom teacher Judith Willis has claimed that surprise in the classroom is one of the most effective ways of teaching with brain stimulation in mind. If students <sup>expose의 올바른 형태</sup> _____ to new experiences via demonstrations or through the unexpected enthusiasm of their teachers or peers, they will be much more likely to connect with the information that follows. Willis has written that encouraging active discovery in the classroom allows students to interact with new information, <sup>move의 올바른 형태</sup> _____ it beyond working memory <sup>memory의 올바른 형태</sup> _____ in the frontal lobe, which is devoted to advanced cognitive functioning. (가)<u>새로움에 대한 선호는, 주의를 이끌고, 지각 체계를 발전시키는 데 자극을 제공하며, 호기심 많고 탐구적인 행동을 충족함으로써 우리를 학습하도록 준비시킨다.</u>

24. 힌트를 참고하여 각 빈칸에 알맞은 단어를 쓰시오.[24]

25. 밑줄 친 ⓐ에서, 어법 혹은 문맥상 어색한 부분을 찾아 올바르게 고쳐 쓰시오.[25]

ⓐ     잘못된 표현          바른 표현

(          ) ⇨ (          )

(          ) ⇨ (          )

(          ) ⇨ (          )

26. 위 글에 주어진 (가)의 한글과 같은 의미를 가지도록, 각각의 주어진 단어들을 알맞게 배열하시오.[26]

(가) exploratory / perceptual / behavior / attention, / learning / stimulation / developing / to / directing / and / and / for / feeding / curious / providing / us / for / novelty / sets / up / systems, / by / Preference

## 33

How hard are you going to try to remember what the neighbor has to say about which wines to buy?

Psychological research has shown that people naturally divide up cognitive labor, often without thinking about it. ( ① ) Imagine you're cooking up a special dinner with a friend. ( ② ) You're a great cook, but your friend is the wine expert, an amateur sommelier. ( ③ ) A neighbor drops by and starts telling you both about the terrific new wines <sup>sell의 올바른 형태</sup> _____ at the liquor store just down the street. ( ④ ) There are many new wines, so there's a lot to remember. ( ⑤ ) Why bother when the information would be better <sup>retain의 올바른 형태</sup> _____ by the wine expert sitting next to you? If your friend wasn't around, you might try harder. After all, it would be good to know what a good wine would be for the evening's festivities. But your friend, the wine expert, is likely to remember the information without even trying.

27. 글의 흐름으로 보아, 주어진 문장이 들어가기에 가장 적절한 곳은?[27]

28. 힌트를 참고하여 각 빈칸에 알맞은 단어를 쓰시오.[28]

## 34

Even companies that sell physical products to make profit are forced by their boards and investors to reconsider their underlying motives and to collect as much data as possible from consumers.

(A) ⓐ Then every company's natural tendency is to minimize its ability to contact subsequence on its own customers because the customers are themselves the new value-creation devises.

(B) They give you loyalty cards with which they track your purchasing behaviors 정확하게 _____. Then supermarkets sell this purchasing behavior to marketing 분석학 _____ companies.

(C) Supermarkets no longer make all their money selling their produce and manufactured goods.

(D) When data and machine learning become currencies of value in a capitalist system.

(E) The marketing analytics companies perform machine learning procedures, slice의 올바른 형태 _____ the data in new ways, and resell behavioral data back to product manufacturers as marketing insights.

29. 다음 주어진 글에 이어질 순서로 바르게 짝지어진 것을 고르시오.29)

① (C)–(B)–(E)–(D)–(A)　　② (C)–(D)–(B)–(E)–(A)

③ (C)–(D)–(E)–(A)–(B)　　④ (D)–(B)–(E)–(C)–(A)

⑤ (D)–(C)–(E)–(B)–(A)

30. 힌트를 참고하여 각 빈칸에 알맞은 단어를 쓰시오.30)

31. 밑줄 친 ⓐ에서, 어법 혹은 문맥상 어색한 부분을 찾아 올바르게 고쳐 쓰시오.31)

| ⓐ 잘못된 표현 | | 바른 표현 |
| --- | --- | --- |
| ( | ) ⇨ ( | ) |
| ( | ) ⇨ ( | ) |
| ( | ) ⇨ ( | ) |
| ( | ) ⇨ ( | ) |

## 35

Academics, politicians, marketers and others have in the past debated whether or not it is ethically correct to market products and services directly to young consumers.  ⓐ This is also a dilemma for psychologists who have been questioned that they ought to help advertisers manipulating children into purchasing more products they have seen advertising. Advertisers have admit의 올바른 형태 _____ take의 올바른 형태 _____ advantage of the fact that it is easy to make children feel that they are losers if they do not own the 'right' products. Clever advertising informs children that they will view의 올바른 형태 _____ by their peers in an unfavorable way if they do not have the products that are advertised, thereby play의 올바른 형태 _____ on their emotional 취약성 _____. The constant feelings of 부적절 _____ create의 올바른 형태 _____ by advertising have suggest의 올바른 형태 _____ to contribute to children become의 올바른 형태 _____ fixate의 올바른 형태 _____ with instant gratification and beliefs that material possessions are important.

32. 힌트를 참고하여 각 빈칸에 알맞은 단어를 쓰시오.32)

33. 밑줄 친 ⓐ에서, 어법 혹은 문맥상 어색한 부분을 찾아 올바르게 고쳐 쓰시오.33)

| ⓐ 잘못된 표현 | | 바른 표현 |
| --- | --- | --- |
| ( | ) ⇨ ( | ) |
| ( | ) ⇨ ( | ) |
| ( | ) ⇨ ( | ) |
| ( | ) ⇨ ( | ) |

## 36

Once we recognize the false-cause issue, we see it everywhere. 연결부사 _____, a recent long-term study of University of Toronto medical students 결론짓다 _____ that medical school class presidents lived an average of 2.4 years less than other medical school graduates. At first glance, this seemed to 내포하다,의미하다 _____ that being a medical school class president is bad for you. Does this mean that you should avoid be의 올바른 형태 _____ medical school class president at all costs? Probably not. Just because being class president correlate의 올바른 형태 _____ with shorter life expectancy does not mean that it causes shorter life expectancy. 연결부사 _____, it seems likely that the sort of person who becomes medical school class president is, on average, extremely hard-working, serious, and ambitious. Perhaps this extra stress, and (가)그에 상응하는 사교와 휴식시간의 부족이—rather than being class president per se—contributes to lower life expectancy. If so, the real lesson of the study is that we should all relax a little and not let our work take over our lives.

**34.** 힌트를 참고하여 각 빈칸에 알맞은 단어를 쓰시오.34)

**35.** 위 글에 주어진 (가)의 한글과 같은 의미를 가지도록, 각각의 주어진 단어들을 알맞게 배열하시오.35)

(가) of / social / lack / corresponding / and / time / relaxation / the

## 37

We commonly argue about the fairness of 과세 _____ —whether this or that tax will fall more heavily on the rich or the poor. But the expressive dimension of taxation goes beyond debates about fairness, to the moral judgements societies make about which activities are worthy of honor and recognition, and which ones should be discouraged. Sometimes, these judgements are 명백한 _____. Taxes on tobacco, alcohol, and casinos call의 올바른 형태 _____ "sin taxes" (가)해롭거나 바람직하지 않은 것으로 간주되는 활동들을 억제하려고 하기 때문에. (나)그런 세금은 이러한 활동을 하는 데 드는 비용을 증가시킴으로써 그것에 대한 사회의 반대를 표현한다. Proposals to tax sugary sodas (to combat obesity) or carbon emissions (to address climate change) likewise seek to change norms and shape behavior. Not all taxes have this aim. We do not tax income to express disapproval of paid employment or to discourage people from engaging in it. (다)일반 판매세 역시 물건을 사는 것의 억제책으로서 의도된 것이 아니다. These are simply ways of raising revenue.

**36.** 힌트를 참고하여 각 빈칸에 알맞은 단어를 쓰시오.36)

**37.** 위 글에 주어진 (가) ~ (다)의 한글과 같은 의미를 가지도록, 각각의 주어진 단어들을 알맞게 배열하시오.37)

(가) or / because / to / activities / discourage / seek / considered / undesirable / they / harmful

(나) in / Such / them / society's disapproval / these / activities / by / of / the / engaging / taxes / raising / of / express / cost

(다) things / a / tax / general / buying / as / is / a / to / sales / intended / deterrent / Nor

## 38

Most beliefs—but not all—are open to tests of verification. This means that beliefs can be tested to see if they are correct or false. (가)<u>믿음은 그 사람의 외부에 있는 객관적인 기준을 통해 진실임이 입증되거나 거짓임이 입증될 수 있다.</u> There are people who believe the Earth is flat and not a sphere. Because we have objective evidence that the Earth is in fact a sphere, the flat Earth belief can be shown to be false. Also, the belief that it will rain tomorrow can be tested for truth by waiting until tomorrow and seeing whether it rains or not. <sup>연결부사</sup> _____, some types of beliefs cannot be tested for truth because we cannot get external evidence in our lifetimes (such as a belief that the Earth will stop <sup>spin의 올바른 형태</sup> _____ on its axis by the year 9999 or that there is life on a planet 100-million light-years away). Also, meta-physical beliefs (such as the existence and nature of a god) present <sup>상당한</sup> _____ challenges in generating evidence that everyone is willing to use as a truth <sup>기준</sup> _____.

38. 힌트를 참고하여 각 빈칸에 알맞은 단어를 쓰시오.<sup>38)</sup>

39. 위 글에 주어진 (가)의 한글과 같은 의미를 가지도록, 각각의 주어진 단어들을 알맞게 배열하시오.<sup>39)</sup>

(가) Beliefs / or / criteria / falsified / person / with / can / verified / external / objective / to / be / the

## 39

Everyone automatically categorizes and generalizes all the time. Unconsciously. It is not a question of <sup>prejudice의 올바른 형태</sup> _____ or enlightened. Categories are absolutely necessary for us <sup>function의 올바른 형태</sup> _____. They give structure to our thoughts. Imagine if we saw every item and every scenario as truly unique—we would not even have a language to describe the world around us. But (가)<u>필요하고 유용한 일반화하려는 본능은 우리의 세계관을 왜곡할 수 있다.</u> ⓐ<u>It can make us mistakenly to group together things, or people, or countries what are actually very similar.</u> ⓑ<u>It can make us to assume everything or everyone in one category is different.</u> And, maybe, most unfortunate of all, it can make us jump to conclusions about a whole category based on a few, or even just one, unusual example.

40. 힌트를 참고하여 각 빈칸에 알맞은 단어를 쓰시오.<sup>40)</sup>

41. 밑줄 친 ⓐ~ⓑ에서, 어법 혹은 문맥상 어색한 부분을 찾아 올바르게 고쳐 쓰시오.<sup>41)</sup>

ⓐ　　　잘못된 표현　　　　　바른 표현

(　　　　　　　) ⇨ (　　　　　　　)

(　　　　　　　) ⇨ (　　　　　　　)

(　　　　　　　) ⇨ (　　　　　　　)

ⓑ　　　잘못된 표현　　　　　바른 표현

(　　　　　　　) ⇨ (　　　　　　　)

(　　　　　　　) ⇨ (　　　　　　　)

42. 위 글에 주어진 (가)의 한글과 같은 의미를 가지도록, 각각의 주어진 단어들을 알맞게 배열하시오.<sup>42)</sup>

(가) world / can / our / to / the / generalize / distort / instinct / necessary / and / useful / view

# 40

When the number they were asked to remember had just two digits, however, 59% opted for the fruit salad.

At the University of Iowa, students were briefly shown numbers that they had to memorize. ( ① ) Then they ~~offer의 올바른 형태~~ _____ the choice of either a fruit salad or a chocolate cake. ( ② ) When the number the students memorized was seven digits long, 63% of them chose the cake. ( ③ ) Our reflective brains know that the fruit salad is better for our health, but our reflexive brains desire that soft, fattening chocolate cake. ( ④ ) If the reflective brain is busy figuring something else out— like trying to remember a seven-digit number—then impulse can easily win. ( ⑤ ) ~~연결부사~~ _____, if we're not thinking too hard about something else (with only a minor distraction like memorizing two digits), then the reflective system can deny the emotional impulse of the reflexive side.

43. 글의 흐름으로 보아, 주어진 문장이 들어가기에 가장 적절한 곳은?43)

44. 힌트를 참고하여 각 빈칸에 알맞은 단어를 쓰시오.44)

# 41-42

Test scores are not a measure of self-worth; ~~연결부사~~ _____, we often associate our sense of worthiness with our performance on an exam. ( ① ) Thoughts such as "If I don't pass this test, I'm a failure" are mental traps not rooted in truth. ( ② ) Failing a test is failing a test, nothing more. (가)그것은 결코 사람으로서의 여러분의 가치를 설명하지 않는다. ~~Believe의 올바른 형태~~ _____ that test performance is a reflection of your virtue places unreasonable pressure on your performance. ( ③ ) Not passing the certification test only means that your certification status has been delayed. Maintaining a positive attitude is therefore important. ( ④ ) If you have studied hard, reaffirm this mentally and believe that you will do well. If, ~~연결부사~~ _____, you did not study as hard as you should have or wanted to, accept that as beyond your control for now and attend to the task of doing the best you can. If things do not go well this time, you know what needs to be done in preparation for the next exam. ( ⑤ ) Talk to yourself in positive terms.

45. 글의 흐름으로 보아, 주어진 문장이 들어가기에 가장 적절한 곳은?45)

46. 힌트를 참고하여 각 빈칸에 알맞은 단어를 쓰시오.46)

47. 위 글에 주어진 (가)의 한글과 같은 의미를 가지도록, 각각의 주어진 단어들을 알맞게 배열하시오.47)

(가) is / of / your / person / a / as / descriptive / value / in / It / way / no

# 43-45

Once upon a time there lived a poor but cheerful shoemaker. He was so happy, he sang all day long. The children loved to stand around his window to listen to him. Next door to the shoemaker lived a rich man. He used to sit up all night to count his gold. In the morning, he went to bed, but he could not sleep because of the sound of the shoemaker's singing. One day, he thought of a way of stopping the singing. He wrote a letter to the shoemaker <sup>ask의 올바른 형태</sup> _____ him to visit. The shoemaker came at once, and to his surprise the rich man gave him a bag of gold. When he got home again, the shoemaker opened the bag. He <sup>never see의 올바른 형태</sup> _____ so much gold before! When he sat down at his bench and began, carefully, to count it, the children watched through the window. There was so much there that the shoemaker was afraid to let it out of his sight. So he took it to bed with him. But he could not sleep for worrying about it. Very early in the morning, he got up and brought his gold down from the bedroom. He <sup>decide의 올바른 형태</sup> _____ to hide it up the chimney instead. But he was still uneasy, and in a little while he dug a hole in the garden and buried his bag of gold in it. It was no use <sup>try의 올바른 형태</sup> _____ to work. He was too worried about the safety of his gold. And as for singing, (가)<u>그는 너무 불행해서 한 음도 낼 수 없었다</u>. He could not sleep, or work, or sing—and, worst of all, the children no longer came to see him. <sup>연결부사</sup> _____, (나)<u>구두 만드는 사람은 너무 불행해져서 그의 금화가 든 가방을 움켜쥐고</u> and ran next door to the rich man. "Please take back your gold", he said. "The worry of it is making me ill, and I have lost all of my friends. I would rather be a poor shoemaker, as I was before". And so the shoemaker was happy again and sang all day at his work.

48. 힌트를 참고하여 각 빈칸에 알맞은 단어를 쓰시오.<sup>48)</sup>

49. 위 글에 주어진 (가) ~ (나)의 한글과 같은 의미를 가지도록, 각각의 주어진 단어들을 알맞게 배열하시오.<sup>49)</sup>

(가) was / miserable / to / he / a / utter / note / too

(나) the  shoemaker / that / he / so / gold / his / seized / of / felt / bag / unhappy

## Answers

1) on
2) recycling
3) working
4) However,
5) occurred
6) Because
7) given
8) putting
9) which
10) 부사적 용법
11) decided
12) know
13) pleasant.
14) starting
15) struggled
16) as though
17) was trapped
18) 현재분사
19) waiting
20) what
21) that
22) Think
23) 형용사적 용법
24) point
25) adopting
26) forcing
27) disassociated
28) what
29) what
30) without
31) what
32) shows
33) how
34) according
35) prior plans
36) than
37) building
38) have
39) run
40) 현재분사
41) principle
42) that
43) minimize
44) 동격의 접속사 that
45) because
46) although
47) that
48) adapt
49) altered
50) examined
51) adaptation
52) taking
53) Before
54) attributed
55) originated
56) that
57) reflecting
58) that
59) when
60) was possessed
61) wrote
62) 명사적 용법
63) instead
64) in
65) 명사절 접속사 that
66) guaranteed
67) However
68) testing
69) produce
70) established
71) uncharted
72) what
73) be called
74) what
75) happen
76) are
77) allowed
78) that
79) reflecting
80) that
81) Because
82) wants
83) makes
84) in
85) 형용사적 용법
86) because
87) inadequate.
88) is
89) as if
90) employs
91) much
92) 부사적 용법
93) simply
94) straightforwardly
95) but
96) 현재분사
97) does
98) calling
99) respectable
100) carries
101) inspiring
102) that
103) remain
104) Listening
105) starting
106) 현재분사
107) evolved
108) because
109) interesting
110) encoded
111) claimed
112) most
113) exposed
114) that
115) written
116) 동명사
117) to interact
118) moving
119) new information
120) which
121) providing
122) shown
123) 현재분사
124) telling
125) being
126) hard
127) what
128) retained
129) sitting
130) what
131) remember
132) make
133) are
134) much
135) manufactured
136) which
137) precisely.
138) slicing
139) 전치사
140) maximize
141) because
142) debated
143) market
144) manipulate
145) advertised
146) taking
147) 명사적 용법

148) feel
149) Clever
150) informs
151) that
152) thereby
153) been suggested
154) fixated
155) that
156) false - cause issue
157) concluded
158) 동명사
159) because
160) that
161) 명사절 접속사 that
162) on
163) contributes
164) that
165) take
166) fall
167) which
168) worthy
169) which
170) are called
171) considered
172) raising
173) engaging
174) 부정사
175) likewise
176) shape
177) paid employment
178) intended
179) raising
180) that
181) if
182) verified
183) 동격의 접속사 that
184) be shown
185) 동격의 접속사 that
186) waiting
187) However,
188) because
189) that
190) spinning
191) Besides,
192) considerable
193) that
194) 동명사
195) for
196) function.
197) 형용사적 용법
198) group
199) that
200) assume
201) unfortunate
202) jump
203) shown
204) 목적격 관계대명사 that
205) were offered
206) were asked
207) however
208) for
209) reflective
210) reflexive
211) reflective
212) figuring
213) On the other hand,
214) reflective
215) reflexive
216) According
217) leads
218) reflexive
219) however,
220) rooted
221) Failing a test
222) Believing
223) status

224) been delayed.
225) Maintaining
226) hard
227) accept
228) to
229) be done
230) rationalizing
231) compound
232) meeting
233) used
234) sit
235) because of
236) 동명사
237) to visit.
238) had
239) much
240) gold
241) that
242) to hide
243) But
244) trying
245) worried
246) to utter
247) so
248) that
249) seized
250) was

Prac 1 **Answers**

1) on
2) recycling
3) working
4) However,
5) occurred
6) Because
7) given
8) putting
9) which
10) 부사적 용법
11) decided
12) know
13) pleasant.
14) starting
15) struggled
16) as though
17) was trapped
18) 현재분사
19) waiting
20) what
21) that
22) Think
23) 형용사적 용법
24) point
25) adopting
26) forcing
27) disassociated
28) what
29) what
30) without
31) what
32) shows
33) how
34) according
35) prior plans
36) than
37) building
38) have
39) run
40) 현재분사
41) principle
42) that
43) minimize

44) 동격의 접속사 that
45) because
46) although
47) that
48) adapt
49) altered
50) examined
51) adaptation
52) taking
53) Before
54) attributed
55) originated
56) that
57) reflecting
58) that
59) when
60) was possessed
61) wrote
62) 명사적 용법
63) instead
64) in
65) 명사절 접속사 that
66) guaranteed
67) However
68) testing
69) produce
70) established
71) uncharted
72) what
73) be called
74) what
75) happen
76) are
77) allowed
78) that
79) reflecting
80) that
81) Because
82) wants
83) makes
84) in
85) 형용사적 용법
86) because
87) inadequate.
88) is
89) as if
90) employs
91) much
92) 부사적 용법
93) simply
94) straightforwardly
95) but
96) 현재분사
97) does
98) calling
99) respectable
100) carries
101) inspiring
102) that
103) remain
104) Listening
105) starting
106) 현재분사
107) evolved
108) because
109) interesting
110) encoded
111) claimed
112) most
113) exposed
114) that
115) written
116) 동명사
117) to interact
118) moving
119) new information

120) which
121) providing
122) shown
123) 현재분사
124) telling
125) being
126) hard
127) what
128) retained
129) sitting
130) what
131) remember
132) make
133) are
134) much
135) manufactured
136) which
137) precisely.
138) slicing
139) 전치사
140) maximize
141) because
142) debated
143) market
144) manipulate
145) advertised
146) taking
147) 명사적 용법
148) feel
149) Clever
150) informs
151) that
152) thereby
153) been suggested
154) fixated
155) that
156) false - cause issue
157) concluded
158) 동명사
159) because
160) that
161) 명사절 접속사 that
162) on
163) contributes
164) that
165) take
166) fall
167) which
168) worthy
169) which
170) are called
171) considered
172) raising
173) engaging
174) 부정사
175) likewise
176) shape
177) paid employment
178) intended
179) raising
180) that
181) if
182) verified
183) 동격의 접속사 that
184) be shown
185) 동격의 접속사 that
186) waiting
187) However,
188) because
189) that
190) spinning
191) Besides,
192) considerable
193) that
194) 동명사
195) for

196) function.
197) 형용사적 용법
198) group
199) that
200) assume
201) unfortunate
202) jump
203) shown
204) 목적격 관계대명사 that
205) were offered
206) were asked
207) however
208) for
209) reflective
210) reflexive
211) reflective
212) figuring
213) On the other hand,
214) reflective
215) reflexive
216) According
217) leads
218) reflexive
219) however,
220) rooted
221) Failing a test
222) Believing
223) status
224) been delayed.
225) Maintaining
226) hard
227) accept
228) to
229) be done
230) rationalizing
231) compound
232) meeting
233) used
234) sit
235) because of
236) 동명사
237) to visit.
238) had
239) much
240) gold
241) that
242) to hide
243) But
244) trying
245) worried
246) to utter
247) so
248) that
249) seized
250) was

Prac 2  Answers

1) behalf
2) association
3) recycling
4) participation
5) recently
6) given
7) messy
8) deal
9) much
10) pleasant
11) advance
12) due
13) crept
14) seemed
15) struggled

16) pressure
17) trapped
18) Gazing
19) challenges
20) characteristics
21) perspective
22) adopting
23) mentality
24) disassociated
25) perspective
26) bonded
27) assessments
28) determine
29) contingencies
30) precisely
31) contingencies
32) how
33) staged
34) mirror
35) shape
36) endurance
37) optimal
38) predetermined
39) assuming
40) based
41) conservationist
42) aim
43) disruption
44) seek
45) maintain
46) idyllic
47) static
48) dynamic
49) endure
50) comparison
51) adapt
52) altered
53) fine
54) adaptation
55) constantly
56) era
57) attributed
58) superhuman
59) novel
60) divine
61) reflecting
62) possessed
63) imitate
64) sacred
65) transcendent
66) pale
67) blindly
68) underlying
69) compromise
70) abstraction
71) accuracy
72) hypothesis
73) guaranteed
74) is supposed to
75) venture
76) uncharted
77) predictions
78) uncharted
79) allowed
80) alleys
81) predictions
82) turn
83) reflecting
84) realize
85) inclusivity
86) inclusivity
87) collaboration
88) majority
89) discussion
90) inclusion
91) exclusivity

92) present
93) inadequate
94) exclusivity
95) inclusivity
96) collaboration
97) objective
98) illustrated
99) taking
100) participate
101) objective
102) static
103) order
104) concentrates
105) drawing
106) emotional
107) straightforwardly
108) objective
109) comment
110) interpret
111) merely
112) unfold
113) impersonal
114) unnoticeably
115) respectable
116) legacy
117) traced
118) primitive
119) formidable
120) aggression
121) assertiveness
122) summon
123) bands
124) dominance
125) predatory
126) evolved
127) unexpected
128) perceive
129) unusualness
130) accordingly
131) claimed
132) stimulation
133) exposed
134) unexpected
135) enthusiasm
136) much
137) likely
138) interact
139) beyond
140) processed
141) devoted
142) cognitive
143) novelty
144) stimulation
145) perceptual
146) feeding
147) Psychological
148) divide
149) cognitive
150) sommelier
151) drops
152) liquor
153) bother
154) retained
155) festivities.
156) trying
157) physical
158) profit
159) forced
160) reconsider
161) underlying
162) motives
163) longer
164) track
165) precisely
166) analytics
167) machine

168) learning
169) slicing
170) insights
171) currencies
172) capitalist
173) tendency
174) maximize
175) surveillance
176) debated
177) ethically
178) dilemma
179) ought
180) manipulate
181) admitted
182) own
183) informs
184) unfavorable
185) thereby
186) vulnerabilities
187) constant
188) inadequateness
189) fixated
190) gratification
191) possessions
192) recognize
193) concluded
194) seemed
195) imply
196) correlated
197) seems
198) ambitious
199) lack
200) per
201) se
202) contributes
203) relax
204) take
205) fairness
206) taxation
207) fall
208) expressive
209) taxation
210) beyond
211) debates
212) recognition
213) discouraged
214) explicit
215) seek
216) harmful
217) undesirable
218) raising
219) engaging
220) norms
221) aim
222) disapproval
223) Nor
224) deterrent
225) revenue
226) verification
227) verified
228) falsified
229) criteria
230) external
231) external
232) evidence
233) existence
234) considerable
235) willing
236) criterion
237) categorizes
238) generalizes
239) prejudiced
240) enlightened
241) unique
242) describe
243) instinct

244) distort
245) mistakenly
246) assume
247) unfortunate
248) jump
249) based
250) unusual
251) briefly
252) memorize
253) offered
254) opted
255) reflective
256) reflexive
257) desire
258) figuring
259) impulse
260) distraction
261) deny
262) intellective
263) load
264) dominant
265) measure
266) associate
267) worthiness
268) rooted
269) descriptive
270) value
271) reflection
272) virtue
273) unreasonable
274) Maintaining
275) therefore
276) reaffirm
277) beyond
278) attend
279) in preparation for
280) rationalizing
281) compound
282) affirming
283) dedication
284) poor
285) cheerful
286) used to
287) once
288) so
289) afraid
290) out
291) sight
292) worrying
293) decided
294) chimney
295) uneasy
296) dug
297) miserable
298) utter
299) seized
300) ill

Prac 2 **Answers**

1) behalf
2) association
3) recycling
4) participation
5) recently
6) given
7) messy
8) deal
9) much
10) pleasant
11) advance
12) due
13) crept

14) seemed
15) struggled
16) pressure
17) trapped
18) Gazing
19) challenges
20) characteristics
21) perspective
22) adopting
23) mentality
24) disassociated
25) perspective
26) bonded
27) assessments
28) determine
29) contingencies
30) precisely
31) contingencies
32) how
33) staged
34) mirror
35) shape
36) endurance
37) optimal
38) predetermined
39) assuming
40) based
41) conservationist
42) aim
43) disruption
44) seek
45) maintain
46) idyllic
47) static
48) dynamic
49) endure
50) comparison
51) adapt
52) altered
53) fine
54) adaptation
55) constantly
56) era
57) attributed
58) superhuman
59) novel
60) divine
61) reflecting
62) possessed
63) imitate
64) sacred
65) transcendent
66) pale
67) blindly
68) underlying
69) compromise
70) abstraction
71) accuracy
72) hypothesis
73) guaranteed
74) is supposed to
75) venture
76) uncharted
77) predictions
78) uncharted
79) allowed
80) alleys
81) predictions
82) turn
83) reflecting
84) realize
85) inclusivity
86) inclusivity
87) collaboration
88) majority
89) discussion

90) inclusion
91) exclusivity
92) present
93) inadequate
94) exclusivity
95) inclusivity
96) collaboration
97) objective
98) illustrated
99) taking
100) participate
101) objective
102) static
103) order
104) concentrates
105) drawing
106) emotional
107) straightforwardly
108) objective
109) comment
110) interpret
111) merely
112) unfold
113) impersonal
114) unnoticeably
115) respectable
116) legacy
117) traced
118) primitive
119) formidable
120) aggression
121) assertiveness
122) summon
123) bands
124) dominance
125) predatory
126) evolved
127) unexpected
128) perceive
129) unusualness
130) accordingly
131) claimed
132) stimulation
133) exposed
134) unexpected
135) enthusiasm
136) much
137) likely
138) interact
139) beyond
140) processed
141) devoted
142) cognitive
143) novelty
144) stimulation
145) perceptual
146) feeding
147) Psychological
148) divide
149) cognitive
150) sommelier
151) drops
152) liquor
153) bother
154) retained
155) festivities.
156) trying
157) physical
158) profit
159) forced
160) reconsider
161) underlying
162) motives
163) longer
164) track
165) precisely

166) analytics
167) machine
168) learning
169) slicing
170) insights
171) currencies
172) capitalist
173) tendency
174) maximize
175) surveillance
176) debated
177) ethically
178) dilemma
179) ought
180) manipulate
181) admitted
182) own
183) informs
184) unfavorable
185) thereby
186) vulnerabilities
187) constant
188) inadequateness
189) fixated
190) gratification
191) possessions
192) recognize
193) concluded
194) seemed
195) imply
196) correlated
197) seems
198) ambitious
199) lack
200) per
201) se
202) contributes
203) relax
204) take
205) fairness
206) taxation
207) fall
208) expressive
209) taxation
210) beyond
211) debates
212) recognition
213) discouraged
214) explicit
215) seek
216) harmful
217) undesirable
218) raising
219) engaging
220) norms
221) aim
222) disapproval
223) Nor
224) deterrent
225) revenue
226) verification
227) verified
228) falsified
229) criteria
230) external
231) external
232) evidence
233) existence
234) considerable
235) willing
236) criterion
237) categorizes
238) generalizes
239) prejudiced
240) enlightened
241) unique

# Answer Keys

242) describe
243) instinct
244) distort
245) mistakenly
246) assume
247) unfortunate
248) jump
249) based
250) unusual
251) briefly
252) memorize
253) offered
254) opted
255) reflective
256) reflexive
257) desire
258) figuring
259) impulse
260) distraction
261) deny
262) intellective
263) load
264) dominant
265) measure
266) associate
267) worthiness
268) rooted
269) descriptive
270) value
271) reflection
272) virtue
273) unreasonable
274) Maintaining
275) therefore
276) reaffirm
277) beyond
278) attend
279) in preparation for
280) rationalizing
281) compound
282) affirming
283) dedication
284) poor
285) cheerful
286) used to
287) once
288) so
289) afraid
290) out
291) sight
292) worrying
293) decided
294) chimney
295) uneasy
296) dug
297) miserable
298) utter
299) seized
300) ill

12) (D)-(C)-(A)-(B)
13) (B)-(A)-(C)
14) (C)-(B)-(A)
15) (A)-(B)-(D)-(C)
16) (C)-(A)-(B)
17) (D)-(C)-(A)-(B)
18) (C)-(A)-(B)-(D)
19) (B)-(A)-(C)
20) (A)-(C)-(D)-(B)
21) (A)-(C)-(B)
22) ③
23) ⑤
24) ⑤
25) ③
26) ①
27) ⑤
28) ①
29) ②
30) ③
31) ④
32) ①
33) ⑤
34) ②
35) ①
36) ⑤
37) ④
38) ④
39) ⑤
40) ④
41) ⑤
42) ②

## QUIZ 2 Answers

1) ⑤, to know ⇨ know
2) ②, started ⇨ starting
3) ⑤, uses ⇨ use
4) ②, what ⇨ that
5) ④, it ⇨ itself
6) ②, reflected ⇨ reflecting
7) ①, guaranteed ⇨ is guaranteed
8) ③, from ⇨ in
9) ③, many ⇨ much
10) ⑤, inferiority ⇨ dominance
11) ⑤, develop ⇨ developing
12) ②, are ⇨ being
13) ②, many ⇨ much
14) ③, played ⇨ playing
15) ⑤, to take ⇨ take
16) ④, buy ⇨ buying
17) ①, what ⇨ that
18) ①, prejudicing ⇨ being prejudiced
19) ②, were opted ⇨ opted
20) ⑤, to rationalize ⇨ rationalizing
21) ④, unhappily ⇨ unhappy

## QUIZ 1 Answers

1) (D)-(A)-(C)-(B)
2) (D)-(B)-(A)-(C)
3) (C)-(B)-(A)
4) (C)-(A)-(B)
5) (A)-(B)-(C)
6) (C)-(D)-(B)-(A)
7) (D)-(C)-(A)-(B)
8) (D)-(C)-(B)-(A)
9) (B)-(A)-(D)-(C)
10) (A)-(C)-(B)
11) (A)-(C)-(B)

## QUIZ 3 Answers

1) 2,3
2) 2,4
3) 2,3,5
4) 1,2
5) 3,5
6) 4
7) 4,5
8) 5
9) 1,3
10) 1,4
11) 1,4
12) 2,4

13) 1,5
14) 1,3
15) 2,3
16) 2,3
17) 1,4
18) 1,4
19) 3,4
20) 2,3
21) 1,5
22) 2,3
23) 1,4
24) 3,4,5

QUIZ 4  Answers

1) ④
2) ②
3) ②
4) ④, ⑤
5) ④
6) ⑤
7) ④
8) ③
9) ①
10) ③
11) ④
12) ④, ⑤
13) ③
14) ③
15) ③
16) ⑤
17) ④
18) ③
19) ⑤
20) ⑤

QUIZ 5  Answers

1)
④ that ⇨ which

2)
① giving ⇨ give
② started ⇨ starting

3)
① how ⇨ what
② if ⇨ whether
③ what ⇨ that
⑤ adapting ⇨ adopting
⑦ disassociating ⇨ disassociated
⑧ uses ⇨ use

4)
① concisely ⇨ precisely

5)
① principal ⇨ principle
② minimizing ⇨ minimize
⑩ adoption ⇨ adaptation
⑪ do ⇨ are

6)
① attributed ⇨ was attributed

② were originated ⇨ originated
⑤ which ⇨ what

7)
① guaranteed ⇨ is guaranteed
② producing ⇨ produce
⑤ allowed ⇨ are allowed
⑥ are ⇨ do

8)
① reflected ⇨ reflecting
② are ⇨ is
③ wanted ⇨ wants
④ is ⇨ are
⑤ which ⇨ in which
⑥ from ⇨ in
⑦ inadequately ⇨ inadequate
⑧ diversity ⇨ exclusivity
⑨ which ⇨ where

9)
① asked ⇨ are asked
② even if ⇨ as if
③ taken ⇨ taking
⑤ is seemed ⇨ seems
⑥ recording ⇨ records
⑦ called ⇨ calling

10)
① carrying ⇨ carries
② traced ⇨ be traced
⑤ Listen ⇨ Listening
⑦ inferiority ⇨ dominance

11)
① been evolved ⇨ evolved
② predicts ⇨ predict
③ intertested ⇨ interesting
④ very ⇨ much
⑤ what ⇨ that
⑥ interacting ⇨ to interact
⑦ moved ⇨ moving
⑧ that ⇨ which
⑨ provided ⇨ providing
⑩ develop ⇨ developing

12)
② are ⇨ being
④ that ⇨ what

13)
① is ⇨ are
② many ⇨ much
③ what ⇨ which
④ market ⇨ marketing
⑤ sliced ⇨ slicing
⑦ them ⇨ themselves

14)
① been seen ⇨ seen

③ played ⇨ playing
⑤ suggested ⇨ been suggested
⑥ become ⇨ becoming
⑦ dissatisfaction ⇨ gratification

15)
② included ⇨ concluded
④ contributing ⇨ contributes

16)
⑥ buy ⇨ buying

17)
③ which ⇨ that
④ awaiting ⇨ waiting
⑥ to spin ⇨ spinning

18)
① prejudicing ⇨ being prejudiced
② be functioned ⇨ function
③ that ⇨ if
④ to group ⇨ group
⑤ to assume ⇨ assume
⑥ being ⇨ is

19)
② asked ⇨ were asked

20)
⑥ for example ⇨ on the other hand
⑦ hardly ⇨ hard
⑪ meet ⇨ meeting

21)
② because ⇨ because of
③ had thought ⇨ thought
④ asked ⇨ asking
⑤ have ⇨ had
⑥ were ⇨ was
⑦ to try ⇨ trying
⑧ unhappily ⇨ unhappy
⑨ did ⇨ was

QUIZ 6 **Answers**

1) put의 올바른 형태 - are putting

2)
ⓐ
worked ⇨ working
been occurred ⇨ occurred

3)
(가) I would like to let you know that you can put out your recycling on Wednesdays only

4) 엄습하다 - crept over // start의 올바른 형태 - starting // Gaze의 올바른 형태 – Gazing

5)
ⓐ
even if ⇨ as though
trapped ⇨ was trapped

6) ⑤

7) bond의 올바른 형태 - bonded // share의 올바른 형태 - shared // look의 올바른 형태 - to look // dissociate의 올바른 형태 - disassociated // risk의 올바른 형태 - risking // 평가 – assessments

8)
ⓐ
how ⇨ what
what ⇨ that

9) 정확히 - precisely // 비상사태 - contingencies // 연결부사 - rather // 지구력 - endurance // 최적의 - optimal // predetermine의 올바른 형태 - predetermined // assume의 올바른 형태 - assuming // predict의 올바른 형태 – predicted

10)
(가) No matter how many mock disasters are staged according++to prior plans, the real disaster will never mirror any one of them

11) ③

12) unchange의 올바른 형태 - unchanged // ~와 비교하여 - in comparison with // 적응하다 - adapt to // 달라지다,변하다 - altered // examine의 올바른 형태 - examined // adapt의 올바른 형태 - adaptation // take의 올바른 형태 - to be taking // mislead의 올바른 형태 - misleading // 정적인 – static

13)
(가) Our planet is dynamic, and so are the arrangements by which its inhabitants live together

14) attribute의 올바른 형태 - was attributed // originate의 올바른 형태 - originated // 연결부사 - In fact // reflect의 올바른 형태 - reflecting // possess의 올바른 형태 - was possessed // 내려가다 - descended // 어설픈,힘없는 - pale // underly의 올바른 형태 - underlying // result의 올바른 형태 - resulting // 타협 – compromise

15)
(가) The artist's job was not to imitate nature but rather to reveal the sacred and transcendent qualities of nature

16) 가설 - hypothesis // guarantee의 올바른 형태 - is guaranteed // 연결부사 - However // suppose의 올바른 형태 - is supposed // establish의 올바른 형태 - established // unchart의 올바른 형태 - uncharted // unchart의 올바른 형태 - uncharted

// allow의 올바른 형태 - are allowed

17)
(가) If we knew what we were doing, it would not be called research, would it

18) reflect의 올바른 형태 - reflecting // be의 올바른 형태 - is // 연결부사 - Yet // make의 올바른 형태 - makes // result의 올바른 형태 - resulting // 연결부사 - Yet // develop의 올바른 형태 - is developed

19)
(가) There is no need for others to present their ideas because they are considered inadequate

20) illustrate의 올바른 형태 - is illustrated // ask의 올바른 형태 - are asked // be의 올바른 형태 - were // 정적인 - static // position의 올바른 형태 - positioning // let의 올바른 형태 - letting // 냉담한,비인격적인 – impersonal

21)
ⓐ
straightforword ⇨ straightforwardly

22)
(가) calling as little attention to itself as possible

23) 훌륭한,존경할만한 - respectable // carry의 올바른 형태 - carries // trace의 올바른 형태 - be traced // make의 올바른 형태 - were made // employ의 올바른 형태 - employed // 강력한,만만찮은 - formidable // 당당함 - assertiveness // 기념비적인 - monumental // 떠올리다,불러일으키다 - summon up // use의 올바른 형태 – using

24) interest의 올바른 형태 - interesting // encode의 올바른 형태 - be encoded // expose의 올바른 형태 - are exposed // move의 올바른 형태 - moving // memory의 올바른 형태 - to be processed

25)
ⓐ
been evolved ⇨ evolved
expected ⇨ unexpected
depending ⇨ depends

26)
(가) Preference for novelty sets us up for learning by directing attention, providing stimulation to developing perceptual systems, and feeding curious and exploratory behavior

27) ⑤

28) sell의 올바른 형태 - being sold // retain의 올바른 형태 – retained

29) ①

30) 정확하게 - precisely // 분석학 - analytics // slice의 올바른 형태 – slicing

31)
ⓐ
minimize ⇨ maximize
contact ⇨ conduct
subsequence ⇨ surveillance
devises ⇨ devices

32) admit의 올바른 형태 - admitted // take의 올바른 형태 - to taking // view의 올바른 형태 - be viewed // play의 올바른 형태 - playing // 취약성 - vulnerabilities // 부적절 - inadequateness // create의 올바른 형태 - created // suggest의 올바른 형태 - been suggested // become의 올바른 형태 - becoming // fixate의 올바른 형태 – fixated

33)
ⓐ
been questioned ⇨ questioned
that ⇨ whether
manipulating ⇨ manipulate
advertising ⇨ advertised

34) 연결부사 - For example // 결론짓다 - concluded // 내포하다,의미하다 - imply // be의 올바른 형태 - being // correlate의 올바른 형태 - is correlated // 연결부사 - In fact

35)
(가) the corresponding lack of social and relaxation time

36) 과세 - taxation // 명백한 - explicit // call의 올바른 형태 - are called

37)
(가) because they seek to discourage activities considered harmful or undesirable
(나) Such taxes express society's disapproval of these activities by raising the cost of engaging in them
(다) Nor is a general sales tax intended as a deterrent to buying things

38) 연결부사 - However // spin의 올바른 형태 - spinning // 상당한 - considerable // 기준 – criterion

39)
(가) Beliefs can be verified or falsified with objective criteria external to the person

40) prejudice의 올바른 형태 - being prejudiced // function의 올바른 형태 - to function

41)
ⓐ
to group ⇨ group

what ⇨ that
similar ⇨ different
ⓑ
to assume ⇨ assume
different ⇨ similar

42)
(가) the necessary and useful instinct to generalize can distort our world view

43) ③

44) offer의 올바른 형태 - were offered // 연결부사 - On the other hand

45) ⑥

46) 연결부사 - however // Believe의 올바른 형태 - Believing // 연결부사 - on the other hand

47)
(가) It is in no way descriptive of your value as a person

48) ask의 올바른 형태 - asking // never see의 올바른 형태 - had never seen // decide의 올바른 형태 - had decided // try의 올바른 형태 - trying // 연결부사 - At last

49)
(가) he was too miserable to utter a note
(나) the shoemaker felt so unhappy that he seized his bag of gold